CHRISTOPHER COLUMBUS'S NAMING IN THE *DIARIOS* OF THE FOUR VOYAGES (1492–1504)

A Discourse of Negotiation

Christopher Columbus's Naming in the *diarios* of the Four Voyages (1492–1504)

A Discourse of Negotiation

EVELINA GUŽAUSKYTĖ

UNIVERSITY OF TORONTO PRESS
Toronto Buffalo London

Toronto Buffalo London
www.utppublishing.com

ISBN 978-1-4426-4746-6

Library and Archives Canada Cataloguing in Publication

Gužauskytė, Evelina, 1975–, author
Christopher Columbus's naming in the diarios of the four voyages (1492–1504) : a discourse of negotiation/Evelina Gužauskytė.

(Toronto Iberic)
Includes bibliographical references and index.
ISBN 978-1-4426-4746-6 (bound)

1. Columbus, Christopher – Diaries. 2. Names, Geographical – Caribbean Area. 3. Names, Geographical – South America. 4. Caribbean Area – Discovery and exploration – Spanish. 5. South America – Discovery and exploration – Spanish. I. Title. II. Series: Toronto Iberic

E118.G89 2014 972.9'02 C2013-907446-5

University of Toronto Press acknowledges the financial assistance to its publishing program of the Canada Council for the Arts and the Ontario Arts Council.

University of Toronto Press acknowledges the financial support of the Government of Canada through the Canada Book Fund for its publishing activities.

Contents

Illustrations

Acknowledgments

This book has been made possible thanks to the generosity of many individuals and institutions. This project was funded by generous grants from the Ministry of Education, Culture and Sports of Spain, the John Carter Brown Library, Escuela de Estudios Hispano-Americanos, Columbia University, and Wellesley College. Faculty Awards at Wellesley College has enabled the advancement the project by giving me time to focus exclusively on writing. The following institutions have kindly granted copyright permissions for illustrations: the John Carter Brown Library, Art Resource Inc., the National Library of France, the British Library Board, the Mappa Mundi Trust and Dean and Chapter of Hereford Cathedral, and the Bavarian State Library. The staff at the American Numismatic Society, Escuela de Estudios Hispano-Americanos, Biblioteca Colombina, the Morgan Library and Museum, and the Universidad Nacional Autónoma de México have been extremely helpful in locating necessary material. An earlier version of chapter 4 appeared as "Stars of the Sky, Gems of the Earth: Place Names Related to 'Planets' and Metals in Columbus's *Diario*" in *Colonial Latin American Review* 18, no. 2 (August 2009): 261–82. I thank the journal for permission to publish a revised and expanded version of the article here.

The support of colleagues, teachers, and mentors was instrumental for the success of this project. For his much-needed mentorship and sound advice, I would like to thank Raúl Marrero-Fente. For her intellectually stimulating feedback on parts of the manuscript and for her invaluable help at times when it was essential, I am especially indebted to Patricia Grieve. You are one of the most inspiring and generous teachers I have had, and I am deeply grateful for your support over the years. For his trust in the project from its very conception, I thank Roberto González-Echevarría, whose work continues to move me. I also wholeheartedly thank Varela Gil and Juan Gil for their professional kindness, valuable suggestions, and unforgettable hospitality. For her timely advice, criticism, and encouragement, I am grateful to Nina Scott. For reading the entire manuscript at a time when a critical eye was very much needed I thank my colleague at Wellesley College Carlos Vega. I am also greatly indebted to Robert Davidson and Josiah Blackmore of the Department of Spanish and Portuguese at the University of Toronto for their interest in the project. The book would not have seen the light of day without the professional guidance of senior editor Suzanne Rancourt during the preparation of the manuscript for publication, for which I am most grateful. I would like to also express my gratitude for their work to my copy editor Miriam Skey and assistant managing editor Lisa Jemison. And finally a heartfelt thank you goes to the anonymous readers for their helpful, constructive feedback. The errors and omissions are all my own.

Colleagues in the Spanish Department and other departments as well as the administrative staff at Wellesley College have been a source of tremendous support and guidance throughout the process of writing the book. In particular, I thank Joy Renjilian-Burgy from the Spanish Department and Wini Wood from the Writing Program for helping me to secure the Jenkins Fund grant at Wellesley College which has funded an important part of the writing process. I am grateful to Carlos Ramos for his mentorship, guidance, encouragement, and also for his great sense of humour. For collaboration opportunities, fruitful exchanges at conferences, feedback, and intellectual stimulation, I thank colleagues at Wellesley and elsewhere, especially Michael Schussler, Marcia Welles, Michael Agnew, Sara Beckjord, Libby Russ, Edward Test, Alicia Zuese, Inela Selimovic, Margaret Ewalt, Larry Rosenwald, Alejandra Osorio, Kathleen Donegan, and Daniela Castelli. For mentorship and moral support, I thank all of my departmental colleagues. I would also like to express gratitude to my students Beatriz Aldereguia and Clair Shea who assisted me with formatting the appendix and worked relentlessly on it for many hours. And my parents, Vilius Gužauskis and Terese Gužauskienė, as well as my sister Kristina Gužauskytė, have helped and inspired me even more than they realize.

While the manuscript was in progress my two daughters were born. Without their unconditional love and without the unfaltering support of my husband during those long nights and days full of discoveries, this ship would have never reached safe harbour. I dedicate this book to the three of you.

Abbreviations

Díaz	Colón, Hernando. *Historia del Almirante*. Ed. Manuel Carrera Díaz. Barcelona: Ariel, 2003.
Millares Carlo	Las Casas, Bartolomé de. *Historia de las Indias*. Ed. Agustín Millares Carlo. Preliminary study by Lewis Hanke. 3 vols. Mexico: Fondo de Cultura Económica, 1951.
Peter Martyr	Anghiera, Peter Martyr d'. *The Discovery of the New World in the Writings of Peter Martyr of Anghiera*. Ed. Ernesto Lunardi et al. Trans. into English by Felix Azzola. *Nuova Raccolta Colombiana*. Vol. 2. Rome: Istituto Poligrafico e Zecca dello Stato, 1992.
Symcox	Las Casas, Bartolomé de. *Las Casas on Columbus: The Third Voyage*. Ed. Geoffrey Symcox. Turnhout: Brepols, 2001.
Varela and Gil	Varela, Consuelo, and Juan Gil, eds. *Cristóbal Colón: Textos y documentos completos*. 3rd ed. Madrid: Alianza, 2003.

CHRISTOPHER COLUMBUS'S NAMING IN THE *DIARIOS* OF THE FOUR VOYAGES (1492–1504)

Introduction

The contract between the Spanish Crown and Christopher Columbus entitled "Capitulaciones de Santa Fe" (17 April 1492), the agreement that established the legal basis for the latter's transoceanic voyages of exploration, mercantilism, and conquest, does not include any place names. Notoriously absent are the names of Asia or the Indies, the supposed goal of Columbus's imminent voyage, and of any places in those vast regions. Absent also are the names of places in Europe, including Castile, Aragon, Catalonia, Andalusia, the Mediterranean lands and waters, and points on coastlines; likewise, absent are the names of mythical or biblical places. All of these are frequently found in medieval *mappae mundi* and later they do make an appearance in the *diarios*. Instead, "Capitulaciones" is defined by its "vacillation in grammar," to use Djelal Kadir's phrase, and by generalizing vocabulary, as when the merchandise to be brought back is described in the broadest terms: "*cualesquiera* cosas y mercaderías de *cualquier* especie, *nombre* y manera *que sean*" (emphases mine).[1] The destination of the voyage – *that* which will be or perhaps, as some have argued, that which already has been discovered – is summed up not with a name of a place but with the most evasive and abstract word in the Castilian language, *lo*: "lo que ha descubierto."[2] In a work of true craftsmanship of diplomacy and intuition, place names are likely omitted to avoid unnecessarily constricting the agreement's scope by situating the objective of the upcoming voyage in any known or hypothetical geography as well as to protect the secrecy of the enterprise. In addition to these objectives, however, the missing toponyms serve another purpose: to lay the ground for naming as an instrument for announcing territorial claims. Furthermore, the silence suggests yet another hypothesis: that Columbus, the king, and the queen admitted the possibility that those territories might already have names, even if they were unknown to the European cosmographers at the time.

Over the next twelve years, Columbian place names would populate the map of the Americas literally and metaphorically. In stark contrast to the missing onomastics in the "Capitulaciones," place names are bursting from the pages of Columbus's *diarios*, the versions of the original ship logs now lost and accessible to the reader as transcriptions that Bartolomé de Las Casas made for his own use. The *diarios* of all four voyages include toponyms Columbus invented in Castilian in addition to numerous references to place names he believed he was hearing from the Taino natives as well as names of places in Asia and Europe, African and Arabic toponyms, and a selection of place names and proper names of mythical and biblical origins. The Columbian naming enterprise would be yet unrivalled in its scope, intensity, and impact, even in comparison with the Catalan conquistadors' acts of naming in the Canary Islands or those of the Portuguese explorers and slave traders in the Atlantic islands and along the African coast.

As both a seminal act in the history of the Americas and as an act of foreshadowing of the destruction of lives, memories, and cultures that was to follow, Columbus's naming of places and the broader subject of European naming of people, places, plants, and animals have both received ample attention by critics. Many of these previous critics have focused on the violent, annihilating effects of naming. Edmundo O'Gorman, José Rabasa, and Eduardo Subirats, among others, consider naming an act that first erases and negates (thus creating vast spaces of *terra nullius*) and then invents a new world based on mental constructs rather than the physical reality. Others, among them Tzvetan Todorov in *The Conquest of America*, Stephen Greenblatt in *Marvelous Possessions*, and Patricia Seed in *Ceremonies of Possession*, explore the more pragmatic aspects of Columbian naming. In the context of the mercantilist, political, and legal objectives of the enterprise, they see the acts of naming as manifestations of power and as a kind of "tools of the trade" in Columbus's dealing with the Other. For Todorov, naming lands is an act of "nomination" which "is equivalent to taking possession."[3] Naming was thus a political act of appropriating and legitimizing as the names of places were inserted into what Greenblatt has called the European "representational machinery." George R. Stewart points out that later conquerors of the Americas were explicitly instructed to assign names to places they were about to conquer, in which context the primary function of naming was to serve as the legal foundation for taking possession: "Arrived there by good providence, first of all you must give a name to the country as a whole, and to the cities, towns, and places."[4] Though many of the critics see naming as a way of instituting a new order, for some it is imposed in an entirely capricious fashion, without the acknowledgment, in the European mind, of any prior cultural and historical activity of the native people. Others admit a relationship, even if clearly biased, calculated, and falsified, between the existing cultural and natural worlds of the Americas and the language of naming that Columbus produced. For some, Columbus's naming in America is an act of writing on a blank page, *terra nullius*, an empty continent, and hence, a linguistic production that is completely disconnected from the reality to which it was directed; for others, it is an act of reading signs, part and parcel not of understanding and affirming, but of appropriating and kidnapping.[5]

The fundamental problem, as far as the essence of Columbian naming is concerned, lies not in the question of whether Columbus approached the lands before him as if they were lacking names entirely (as Subirats has put it, "los infinitos desiertos sin nombre de un continente vacío" [infinite deserts without names in an empty continent]), or whether he quickly became aware that the lands before him did have names already.[6] Rather, it is rooted in the fact that for many critics Columbian naming still draws a clear and abrupt line between American physicality and European verbality. The New World is often presented in criticism as though perceived by Columbus strictly as a world consisting of physical signs: luscious nature, naked bodies, and ornaments made of gold. And the Columbian naming enterprise then is seen as an act of fitting existing Castilian words onto objects, people, and places that Columbus perceived as lacking names as well as any verbal expression or knowledge. This book challenges the idea that the language of Columbian naming stemmed exclusively from the political power and cultural vocabulary imposed via European institutions and technologies, and that it carved, unerringly, the shapes of European visions onto silent and passive landscapes of the Americas.

The tension between the acts of naming and the physical spaces on which the names were imposed is born from an analogy that has been evoked frequently: one between Columbus's naming of places and Adam's naming of animals. For example, Todorov writes: "Like Adam in the midst of Eden, Columbus is profoundly concerned with the choice of names for the virgin world before his eyes; and as in his own case [that is, in the case of Columbus's own name], these names must be motivated."[7] The lure of the analogy lies, among other things, in contemporary historians' insistence on Columbus's role as the carrier of God's Word encoded even, as Las Casas and Ferdinand Columbus claimed, in his first and last names: Cristoferens, "Christ-carrier," and Colombo, "dove," the symbol of divine wisdom. It also lies in the trope of Paradise articulated by Columbus himself and propagated, at least initially, by Las Casas.[8] However, the reliance on the analogy between the Adomite and the Columbian naming, however historically accepted, becomes an obstacle to a deeper inquiry into the processes that underpinned Columbian naming. The principal problem associated with the Adomite metaphor is that it perpetuates the idea of the linguistic and political "virginity" of the Americas and of Columbus's view of the Indies as such.

Another form of appropriating, intimately related to naming, was and is mapping. In the prologue to the *Diario del primer viaje*, Columbus presents to his readers, the king and the queen, two principal instruments for documenting the discoveries made during his first voyage: the written log and the map. The prologue culminates with a formulation of the commitment to these two instruments. First, Columbus would write down everything very punctually: "y para esto pensé de escrevir todo este viaje muy puntualmente, de día en día todo lo que yo hiziese y viese y passasse, como adelante se veirá."[9] And he would also make a new navigational chart or map, "carta nueva de navegar": "También, Señores Prínçipes, allende de escrevir cada noche lo qu'el día passare y el día lo que la noche navegare, tengo propósito de hazer carta nueva de navegar, en la cual situaré toda la mar e tierras del mar Occéano en sus proprios lugares, debaxo su viento, y más componer un libro y poner todo por el semejante por pintura, por latitud del equinocial y longitud del Occidente."[10] The use of these two forms in the production of personal observations made while navigating ("y sobre todo cumple mucho que yo olvide el sueño y tiente mucho el navegar") is consistent with the mapping practices in the *portolano* and *roteiro* traditions.[11] The intent to record these observations in two formats – text and drawing on the map, "por pintura" – is also consistent with the medieval *mappa mundi* tradition according to which written lists of locations, including the names of the places and their coordinates or distances relative to another location, were made in addition to drawing the map. The use of the two forms for recording geographic knowledge is also based on Ptolemy's *Geography*, which consisted of both the list of localities as well as drawings of maps. Furthermore, the fact that in the prologue a reference is made not just to a single navigational chart but to a collection of them in the form of a book ("y más componer un libro y poner todo por el semejante por pintura") suggests that one of Columbus's goals was to contribute to the cosmographic knowledge of the time and to produce a work that dealt with the *mar Occéano* and the lands surrounding it in as complete a fashion as possible, similar to how Ptolemy had dealt with the land masses and the surrounding seas known to ancient scholars at the time.[12]

Columbus's cosmographic interests would soon result in imperial acts of taking possession since mapping is in itself an act of appropriation. "*Possession* cannot do without the preparation of, or recourse to, a map or chart," says Rolena Adorno in her brilliantly argued book *The Polemics of Possession in Spanish American Narrative*.[13] In this sense, Columbus's contributions to the "cartographic literature" and the art of map making of his time would propel the Spanish colonization of the Americas, as Ricardo Padrón argued convincingly in his *The Spacious Word: Cartography, Literature, and Empire in Early Modern Spain*.[14] Recently, various invigorating studies about cartography and mapping have underscored the ability of maps to function as rhetorical discourses, ideological instruments, and subjective constructs. Since the work of the historian of cartography John Brian Harley, a map can no longer be thought of as a disengaged representation of facts but rather as "a form of political discourse concerned with the acquisition and maintenance of power."[15] In this context Nicolás Wey Gómez's *The Tropics of Empire: Why Columbus Sailed South to the Indies* has also been important for an understanding of the cultural geography of late medieval Europe and Columbus's "invention" of the tropics to its south.[16] However, we cannot forget that the Tainos, the Island Caribs, and other native cultural groups in the Caribbean Basin also had functional onomastic systems and that they also made maps. The Tainos showed Columbus some of these maps on tree bark and they also drew directions for him in the sand. Just like European medieval and early modern mapping practices, those performed by the Taino and other indigenous groups were likewise highly symbolic and ideological constructs. Furthermore, their acts of showing Columbus existing maps or drawing directions for him in the sand were in themselves acts of exerting influence.

One of the things this book does to address the points outlined above is analyse the drastically different ways in which the Columbian naming enterprise is represented in the *diarios* transcribed from the original ship logs – which had been meant for Columbus's, and perhaps the king's and queen's eyes, only – on the one hand, and two letters crafted for public dissemination, on the other. Of the two letters, which contain almost identical text and are both dated 15 February 1493, one is addressed to Luis de Santángel, *escribano de ración* (notary and accountant) to King Ferdinand, and the other to Rafaél (Gabriel) Sánchez.[17] The letters were published in various editions in Castilian, Latin, and German, and disseminated throughout Europe. Antonio Rumeu de Armas has speculated that Columbus wrote these letters, as well as a letter dated 4 March 1493, whereas Demetrio Ramos Pérez contends that someone else, probably Santángel himself,

0.1. *De insulis inuentis: Epistola Cristoferi Colom* (Basel, 1493). Courtesy of the John Carter Brown Library, Providence, RI.

wrote the letter to Santángel based on another letter sent to him by Columbus, which most likely was the letter of 4 March to the sovereigns, a thesis that Zamora also supports.[18] Regardless of the authorship of the letter to Santángel, many critics have quoted these lines from this letter as the sentence that summarizes the Columbian naming project: "A la primera que yo fallé puse nonbre Sant Salvador a comemoración de su Alta Magestat, el cual maravillosamente todo esto a[n] dado; los indios la llaman Guanahaní. A la segunda puse nombre la isla de Santa María de

Concepción; a la tercera, Ferrandina; a la cuarta la Isabela; a la quinta la isla Juana, e así a cada una nombre nuevo."[19] Perhaps the extent of the Columbian naming project as it was presented to the European public could indeed be summarized by the above sentence since the ship log was never meant to be made public while the letter to Santángel was published in many editions; one of these, the Basel edition, even contained a woodcut illustration that was one of the early European attempts at mapping the Americas while using the Columbian place names propagated in the letter (figure 0.1). Hence, some critics have referred to these sentences and to the place names listed in them to argue that the Columbian naming project was ideologically charged from the beginning and that it was based on preconceived notions of order and hierarchy. For example, Seed argued that the "first" six place names listed in the letter to Santángel were manifestations of the political intent present in the Columbian discourse. However, the view here is that focusing attention on the place names listed in the letter to Santángel or, in some other cases, to a small handful of selected place names, has been detrimental to a broader and deeper understanding of the nature, the driving forces, and the implications of the Columbian naming enterprise as a whole. The first serious problem has to do with the uncertain authorship of the letters to the court officials Santángel and Sánchez. If Columbus did not write these two letters himself or, at the very least, if there was, as Zamora has argued, *some* intervention in the composition of the letters by the Crown, an intervention that is quite understandable since the letters would represent an important state enterprise to its European rivals, then the list of six toponyms is entirely arbitrary. In this case, the short list does not capture the nature and the purpose of the Columbian naming project as a whole nor does it represent the much more extensive list of Columbian place names found in the *diarios* edited by Las Casas or those that Columbus had recorded in his original ship logs, now lost. Even if Columbus did himself write the letter to Santángel based on the letter of 4 March, as Rumeu de Armas argued, in this case too it represents a mediated, selective, and strategic rewriting that presents a desired official vision by truncating and dissecting the original toponymic discourse. Though the *diarios* are also products of editing by another individual, namely Las Casas, the material concerning the acts of Columbian naming they include is significantly more copious and detailed. Lacunae, alterations, and in some cases even insertions notwithstanding, the *diarios* provide a much greater amount of material from which the changing nature and the shifting course of the Columbian naming can be approximated. Furthermore, the letter to Santángel formulates the initial intent and the results of the

Columbian naming enterprise with a public audience in mind that is not necessarily representative of the way Columbus conceived and carried out his naming practices. Two essential differences between the ways in which naming is presented in the letter and in the *diarios* show that naming served different purposes to different audiences. While naming was perceived as a potentially powerful instrument for asserting Spanish imperial influence, Columbus did not consistently use it in such a way nor did he necessarily intend to use it thus originally.

The first difference between the presentation of the Columbian naming enterprise in the letter to Santángel and the *Diario del primer viaje* concerns the identification of the first five toponyms that Columbus pronounced. According to the letter to Santángel (and the letter to Sánchez), they were *San Salvador*, *Santa María de Concepción*, *Fernandina*, *Isabela*, and *Juana*. While the *Diario del primer viaje* also introduces the first four of these in this order on 14 and 15 October, the fifth toponym in it is not *Isla Juana* but a much less ideologically charged *Cabo Hermoso*. Should the argument be made that the letter to Santángel only lists names of islands, which is indeed the case, and not their parts, such as capes and bays, then it should be useful to point out that the next toponym referring to what Columbus believed to be a group of islands was also the very earthly sounding name of Sandy Isles, *Islas de Arena*, introduced in the *Diario* on 27 October.[20] In fact, before naming *Isla Juana*, Columbus had already pronounced twenty-five other place names in Castilian, including *Río del Poniente* (12 November), *Puerto de Santa Catalina* (24 November), *Isla Llana* (24 November), and *Cabo de Campana* (26 November), to mention just a few, in addition to incorporating into his discourse various Taino and hybrid place names as well, including *Tierra de Bohío* (21 October) and *Cabo de Cuba* (12 November). *Isla Juana* does not make an appearance in the *Diario del primer viaje* until 5 December, which makes it the twenty-sixth (!) toponym in the sequence of Castilian place names. On 5 December, it is introduced in the *Diario* together with the Taino name of the island, *Cuba*: "diz que los de Cuba o Juana." It is unlikely that Las Casas's editing is to blame for its earlier absence in the *Diario*, since the friar's comment in the margin confirms that Columbus named *Isla Juana* on 5 December rather than almost two months earlier: "Aquí parece que debía de haber puesto nombre a Cuba, Juana."[21] Until then, the *Diario* refers to the island with its Taino name, *Cuba* or *Colba*, beginning with its first mention on 21 October: "que creo que deve ser Çipango, según las señas que me dan estos indios que yo traigo, a la cual ellos llaman Colba."[22]

The articulation of the five-toponym sequence in the letter to Santángel is consistent with the intention to project the naming enterprise as reflective of the official vision of the enterprise of the discovery, in which Providence and the Crown are its ultimate overseers. Less grand-sounding place names, such as *Islas de Arena* and others similarly lacking imperial connotations, such as *Isla Llana* or *Isla de la Tortuga*, would have made a much more modest statement about the expanding powers of King Ferdinand and Queen Isabel than the place name presumably dedicated to the heir of the Crown, Prince Juan. However, according to the *Diario del primer viaje*, Columbus did not dedicate an island to Prince Juan immediately after he had dedicated islands to Christ, the Virgin Mary, the king, and the queen. Even more doubts are shed regarding the meaning of the name of *Isla Juana* in the Castilian translation of Ferdinand Columbus's history of his father's navigation, where the same spelling, *juana*, is used to refer both to the island and to the large iguanas his father had spotted on the Fernandina.[23] Even if the mistake was introduced by a copyist or a translator, the discussion of both meanings of *juana* in two subsequent paragraphs of chapter 25 of Ferdinand Columbus's *Historia del Almirante* taints the strictly European and imperial meaning of a name dedicated to the Crown's heir.[24] Perhaps this was simply a technical error made during the processes of translation or copying; or, perhaps Columbus's son himself had used the word *juana* to mean "iguana," which would further undermine the political meaning of the names of the island. In either case, as these examples begin to illustrate, the subtleties of Columbian naming recorded in the *diarios* and other contemporary documents have been cleaned out of the letter to Santángel to present a clear Christian imperialistic vision.

The second important difference between the letter to Santángel and the *Diario del primer viaje* lies in the introduction of the first Taino place name, *Guanahaní.* As noted above, the first place name in the letter to Santángel is the Castilian *San Salvador*, which is followed by the Taino name of the island, "los indios la llaman Guanahaní" (Indians call it *Guanahaní*). While the letter does acknowledge the Taino place name instead of erasing it altogether, a fact that is significant in itself, it nevertheless clearly gives greater importance to the act of naming places in Castilian. Such is not the case in the *Diario del primer viaje*. In the 11 October entry, the very first toponym referring to the Caribbean is *Guanahaní*, the toponym the Lucayo Tainos routinely used: "el día viernes que llegaron a una isleta de los lucayos, que se llamava en lengua de indios Guanahaní."[25] The toponym Columbus invented in Castilian is introduced only on 14 October, *three days later* and after several pages of descriptions of Columbus's and his crew's exploration of the island and encounters with its people. Whether or not this omission has anything to do with Las Casas's editing of the original ship log is difficult to know, but it is unlikely that such was the case. Similarly, in the case of *Isla Cuba*, the Taino place name was used in the *Diario del primer viaje* extensively before the Castilian *Isla Juana* was introduced almost two months later; in this case Las Casas himself noted its late introduction in the margin. There was no good reason for Las Casas to fail to mention such an essential detail as the first act of naming an island with a Castilian place name. Zamora noted that such an early mention of *Guanahaní* in the *Diario del primer viaje* is "an anachronistic intrusion" inserted by Las Casas.[26] Even if that may be so, the absence of *San Salvador* until 14 October remains significant, and the introduction and repeated use of both *Guanahaní* and *Cuba* before their Castilian counterparts, *San Salvador* and *Juana*, are introduced significantly later, indicates that not only Las Casas but also Columbus in his original ship logs granted significant importance to the names by which local inhabitants called islands and places in them. Yet another reference to the place names Columbus had learned from the local inhabitants is made before the first mention of *San Salvador* at the end of the 14 October entry: "Y aquellos hombres que yo tenía toma[n]do me dezían por señas que eran tantas y tantas [islas] que que no avía número *y anombraron por su nombre más de ciento.*"[27] Though none of the actual names are actually listed, this reference reveals the repeated exposure to indigenous onomastics and a conscious interest in learning place names in local languages. Ferdinand Columbus, who presumably worked with his father's original ship logs, also introduces the Taino toponym *Guanahaní* before the Castilian one. When correcting the misconception ("falsedad") that the first island his father had discovered was Española, he also refers to both the Taino and the Castilian names of the island: "Se trató, por el contrario, de Guanahaní, a la que el Almirante llamó San Salvador."[28] The toponyms *Guanahaní* and *Cuba* are examples of the exchanges that occurred between the Taino natives and Columbus, and the tenuous nature of some of these exchanges is shown in another woodcut illustration of the Basel edition of the letter to Santángel (figure 0.2). The relative absence of indigenous place names as well as of Castilian place names unrelated to the imperial ideology suggests that the letter to Santángel viewed the naming in Castilian as an authoritative act that imposed imperial ideology from the onset. In contrast, the *Diario del primer viaje* provides a more inclusive account and one that acknowledges the immediate effects that the encounters with the local inhabitants had on

Columbus, before the latter even began his naming and colonizing enterprise. In other words, the linguistic and thematic variety of place names in the *Diario del primer viaje* reveals that Columbian naming acts were acts of translation and negotiation as the information acquired during the voyages was absorbed and integrated into Columbus's discursive and cartographic outputs.

It may be redundant to say that the Americas, including the lands and the waters of the Caribbean Basin, had been long exploited by the peoples that lived there and therefore they were filled with places and things that had been "read," appropriated, and kidnapped for thousands of years. Renaming territories and giving new names to individuals to mark a new stage in their lives was a common practice among the various peoples of the Caribbean and continental Americas such as the Tainos, the Igneri, and the Island Caribs. People had been living on the Caribbean islands for nearly 6,000 years.[29] These people had developed a highly structured approach to exploiting territories through building, making villages, practising agricultural techniques, and developing political organizations. At the time of Columbus's arrival, the Tainos "were organized into a series of complex chiefdoms, polities encompassing as many as one hundred villages and tens of thousands of people."[30] They were avid travellers and had named places nearby and far.[31] And they knew where the resources of their lands could be found. The assumption that Columbus ignored entirely the existence of all this information and of the extensive indigenous onomastic system is contradicted by the numerous Taino and other indigenous toponyms, words, and word fragments that populate the pages of the *diarios* together with the new names in Castilian.[32] Some critics have acknowledged the persistence of the Taino language and culture documented in the toponyms still used today: "In spite of the efforts by the Spaniards to give these islands Christian names, a surprising number of the original Taino names have survived to the present day."[33] Scholars such as Nancie L. Gonzalez, Samuel M. Wilson, Garnette Joseph, Antonio M. Stevens-Arroyo, and José Juan Arrom, among others, have written about the resistance and the survival of the various indigenous groups of the Caribbean.[34] For example, Arrom writes: "The Taínos were not exterminated. There were survivors of the great decimation who were gradually assimilated into the dominant culture, and after contact these survivors transmitted not only their genes, but also the principal achievements of their culture."[35] Currently, new exciting research is being produced, only one example of which is Gene Rhea Tucker's dissertation entitled "Place-Names, Conquest, and Empire: Spanish and Amerindian Conceptions of

0.2. *De insulis nuper in mari Indico repertis* (Basel, 1494). Courtesy of the John Carter Brown Library, Providence, RI.

Place in the New World" (2011). In it, Tucker studies the naming of places in Castilian as well as the continued use of Amerindian place names in the context of the Spanish conquest from Columbus through the eighteenth century. Tucker argues that the imposition of names in Castilian "only accounts for a portion of the toponyms used in the Spanish New World" and that "Amerindians continued using their own place-names and contributed many of them to the Spanish, who adopted and adapted them."[36] Such adoption and adaptation of indigenous place names is clearly notable in the *diarios* (see the appendix for lists of place names of indigenous origins).

Nevertheless, the impact that the Taino language and toponymy had on Columbus's exploration of the lands and his acts of naming has been largely ignored by the majority of colonial and postcolonial critics. Many still perceive Columbian acts of naming in Castilian as an act that is disconnected from the previous acts of mapping and native linguistic practices in the Caribbean Basin. Frequently, critics cite only the toponyms in Castilian as examples of the names Columbus assigned in the Caribbean, and sometimes they focus only on the names taken from the letter to Santángel. For example, Todorov views Taino toponymy as having had little significance in the context of the Columbian naming enterprise which he sees as consisting solely of acts of naming in Castilian: "Hence Columbus knows perfectly well that these islands already have names, natural ones in a sense (but in another acceptation of the term); others' words interest him very little, however, and he seeks to rename places in terms of the rank they occupy in his discovery, to give them the *right* names."[37] For Todorov, awareness does not equal interest or engagement. However, Columbus not only knew that the lands had names, but he was also keenly interested in learning those names for various practical, scientific, and political reasons: for finding his way, communicating with the local inhabitants, locating the desired resources, and understanding the landscape so that he could reproduce it on a navigational chart. The Tainos gave Columbus directions on how to reach specific islands and places with the help of signs and gestures, and they drew rudimentary maps for him in the sand. On numerous occasions in his *diarios*, Columbus acknowledges the information he received from the native inhabitants and the influence that they exerted on him. He claimed he heard numerous Taino place names when he made the note in his ship log of the more than hundred indigenous place names, "y anombraron por su nombre más de ciento."[38] The *diarios* also contain numerous hybrid toponyms, such as *San Telmo de Xamaná* and *Cabo de Cuba*, which consist of verbal elements of both Castilian and Taino or other origins. Furthermore, toponymic variations, such as *Cuba*, *Cibao*, and *Çipango*, speak to the conflating of Asia and the Americas in the Columbian toponymic discourse. To assume that all these toponymic borrowings, adaptations, and translations did not have a significant impact on the Columbian itineraries and strategies as well as on his naming in Castilian would be to dismiss a glaringly evident aspect of his strategy and method. Hence, this book aims to present a fuller, more comprehensive understanding of Columbian naming in the Americas, one of the desired outcomes of which is to allow those voices, visions, and landscapes that have been largely edited out of the historical record back into it.

The term "Columbian toponymic discourse," which I use throughout the book, reflects my view that Columbian place names should be approached not as a collection of disconnected utterances, but as a discourse, in the Foucauldian sense of the word, in which the relationships among the toponyms rather than single toponyms alone create their meaning as a whole. Understanding of a discourse is derived here from Foucault's studies of the relations between discourse, knowledge, power, and representation, according to which a discourse consists of a group of statements that allows groups of signs to exist "in relation with a domain of objects and [prescribe] a definite position to any possible subject."[39] Based on this definition, this book seeks to uncover the development of ideas, the fabrication of a rhetoric, and the formation of a climax in the Columbian toponymy as in a discourse that constructs a particular version of the reality that is fictional and persuasive. Through the examples examined in the chapters that follow, this book questions the essence of Columbian naming as one built strictly, or perhaps even at all, on the preconceived idea of structure and order (even though that was something that Columbus himself had promised he would attempt to achieve through his naming).

Recent studies in toponymy and place naming have voiced an urgent need to theorize what has been an overwhelmingly descriptive field of the study of toponymy. Over the last couple of decades, Wilbur Zelinsky – a pioneer in the critical studies of toponymy, a geographer by training, and a specialist in the demographic, social, and cultural geography of North America – has strongly advocated for the need to theorize the studies of the far-reaching phenomenon of naming. Among other things, he sees the development of classification schemes for names, something that he sees as the "Linnean Phase" of the discipline involving "cataloguing and arranging all the objects under investigation into some logical, coherent classificatory scheme," as an important step in the direction of developing the much-needed theories and a rigorous definition of what constitutes a name.[40] This book is an attempt to have a more complete look at the totality of the Columbian place names in Castilian, which are seen here as being inseparably interwoven with Taino onomastics. I argue that behind the projection of control apparent in some of the symmetrical and hierarchical toponymic progressions notable in the Columbian toponymic discourse lay a web of complex influences that the Tainos exerted on Columbus. The appropriation of Taino proper nouns as place names, as in the case of *Bohío* (meaning house) and *Guanín* (meaning an alloy of copper and gold), reinforces Zelinsky's contention that "the conventional place-name stands at the terminus of a long, interesting spectrum, or continuum, of words and names, one that reaches all the way from terms totally dissociated from any form of territoriality to those that are firmly anchored in unique places."[41] This is only one example in which the Taino view of the world, registered in their language, interrupts and shapes the Columbian acts of naming as it alters the very nature of what place names normally were. The list of Columbian place names is filled with names that are not even names at all, if viewed from a traditional perspective. Instead, they consist of elements in Castilian, Taino, and other languages, and they are built not on the steady base of nouns but on words, the meaning of which Columbus probably did not even understand, as well as on fragments of speech, syllables, and combinations of words, the meanings of which were extracted from signs, objects, and visions. Furthermore, Columbian place names were influenced by the multicultural heritages that surrounded both Castilian and the Taino language, including Arabic, Jewish, African, Asian, classical, Island Carib, and perhaps other native language influences. In this context, I also argue that native Taino, Castilian, Asian, and other toponyms should not be viewed as strictly separate entities, one imposing on the other, but rather as elements that participated in a process that was complex and multidirectional. In this sense, I agree with the central idea in a recent volume entitled *Critical Toponymies: The Contested Politics of Place Naming*, edited by Lawrence D. Berg and Jani Vuolteenaho, that naming is a contested practice, the study of which needs to be carried out from theoretically sound, critical perspectives that should account for "the intersection of naming, place-making, and power."[42] Throughout this book, I argue that the verbal artefacts, which I call Columbian place names, must be thought of as products of multiple collisions between the Castilian and native languages and epistemologies. This book, therefore, offers a different way to think about the earliest encounters between Europe and the Americas, not only as a series of acts of unidirectional imposition of power, but as a process through which power was continuously negotiated.

The subject matter examined here is the known corpus of place names, or toponyms, that Columbus pronounced during the course of his four voyages to the Americas, which spanned a period of twelve years (1492–1504). Rather than thinking about Columbian naming as a series of acts performed exclusively in Castilian, as has been a common practice in criticism, I define the corpus of Columbian place names as one consisting of both the place names, or toponyms, that Columbus invented in Castilian and those he incorporated into his repertoire based on native verbal expression – in particular, Taino toponyms and lexicon. In addition to Taino toponyms, this also includes the toponymies and vocabularies of the various ethnic groups in the Caribbean Basin, names of people and deities, and fragments of them all (including individual syllables, exclamations, curses, and cries), which Columbus appropriated, translated, or just repeated in an attempt to register them. Thus, I consider *Guanahaní* as part of the Columbian toponymic discourse for two reasons: because this name is a result of Columbian interpretation of the words pronounced to him by the natives and because his awareness of it had a significant impact on his mapping of spaces, no less (or possibly more) than the Castilian names he was pronouncing. Likewise, this book considers the Columbian toponymic discourse to include place names Columbus invented that incorporate in some way the rich and complex toponymic heritage that includes references to Asian, African-Portuguese and Atlantic-Portuguese, Andalusian, Castilian, and Arabic toponymies, as well as to classical place names and to mythical and spiritual places. To summarize, this book views place names in the Columbian toponymic discourse as rhetorical tools through which persuasion, control, and dominance were channelled. But it allows for that persuasion to flow in more than one direction.

It is important to note that we do not have access to a complete list of names that Columbus invented nor do we know with certainty that he authored all of the place names included in the *diarios*. In thinking about the issue of authorship in Columbian texts, I am indebted to Margarita Zamora's interpretation of this subject in *Reading Columbus* and Elise Bartosik-Vélez's analysis of the rhetorical strategies of Columbus's writing in "The Three Rhetorical Strategies of Christopher Columbus." Perhaps an alternative solution would be not to speak of "Columbian naming" at all. Awareness of the weakness of a similar term, "Columbian writing," in the light of the heavy editing of the *diarios* by Las Casas, has been adequately recognized, in particular in Zamora's work. If there is no such "Columbian writing," there is also no "Columbian naming," and I use this term for lack of a better one. When thinking about the naming phenomena, we must keep in mind questions of authorship and of editing, both by Las Casas and by Columbus himself. Deletions and omissions of names in the written text of the *diarios* and later changes of names sometimes make the fabric of naming warped and disorderly. Other members of Columbus's crew may have suggested some of the names. And finally, Taino names and influences both belonged to Columbus and escaped him, and they were also both kidnapped by him and engaged him in the active kidnapping of his own language, to use Stephen Greenblatt's well-known phrase.

One more observation needs to be made regarding the uncertain authorship of the place names being studied here. The legend of the unknown pilot who, just before expiring on his deathbed, told Columbus about the lands unexplored by Europeans he had reached, which has been perpetuated in sources since the sixteenth century, brings another important dimension to the question of the nature of Columbian names. The most extensive study of this legend and the theory of prediscovery, according to which Columbus in fact knew where he was headed, is in Juan Manzano Manzano's book *Colón y su secreto*. Despite the minute analysis in Manzano Manzano's book, generally scholars have not been convinced by the theory. Even if we were to accept Manzano Manzano's thesis that Columbus had some knowledge about where he was headed, in which case we would have to admit the possibility that he had already heard about some of the important landmarks and perhaps even heard some place names, should this change our view of Columbian naming altogether? While the acceptance of this theory would raise further questions about the authorship of at least some of the Columbian names as well as about their referentiality, the view here is that whether or not in Columbus's mind these toponyms referred to a land previously visited by an anonymous pilot does not significantly change the nature of most of his naming acts which would still likely have been acts of inventing new names. Similarly, this theory would not change the fact that Columbian place names contain evidence about Columbus's dependence on verbal information with the native inhabitants.

Some place names that appear to be in Castilian are, in fact, based on the Taino language and onomastics. For example, I argue that the very Castilian-sounding Columbian toponym *Isla Caracol* is in fact an adaptation of the difficult-to-pronounce Taino place name *Chacachacare*. Such acts of transforming a native name into a Castilian name based on incorporating its representative sounds can be found throughout the *diarios*. Transforming *Chacachacare* into a Castilian name is only in part an act of imposition of an imperialistic language. It also reveals a reliance on the language of the peoples whose hermeneutics and memories the imperialistic language tried to erase. Following the proposition of Robin Kearns and Lawrence Berg that resistance to naming can occur through the creation of alternative names and "the use of alternative pronunciations for established names,"[43] Columbus's creation of an alternative pronunciation of an established Taino place name puts him in the position of someone who is responding rather than imposing. The persistence of *Chacachacare* in the form of the Castilian *Isla Caracol* can also be seen as an act of silent resistance. As this book takes note of the influence, manipulation, and subversion that the Taino inhabitants exerted on Columbus and his crew, it acknowledges the impact they had on his itineraries, strategies, and views, all of which were expressed in his acts of naming.

The portion of my work related to the Taino and other indigenous contributions to the Columbian toponymic discourse relies on the studies of the Taino language and the linguistics of the Caribbean Basin by scholars such as Samuel M. Wilson, José Juan Arrom, Antonio M. Stevens-Arroyo, Douglas Taylor, and Arnold R. Highfield. In addition, my discussion of the native contribution and resistance builds on the works of scholars such as James Lockhart, Miguel León-Portilla, Karen Spalding, and Rolena Adorno, among others, whose studies of linguistic, textual, and archival material have dramatically changed our understanding of the response of the native people to the arrival of the Europeans in the Caribbean Basin and in all of South America. Furthermore, Peter Hulme, Philip P. Boucher, Carlos Jáuregui, Reniel Rodríguez Ramos, Kathleen Deagan, and José María Cruxent have made significant contributions to resisting the European stereotyped visions of native peoples by helping us understand the complex grid of their ethnic identities and the impact, even if indirect, they had on the emergence of Western philosophical traditions. My work builds on these and other studies with the hope of contributing to the growing field of literature that articulates the voices of resistance.

Following are some definitions of the terms related to the indigenous languages and cultures used in this book. The vast majority of indigenous toponyms incorporated into the Columbian toponymic discourse were from the Taino language and onomastics. Works by scholars such as Cayetano Coll y Toste, Rodolfo Cambiaso, and Rafael García Bidó provide valuable information for recovering the meanings of many of these. In addition to assigning a great number of place names to the islands, rivers, bays, mountains, and other places in the Greater and Lesser Antilles as well as further out,[44] the Tainos also had names for other peoples; for example, *Ciboney* is a Taino word that describes a non-Taino group of peoples who lived in the caverns in the more remote regions of the Antilles. I refer to all these toponyms incorporated into the Columbian toponymic discourse as "Taino" toponyms or "toponyms of Taino origins." I have also chosen the term "Taino" to refer to the language of the native people Columbus met during his first and later voyages. Though other terms to describe the predominant language, such as "Arawak" and "Island Arawak," are also in use, "Taino" has been generally accepted and it refers to the pre-Columbian language from the Arawakan or Arahuacan language family used by the pre-Columbian peoples. The term "Taino" avoids any confusion with the modern Arawakan languages spoken throughout South America. My use of the term "Taino" in this book to refer to the peoples inhabiting the lands reached by Columbus stems from Irving Rouse's study which defines the Taino as the central group who inhabited the Bahamas and all of the Greater Antilles except western Cuba. According to Rouse's definition, the term "Taino" includes several different ethnic groups that inhabited different islands, such as the Lucayo (those living in the Bahamian Archipelago, the group Columbus met first) and the Borinquen (living in what is now Puerto Rico). Rouse also distinguishes the Taino from the Island Caribs and from the mainland indigenous groups, the Arawaks.[45]

In addition to Taino, two other major languages were spoken in the Caribbean Basin: Igneri, which belonged to the Arawakan language family like Taino, and Island Carib. Other languages that were spoken throughout the islands of the Greater Antilles were the Ciguayo and the Guanahatabey languages, about which very little is known.[46] Research shows that many different ethnic groups were spread out through the Lesser Antilles, Greater Antilles, and Bahamas.[47] In the cases of some place names of clearly indigenous origins, it is difficult to know whether their origins lie in the Taino language or perhaps in another indigenous language such as Igneri, Island Carib, or another minor language or dialect such as the Ciboney or the language of the Guanahatabey in Cuba. Columbus may have acquired some non-Taino toponyms via his communications with the Tainos, rather than through direct contact with other groups. There is little evidence in the *diarios* that Columbus borrowed toponyms from the Igneri peoples or from other minor languages. In most cases, the indigenous toponyms documented in the *diarios* are of Taino origin. In some cases, they are Island Carib toponyms that have been incorporated into the Taino language, such as the word *carib* and the place name *Matininó*. When it is clear that Columbus incorporated a toponym from the language of the Island Caribs, I will be using the term "Island Carib" to refer to this form of speech in use by the Carib men at the time of Columbus's arrival. Since primary sources generally do not document the precise indigenous origins of toponyms, when these are not clear I indicate so by saying that the toponyms are of "indigenous," rather than Taino or Island Carib, origins. These terms and the linguistic situation in the Caribbean region are explained in greater detail in chapter 3 of this book.

Another important point in this book has to do with the portrayal of the Earthly Paradise and the infernal imagery in the context of the toponymy and the narrative of the *diarios*. One of the Crown's fundamental purposes was to bring Christianity to the "infidels," and the narratives documenting the Columbian naming enterprise are full of spiritual references. The act of naming itself is intimately related to the Christian ceremony of baptism, one of the elements of which is the act of blessing the child by giving him or her a new Christian name. This motif is well-worn in Western lore, such as in the case of Jacob who is renamed Israel.[48] Zamora argues that some place names occurring in Columbus's *diarios*, such as *Çipango*, *Zaitón*, and *Quinsay*, mark "an objective, practical, materialistic geography," while others, such as "San Salvador, Santa María de la Concepción, Monte Christo, río de Gracia, Cabo Sancto, Valle del Paraíso, and Mar de Nuestra Señora name a topography characterized by its edenic qualities."[49] The intent to baptize the infidel can be seen as an extension of the religious struggles over territories in the Iberian Peninsula between Muslims and Christians and the completion of the reconquest of Al-Andalus initiated by the Christians after the overrunning of the peninsula in 711 AD. Hence, renaming the lands in the Americas with Christian names was a metaphoric act that was intended to bring salvation to the infidel. Naming with religious toponyms was also an act of voicing a prophetic vision of Christian millenarianism and eschatology, the interest in both of which Columbus recorded not only in his *diarios* but also in his *Libro de las profecías*. However, in the accounts of the last two voyages, Columbus's descriptions of spiritual salvation and of the Earthly Paradise became tainted by infernal imagery. Chapter 6 explores this transformation in his perception of the world surrounding him and his own role in it through an analysis of the toponymic discourse of the third and the fourth voyages.

Furthermore, the influence and manipulation of the Taino people and other indigenous groups and Colombus's perception of the natural world seem to be, at least in part, related. Greenblatt argues: "Columbus may have thought that he was near to Paradise, but he also knew that he was the inheritor of Adam's sin through which, as Luther remarks, we lost Paradise as well as this power to bestow primal names and to compel through naming. In his letter, moreover, Columbus makes it clear that he is encountering not a world that has never before been named but rather a world of alien names: 'the Indians call it Guanahaní.'"[50] It seems that Greenblatt is not intentionally making a parallel between Adam's sin, Luther, or Paradise lost and the Taino toponym *Guanahaní*. However, in my analysis in the final chapter of the book I will argue, precisely, that the proliferation of Taino toponymy and the demonization of the indigenous peoples, together with the unusual natural phenomena and Columbus's exhausted physical and mental state, contributed to the increasing fragmentation of the Columbian toponymic discourse. Furthermore, I will argue that due to these factors, Columbus became increasingly uncertain about whether, instead of the Earthly Paradise, he may have instead reached the gates to Hell.

To continue discussing the complex, multidirectional relationships of power and of authority that took place during Columbian naming, this book borrows Gérard Genette's notion of mimology as "a relation of reflective analogy (imitation) between 'word' and 'thing' that motivates, or justifies, the existence and the choice of the former," which he defined in his *Mimologics*, the monumental work on the centuries of debates about the relationships between words and things.[51] This notion is useful and, at the same time, it can be only a starting point for considering Columbian naming. Columbus's decisions were not strictly acts of naming; rather, they were acts of un-naming, re-naming, translating, and mimicking. As a result, toponymies, cultures, visions, and landscapes were desecrated, fragmented, joined, and reinvented as the shapes of both words and things morphed and were broken to produce a new toponymy. For these reasons, thinking of Columbian naming as being fuelled primarily by resemblance is equally misleading.[52] Resemblance implies that names were fitted, rather comfortably, on the contours of the foreign landscape; instead, I will argue that these names were stretched, reshaped, broken down, and reassembled to fit the forms that they were not at all intended to fit.

Only when the uncomfortable nature of the unions that Columbian naming involved is recognized can we begin to question the authority of the European discourse and to allow fragments of the heritage of the Caribbean peoples, as well as of the shapes, aromas, tastes, and sounds of their lands, to seep through, recognizing that they altered decisively its very constitution. These theoretical elaborations have very concrete implications. The analogy between Adomite and Columbian naming, ironically, reinforces the very idea of nothingness that we write to denounce; as it negates the presence, even if subdued, of the voices and visions of the American native peoples, it recreates the emptiness of the continent and it emphasizes destruction over permanence. Can we really fathom that this metaphoric emptiness existed even in Columbus's mind at the time of writing in the ship logs? Invention did not occur in a vacuum simply because language was (and is) a space crowded with cultural and cross-cultural meanings and intersections. In this regard, Paul Carter's words about Cook's naming of places along the Australian coastline are pertinent here:

> The significance of this overdetermination of meaning does not lie in the direction of Cook's psychology, but in the revelation of the fact that Cook moved in a world of language. He proceeded within a cultural network of names, allusions, puns and coincidences, which, far from constraining him, gave him, like his Pacific Ocean, conceptual space in which to move. His was not the definitive univocal language of the dictionary. Unlike dictionary definitions, Cook's place names remained to be defined: they certainly claimed no finality or universal validity.[53]

Likewise, Columbus moved in a world in which words in the Castilian language had complex cultural, political, legal, and spiritual meanings that were the results of multiple intersections. The multi-referentiality of his place names is further reinforced by Columbus's own multi-linguistic background as well as his uncertain nationality, place of birth, and biography (such as his educational level). Not to be forgotten are his previous experiences in navigation which exposed him to the varied and likewise contested practices of naming by the Portuguese and the Catalans along the African coast and in the Atlantic. Moreover, the inevitable intersections between Columbian naming in Castilian and the Taino onomastics, the latter being also tainted with streaks of imperialistic use of language through which territories were appropriated and the self and others were defined, simply cannot be dismissed. Therefore, the rejection of the metaphor of Adomite naming in the Americas opens doors to the possibility that the imperialistic discourse was warped by subversion, that the evangelizing vision was not only imposed on the landscape and its people but also inspired and manipulated by them, and that the discourse of resemblance was fragmented into countless pieces that produced a mosaic from which entirely new pictures emerged.[54] As a whole, my reading does not reject entirely either the metaphor of the empty continent (Subirats) or that of kidnapping language (Greenblatt), both of which present insightful ways of thinking about the circumstances under which the European discourses changed the face of the Americas. It does aim, however, to supplement these interpretations by probing into those moments of vacillation and shadows of doubt clearly visible when Columbian naming is studied more closely, in which negotiation, translation, and confrontation can be witnessed.

The first question to ask, therefore, is not whether or not the analogy between the two moments of naming, the biblical and the Columbian, can be sustained at all but how the question of the origin of language can be adapted so it becomes relevant to the examination of the latter. There is no single way of thinking about naming, as Genette demonstrates in his long history of the intellectual debates on the subject of the relationship between words and things, beginning with his study of Plato's *Cratylus*, the first work dedicated exclusively to this subject, and ending with twentieth-century writers.[55] From among these various ways of thinking about the function of names in texts, one phrase seems particularly suggestive for my consideration of Columbian naming. It concerns a writer that Columbus could not have known and a way of writing that had nothing to do with the way Columbus wrote; perhaps the only thing they did have in common was a deep fascination with place names and with their functions in discourses. Genette's idea of "mutual contagion," which he uses to describe the relationship between names and things in Marcel Proust's fiction, helps us better understand the phenomenon, both invasive and evasive, that we think of as Columbian naming. "The mutual contagion of the name by the idea and the idea by the name" reflects, for the purposes of this book, what the term "naming" does not: the porous nature of Columbian naming and its anxious character as boundaries – geographic, linguistic, epistemological – were being uncomfortably broken, allowing organisms to travel.[56] Just as microbes, germs, and viruses were exchanged through air, water, clothing, and bodily fluids impacting fleshy substances of human, zoological, and botanical matter, similarly, place and proper names, words, gestures, signs, sounds, and manifestations of power were passed on, impacting the verbal, the epistemological, and the physical matters. Indigenous toponymy and language is only one element, though one of enormous significance, through which the mutual contagion between names and things, as well as between names and names, can be witnessed. The experiences had in the Americas as well as the visual, olfactory, and otherwise sensory features of the landscapes, shaped Columbian naming as well. A particularly powerful vehicle for the transfers of meaning was the visual, which, rather than being subject to the power of the gaze, exerted its own power on the gazer as it formed inescapable mental images.

If "mutual contagion" signifies an exchange, this exchange is enabled by a coming-together of two things or concepts, which, in its turn, occurs when a gap between them is erased or lessened. The first impulse for this book was born from my observation of the decided contrast between the namelessness of abstract territories in the "Capitulaciones" and the multiplicity of names in the *diarios* as one that may provide a clue about the motivation behind this tireless sequence of naming acts. During the writing of this book, various other pulsating, vivacious, inerasable gaps turned out to be likewise productive: those between the names already in existence and those being pronounced, between the king's and queen's expectations and Columbus's desires, between the Crown's ideology and the pragmatics of voyages, and between the orderly presentation of toponymy in the letter to Santángel and the cacophony of place names in the *diarios*.

The chapters in the book are organized both thematically and chronologically, and they follow the transformations of the Columbian toponyms viewed as a fluid and reactive discourse. Chapter 1, entitled "'Named Incorrectly,'" asks the question, what did historians around Columbus's time use as the basis for judging the "rightness" of a name? To shed some light on this question, the chapter delineates the historical context in which Columbus and his contemporaries addressed and debated the question of the "correctness" of a name as it considers the comments that Queen Isabel, Las Casas, Peter Martyr d'Anghiera, Gonzalo Fernández de Oviedo y Valdés (Oviedo), and Ferdinand Columbus, among others, made about the meaning of toponyms in legal, historical, and religious contexts. The chapter also considers two theoretical models – Ptolemy's instructions on drawing a map of the *oikoumenē* and Saint Augustine's semiotic interpretation of Adam's name – to understand two distinct ways in which Columbian naming can be approached: as a practical step for drawing a new navigational chart and as an act full of ideological significance. Chapter 2, "Words and the World," seeks to uncover some of the patterns and progressions in the Columbian toponymic discourse that were based on the principles of hierarchy, symmetry, and centre in medieval European culture. It provides an overview of Columbian place names from all four voyages, and it examines the various kinds of patterns that create an impression of order and control.

Chapter 3, "Y saber dellos los secretos de la tierra," demonstrates how expectations that Columbus had set up for his naming to institute a symbolic order were compromised as they clashed with the reality of the world he was confronting and, in particular, with the already existing onomastic structure of the Tainos. This chapter focuses on the place names that Columbus invented, based on the Taino toponymy and language, as well as the ways in which the indigenous inhabitants influenced, manipulated, and altered his views and his itineraries. The chapter also deals with the way documents, including the *diarios*, presented these conceptual and linguistic clashes, and how early modern redactors used editing techniques to recreate the symbolic order Columbus had failed to institute through his naming. This chapter points out some of the many instances in which Columbus expressed an interest in indigenous onomastics and the ways in which he sought to secure knowledge of it. It addresses the instances in which Columbus used physical force to compel the natives to provide him with knowledge about the lands, as well as the instances in which the latter shared this information willingly and even purposely manipulated him.

The final three chapters delineate the development of the rhetoric of the Columbian toponymic discourse by focusing on specific groups of toponyms organized according to their changing thematic focus. Chapter 4, "Heavenly Bodies and Metallurgy in Columbian Toponymy" addresses Columbus's interest and familiarization with alchemy and astrology evidenced by Columbus's naming of places after planet/metal pairs and by placing "gold" in the middle of the sequence to emphasize its supremacy among the metals. The chapter focuses on a group of place names from the first voyage connected thematically and named in geographic and temporal proximity – what I call a toponymic cluster – that was inspired by celestial bodies and metals. It argues that Columbus's two-month-long gold hunt placed serious challenges for his attempt to create symbolic order in his toponymy. The chapter also examines how the Taino manipulated Columbus's views and his altered itinerary by providing him with false geographic information connected to the place name *Isla Baveque*. It analyses Columbus's obsession with Baveque, the island where, according to native informants, enormous amounts of gold were to be found, and his long and ultimately unsuccessful search for it. The chapter argues that this obsession was a result of the conscious manipulation that the local inhabitants were able to exert on him and on his actions, itineraries, and process of naming.

The translation of signs and the circular transatlantic shifts between the Caribbean and the Andalusian landscapes is at the centre of chapter 5, "Iguana and Christ." Focusing on the toponym *Cabo de Sierpe*, or "Cape of the Iguana" in English, and its toponymic cluster, the chapter follows the route suggested by the toponyms, which begins with an iguana on the Caribbean beach and ends with a vision of Christ crucified on the mountain, passing through various visions in between. The chapter revisits the notion of resemblance that has been frequently evoked to describe

Columbian naming, and refutes it as one that fails to account for the multiple, intersecting correspondences between the European and American worlds. The analysis reveals how even a scene as deeply imbedded in the Christian tradition as that of the Crucifixion cannot be addressed independently of the tropical reality Columbus witnessed. As it examines the dialogue between the Caribbean and the Andalusian landscapes, the latter of which was frequently evoked through comparisons and adoptions of its toponyms, and the moulding of the contours of each to fit the other, the chapter argues that the visual image created as a result of this negotiation should not be viewed as an imposition of one landscape or vision on the other but rather as a disintegration of both, resulting in the creation of a third, hybrid, and grotesque, landscape.

Chapter 6, "Infernal Imagery," is centred on three toponyms invented during the third and the fourth voyages: *Boca de la Sierpe*, *Boca del Drago*, and *Isla de las Bocas*. This chapter reveals the ways in which the toponymic discourse of the third and fourth voyages becomes a record not only of Columbus's shortcomings as an colonizer and administrator, but also of his inability to establish, through language, the symbolic order he had promised to establish at the start of his voyages and writings. This failure is evidenced in the proliferation of Taino and other native toponyms and in the growing fragmentation of naming patterns during the last two voyages. The chapter addresses the complex image of the dragon as one having roots in indigenous, Asian, and European languages and mythologies. This image spans the various components that can be seen as forming part of the meaning of the toponyms *Boca del Drago* and *Boca de la Sierpe*, including the imagery of sea monsters on European maps of the time, the Apocalyptic discourse, and the figure of Hercules, who had fought monsters according to classical mythology. The chapter argues that *Boca del Drago* and *Boca de la Sierpe* showcase Columbus's failed effort to take possession of the landscape because of his failure to insert his own name onto it, and that they testify to Columbus's fear of being metaphorically, and literally, devoured by the very landscape he was attempting to subdue. I also argue that, contrary to the image of Paradise on which the narratives of the *diarios* of the last two voyages focus, the toponyms *Boca del Drago* and *Boca de la Sierpe* suggest he believed he had, instead, reached the gates to Hell.

This book is built on the framework of the comprehensive list of Columbian toponyms that I have compiled from various sources that document his four voyages to the Americas, which he called, until the very end of his days, the Indies, *Las Indias*. As explained earlier, I define the corpus of Columbian place names as consisting of both the place names he invented in Castilian and those he borrowed, translated, and otherwise incorporated from indigenous languages and toponymies. He subsequently imposed these names on places in the Caribbean and the coast of South America during his acts of verbal mapping that took place during his four transatlantic voyages. The sources I used for compiling the list, included in the appendix, are the following: Consuelo Varela and Juan Gil, editors, *Cristóbal Colón: Textos y documentos completos*, both the 1982 and 2003 editions; Ferdinand Columbus (Hernando Colón), *Historia del Almirante*, edited by Manuel Carrera Díaz; Bartolomé de Las Casas, *Historia de las Indias*, edited by Agustín Millares Carlo; Bartolomé de Las Casas, *Las Casas on Columbus: The Third Voyage*, edited by Geoffrey Symcox; Peter Martyr d'Anghiera (Pedro Mártir de Anglería), *The Discovery of the New World in the Writings of Peter Martyr of Anghiera*, edited by Ernesto Lunardi et al., and translated into English by Felix Azzola. In the appendix, the toponyms are listed in chronological order according to the dates on which they were introduced in the *diarios*, and they are accompanied by comments that Columbus, Las Casas, or other contemporary historians made about these place names in the primary sources. Such a listing appears here for the first time.

The exact number of place names that Columbus invented in the Caribbean and along the north coast of South America is unknown because the original ship logs have been lost and the estimates provided in contemporary accounts vary significantly. The letter to Santángel, for example, includes only six place names Columbus invented in Castilian; some historians, on the other hand, have claimed that Columbus pronounced as many as seven hundred toponyms during the first voyage alone.[57] Collectively, the *diarios* and letters and documents to and by Columbus, complemented by Las Casas's *Historia de las Indias*, Ferdinand Columbus's *Historia del Almirante*, and Peter Martyr d'Anghiera's *Decades of the New World* (*Décadas del Nuevo Mundo*), provide the great majority of known place names that Columbus invented and they have been used as the basis for this study. Most of the Columbian toponyms found in Fernán Pérez de Oliva's *Historia de la invención de las Indias*, Fray Ramón Pané's *Relación acerca de las antigüedades de los indios*, and Oviedo's *Historia general y natural de las Indias* are repetitions of those appearing in the texts by Columbus, Las Casas, Peter Martyr, and Ferdinand Columbus; the exceptions are the Taino names of places, people, and deities included by Pané, which are not included in the list in the appendix but which are accounted for in chapter 3. While this might not encompass every single Columbian toponym that has been registered in writing, it accounts for the great majority of them. Chasing any place names that may be lurking in the pages of other historical narratives or documents could easily turn into an endless endeavour, which most likely would not alter significantly the points made here. Since this is the first time that such a list has been compiled and published anywhere, I hope it will open doors to further studies of the implications and the nature of European naming acts in the Americas.

A few notes need to be made regarding the titles of the Columbian texts and the spellings of authors' names and place names used in this book. To distinguish between the original ship logs Columbus composed while on his voyages and the transcriptions that Las Casas made of them later, I use the term "ship log" or "ship logs" when referring to those original logs, which have been lost, and the complete text of which is hence unknown to us. When referring to the transcriptions Las Casas made of the original ship logs, which are the texts we use today when studying Columbus's writing about his voyages, I use Varela and Gil's 2003 edition of Columbus materials. To refer to the texts of the ship logs transcribed by Las Casas of the first, second, third, and fourth voyage, respectively, I use Varela's headings: *Diario del primer viaje*, *Relación del segundo viaje*, *Relación del tercer viaje*, and *Relación del cuarto viaje*; to refer to the composite of the transcriptions of all four voyages together, I use the plural *diarios*. Throughout the text, I use the following two names of authors as they are usually known in English: Peter Martyr (short for Peter Martyr d'Anghiera) and Ferdinand Columbus.

The spelling of the place names that Columbus invented in Castilian as well as of those he appropriated from the indigenous inhabitants, primarily the Taino, follows the version most consistently used throughout the *diarios* (thus, *Guanahaní* and not *Guanafaní*) and the variations are listed in parentheses in the appendix. The definite articles at the beginning of the toponyms have been deleted as they are not used consistently (thus, *Monte Cristo* and not *El Monte Cristo*); they have been preserved in the few cases in which they seem logically necessary (as in *Los Dos Hermanos*). All of the words (except for the articles and prepositions) have been capitalized in the toponyms, as would be customary in English despite the variations in this regard in the *diarios* and other primary sources (thus, *Cabo del Bezerro* and not *Cabo del bezerro* or *cabo del Bezerro*, although all such forms are used in the *diarios*). Throughout the book, the toponyms are italicized when they are used to refer to the name of the place rather than the place itself; they are not italicized when they refer to the place itself: hence, Isla Caracol is the largest island inside the Boca del Drago, while *Isla Caracol* is the place name that Columbus invented. In the case of the island of Hispaniola, I use "Hispaniola," the use of which is prevalent in criticism, to refer to the island itself, while I use *La Española* to refer to the name that Columbus invented since it is consistently used thus throughout the *diarios* and since it captures best Columbus's intended meaning.

1 "Named Incorrectly": The Geographic and Symbolic Functions of Columbian Place Names

Columbus finished the prologue to the *Diario del primer viaje* with a promise: "También, Señores Prínçipes, allende de escrevir cada noche lo qu'el día passare y el día lo que la noche navegare, tengo propósito de hazer carta nueva de navegar, en la cual situaré toda la mar e tierras del mar Occéano en sus proprios lugares, debaxo su viento."[1] Traditionally, this promise has been interpreted as an expression of the desire to make a new map and to mark on it the correct locations of places ("situaré ... en sus proprios lugares"), corresponding to their correct coordinates ("debaxo su viento").[2] The prologue either articulates Columbus's intention or, more likely, it sums up the actions already performed since it was probably written after the first voyage had been completed, as Zamora has argued.[3] As the *diarios* testify, Columbus made a long and detailed list of new and existing toponyms that indeed would have been useful for making a new navigational chart; many were soon made. And though none have survived, Columbus himself likely drew navigational charts which would have been kept in great secrecy. At the same time, he imbued his naming with spiritual, political, and ideological meanings. The promise articulated at the end of the prologue can also be interpreted metaphorically as an expression of the desire to create a new symbolic order in the unknown lands, with the help of the rhetoric of new place names. The acts of naming were also acts of imposing a new order, and the meaning of the new names, in relation to the existing names Columbus wove into his narrative, created an ideological vision of a world in which places were positioned in relation to the significant points in the tradition of medieval spiritual mapping, in particular, Jerusalem and the Earthly Paradise. These two uses of place names could be summed up as serving two distinct, though interrelated, goals: scientific / practical and ideological / spiritual.

The major cartographic traditions that inform these two functions of Columbian place names are portolan charts and medieval *mappae mundi.* The primary function of portolan charts was to record practical geographic information collected by seafarers during their voyages in a way that was most useful to future navigators. In the words of the scholar of cartography Tony Campbell, the portolan chart is "the clearest statement of the geographic and cartographic knowledge available in the Mediterranean."[4] Due to their intended pragmatic function according to Zamora, portolan charts were categorized by "austere realism."[5] Since portolan charts were concerned not with the depiction of spatial dimensions, but with navigational routes based on distances between points along the coast, they relied heavily on the use of toponymy. Toponymy, according to Campbell, was "the lifeblood of the portolan charts."[6] For today's historians of cartography, studying the toponymy registered in portolan charts has provided invaluable tools for understanding them, including dating individual charts and determining the interrelations among several of them.[7] In contrast, the goal of the medieval *mappa mundi* was the ideological mapping of geographic and mythical space. According to the historian of cartography David Woodward medieval *mappae mundi* have been long misunderstood as geographically inaccurate when in reality their intended function was not to provide an accurate representation of the space based on observation but rather to create ideologically meaningful landscapes.[8] According to Campbell, the differences between the two cartographic traditions formed a great "gulf [which] divided the portolan charts from the medieval *mappae mundi*, the cartographic content of which was largely shaped by their theological message."[9] The geography of the *mappa mundi* was framed by Christian concepts. In one type of the medieval *mappae mundi* known as T-O maps, the Earthly Paradise was typically located either in the east or in the north, and Jerusalem commonly marked the centre, despite the fact that it was well known that these were not their actual geographic locations on the physical landscape. To reinforce the theological message, the figure of Christ sometimes framed the image, as in the Ebstorf map (c. 1240), in which Christ's head, hands, and feet point to the four cardinal directions.

Ideology was of course not the sole purpose of medieval *mappae mundi.* In addition to representing visions of spiritual symbolism on landscapes, they also included accurate geographic information based on the knowledge available at the time. In his chapter titled "Medieval *Mappae mundi*," published in the founding multivolume work *The History of Cartography*, edited by J.B. Harley and David Woodward, Woodward addresses these various purposes of the European *mappae mundi* including their realistic and symbolic functions. Woodward refers to a series of articles in German by Anna-Dorothee von den Brincken in which she listed the place names appearing on twenty-one maps to demonstrate that medieval *mappae mundi* fulfilled both spiritual and historical functions. Among these, "in addition to the expected frequent occurrence of the centers of Christianity (Jerusalem, Rome, Constantinople, Antioch, and Patmos), a surprising number of secular places of historical interest are found – such as Olympus, Taprobane, and Pergamon – together with several secular places of particular interest at the time, such as Kiev, Novgorod, Samarkand, and Georgia."[10] Brincken concludes that this reveals the multiple functions that these *mappae mundi* fulfilled.

Both the portolan and the medieval *mappa mundi* traditions informed Columbus as he formulated his own goals related to the making of a new navigational chart or map. As a whole, the Columbian toponymic discourse manifests the coexistence of two different kinds of mapping. Many Columbian place names were assigned to places large and small, including islands as well as smaller geographic places such as promontories, bays, hills, and islets, and thus prepared the ground for making a practical navigational chart. At the same time, many of his acts of naming imbued this landscape with ideological and symbolic meaning similarly to the *mappa mundi* tradition. They did so through both the individual meaning of the place names he assigned and the collective meaning of the combinations of place names that created references to well-known narratives and visual sources and hence articulated theological and political messages. Chapters 5 and 6 of this book explore the re-creation of the imagery of the Earthly Paradise and Hell on the Caribbean landscape through naming of the scene of the Crucifixion. Among the Columbian place names, the spiritual / ideological category is also understood to include names of imaginary or mythical places whereas the current / historical category includes existing toponyms from Asia, Africa, and Europe as well as historical names of places. The Columbian toponymic discourse recorded in the ship logs and rendered at least partially in Las Casas's transcriptions incorporates names of concrete places known to the navigators and travellers from navigational charts, maps, and travel narratives, such as Japan (*Çipango*), Ireland (*Yrlanda*), and Arabia (*Aravia*). It also includes names for places along the coastline that Columbus was mapping, including names in both Taino and Castilian such as *Punta Aguda* and *Haiti*. At the same time, it incorporates numerous spiritual or ideological names which include some originating from the Old World with important spiritual or mythological significance, such as Jerusalem, the Earthly Paradise, and Mount Sion, and some ideologically charged names that Columbus invented in the Caribbean, such as *Isla Sancta* or *Isla Fernandina*. Moreover, the Columbian toponymic discourse also shows the fading boundaries between the two since, through his acts of naming, Columbus made ideological statements and also situated the places on the physical landscape and, possibly, on a physical navigational chart if he indeed made one. A name could both refer to a real place and have important ideological meaning, as in the case of Jerusalem and various names that Columbus invented in the Caribbean. Many Columbian place names should be viewed not as belonging to either the ideological or the empirical category as two mutually exclusive subsets, but rather as signs through which Columbus's ideological views are translated into points on a map. Through his acts of naming, Columbus created practical navigational directions and trade-route itineraries based on current geography while at the same time translating the earthly map into a mapping of a spiritual philosophy.[11]

Furthermore, two classical authors exemplify two distinct traditions for interpreting place names: Ptolemy (born c. 100 AD) and Augustine (354–430). For Ptolemy, names were practical instruments necessary for the technical process of drawing a map of the known world; for Augustine, the name of Adam was a coded, all-containing symbol that held in its very composition the divine wisdom about the entire world. For Ptolemy, names were a part of a map; for Augustine, the name of Adam was a map in itself. Columbus was familiar with writings by both of them. He made references to both Ptolemy and Augustine in his *diarios* and his letters, including the reference to Ptolemy in his well-known discussion about the shape of the earth resembling a woman's breast, as well as the reference to the *City of God*, in "Carta a los Reyes" of 1501,[12] and various other instances. Columbus had read Mark's Gospel and at least some of Augustine's commentaries on the Gospels. He also had transcribed selections from *The Homily of Saint Augustine on the Gospel according to Matthew*, *Of the Word of the Lord*, and *On the City of God* in the *Book of Prophecies*. Ptolemy and Augustine approached names and knowledge in radically different disciplinary contexts: geography and cartography, in the case of the former; theology, Christian exegesis, and semantics, in the case of the latter. The objectives that led the two authors to consider names were also different: development of scientific methods, in the case of the former; the search for the truth through commentary and symbolic interpretation, in the case of the latter. Names themselves fulfilled distinct functions in their works:

they served, for the former, only as rudimentary tools or as raw material, out of which a larger instrument for organizing existing geographical knowledge (a map) could be built; the latter identified the name of Adam as an object of interest in itself, and saw that it could be broken down into smaller pieces, each one of which contained part of the divine truth.[13] Exemplifying two different streams of thought and two distinct disciplinary and philosophical approaches to names, these two models shed light on the traditions that informed Columbus's naming in the Americas.

Ptolemy's *Geography* had an enduring influence on ancient, medieval, and early modern science. Ptolemaic maps are trapezoidal in shape, and they represent the *oikoumenē*, or the known part of the world spread out on a grid. The purpose of this map was practical, rather than ideological, as Samuel Edgerton commented: "No part of Ptolemy's map was emphasized as having ideological significance. It was completely ecumenical and nonmystical."[14] According to Ptolemy's instructions on how to draw a map of the *oikoumenē*, three distinct steps were necessary. The first step consisted of composing a detailed list of the names of all the places to be marked on the map later, including the names of provinces, cities, rivers, bays, and mountains. The other two steps were writing down their "accurate locations," that is, the degrees in longitude and latitude that describe the position of each, and finally, marking the localities on a map or a globe.[15] Of the three parts that comprise *Geography* itself, the second is made up solely of a very long list of place names accompanied by their coordinates in latitude and longitude, which were to be inscribed on the world map. The first part contains the instructions for drawing a world map on a globe and on a flat surface, while the third consists of captions or descriptive labels (*hypographē*) to be inscribed on the map.[16] Place names for Ptolemy served a pragmatic function: they were the labels that represented the known places on earth. "An imitation through drawing of the entire known part of the world together with the things that are, broadly speaking, connected with it" was achieved through a transfer of a written list of place names with their coordinates to a world map on a plane surface or a globe.[17] This process was governed by technical principles such as perspective, mathematical methods, and drawing technique. The correct placement of toponyms was based on the knowledge accumulated through various practices of scientific methods, including mathematical modelling, astronomical observation, and astrological speculations. It was also based on the empirical observations travellers had recorded in their accounts.[18] The meaning of the place names themselves was not important; for Ptolemy, place names allowed for communication and preservation of geographic knowledge. Moreover, each individual toponym and its placement on the map delivered only incremental value, for in itself it was only a tiny fraction of the parts of the map that made up the representation of regions. These representations taken all together made up the representation of the whole world. In Ptolemy's model, the toponyms collectively and the spatial relationships among them transmitted the wealth and complexity of accumulated geographic knowledge.

On the opposite end of the spectrum, for Augustine, names fulfilled an entirely different function.[19] He believed that a single name – that of Adam – contained ciphered in its very composition the divine wisdom about the composition of the entire world. In his commentary on Psalm 96, Augustine gave his readers a semantic analysis of Adam's name:

> For with righteousness shall He judge the world: not a part of it, for He bought not a part: He will judge the whole, for it was the whole of which He paid the price. Ye have heard the Gospel, where it saith, that when He cometh, He shall gather together His elect from the four winds. He gathereth all His elect from the four winds: therefore from the whole world. For Adam himself (this I had said before) signifieth in Greek the whole world; for there are four letters, A, D, A, and M. But as the Greeks speak, the four quarters of the world have these initial letters, 'Ανατολή, they call the East; Δύσις, the West; Άρκτος, the North; Μεσημβρία, the South: thou hast the word Adam. Adam therefore hath been scattered over the whole world. He was in one place, and fell, and as in a manner broken small, he filled the whole world: but the mercy of God gathered together the fragments from every side, and forged them by the fire of love, and made one what was broken.[20]

While according to Ptolemy's model, names had meaning when used collectively, for Augustine, a single name – that of Adam – encapsulated in its composition the meaning of the entire world. Its individual parts – the letters or signs – joined to form a complex sign, similar to how parts of the world had joined to form the world forged together "by the fire of love." The name of Adam was, for Augustine, a complex semantic symbol, the integral components of which represented the four parts of the world and the four directions (east, west, north, and south) that God had brought together during Creation. Though made up of only one word, Adam's name contained profound intuitive knowledge about God's love and Creation as well as about the basic geography of the world. The name was, therefore, a symbol that needed to be deciphered to access the divine truth it contained.

The consideration of names by Ptolemy and Augustine in addition to the cartographic traditions of portolan charts and medieval *mappae mundi* shed light on the different (though often overlapping) functions of the place names Columbus assigned throughout the four voyages. The lengthy list of place names and the descriptions of their location relative to other places already mentioned earlier is not unlike the catalogue of names Ptolemy had composed in preparation for the drawing of the map of the known part of the world. The most appropriate format for including all of the points marked by the place names Columbus invented in Castilian would have been on a navigational chart in the tradition of the portolan charts. At the same time, given the ideological and spiritual meaning of many of the names Columbus invented and the context of the existing names imbued with profound spiritual meaning he incorporated into his narrative, the pictorial representation resulting from transferring them onto paper could also have easily taken the form of a *mappa mundi*. Some of the place names Columbus assigned seem to have little significance besides the fact that they mark points on the geography, similar to the function of place names in Ptolemaic maps. Others are charged heavily with political or theological meaning becoming the axes of Columbus's ideological mapping through which a new symbolic order was created.

Given these various cartographic and philosophical traditions concerning the nature and the use of names, it is not surprising that both naming and the interpretation of names was during Columbus's time quite a contentious practice. Above all, interpreters seemed to share an anxiety about figuring out whether or not a given name was "right" and about whether an existing name was being interpreted correctly. Striking is the sheer number of instances in which contemporary authors scrutinize the meanings of place names, formulate their disapproval of those that appear to them poorly chosen, and express a desire to know more about names of places and proper names. Columbus himself voiced his opinion that place names could be chosen correctly and incorrectly and hence that they could be true or false, when he declared that the name of *Cabo Verde* (Cape Verde) was false: "Y llegado a las islas de Cabo Verde, de falso nombre, porque son atán secas que no ay cosa verde en ellas, y toda la gente enferma, que no me osé detener en ellas."[21] Ferdinand Columbus used a similar rationale to criticize *Buenavista*, the name of an island in the Cape Verde group: "se acercó a otra isla llamada Buenavista, nombre ciertamente alejado de la verdad, puesto que es melancólica y pobre."[22] Given that there were no written instructions on how names had to be chosen or who had the right to choose them, what did Columbus and his contemporaries use as the basis for judging the "correctness" or "incorrectness" of a name? Columbus's interpretation of the name *Cabo Verde* and his son Ferdinand's interpretation of *Buenavista* as false names were both based not just on one possible interpretation of the name but on a whole set. *Cabo Verde* failed to capture three specific features of the islands: the literal lack of greenery ("no ay cosa verde en ellas," which points to the failure of the name to provide a faithful description of the landscape), the dryness of the lands ("atán secas," which is a comment on its natural property), and even the sickness of the local inhabitants ("toda la gente enferma," which reveals the characteristics of the people that inhabit the place). *Buenavista* failed to encapsulate the feeling of melancholy ("melancólica") that the place inspires (presumably in those who visit it) and its overall poverty ("pobre"), though it is not specified whether this refers to its nature, people, or landscape. But why did the correctness of the name matter at all? In other words, what functions were those place names that had been chosen appropriately expected to fulfil?

It appears that the correctness of the name depended largely on the view of the interpreter, on the context in which the name was being discussed, and on the purposes for which the commentary of the name was being performed. The range of arguments, proofs, and narratives in contemporary historical and documentary sources in which place names are used as cornerstone evidence is quite astounding. In contemporary literature, place names are used in the context of arguments and discourses of legal, political, historical, theological, philosophical, and lyrical nature. Names were sometimes perceived as sources of specific historical information while at other times as rhetorical constructs useful for mapping an ideology or providing support for what might be a subjective argument. Sometimes their meaning was treated as literal or descriptive, while at other times it was interpreted in a symbolic fashion. Sometimes a commentary on a place name was included for the sheer narrative pleasure, even when it did not serve any particular goal. For example, Ferdinand Columbus inserted into his historical writing a belletristic interlude in which he deliberated upon the various possible meanings of *Cabo de Buena Esperanza*.[23] At other times, it served a specific rhetorical function like a springboard for propelling an argument in the desired direction, as when Las Casas used place names to support his argument about the need for spreading Christianity across the New World. Place names were even viewed as evidentiary material based on which proof could be built, as in the case of Oviedo and Ferdinand Columbus, both of whom used the name of the Hesperides Islands to argue Spain's ancient ownership rights to the Americas. The seriousness with which the interpretation of names and the acts of naming were treated and the privileged place they often received within historical texts shows that place names were viewed as powerful verbal paradigms.

In contrast to *Cabo Verde*, which Columbus viewed as poorly chosen, another name encapsulated for him geographic and ideological truths all in one. *Libro de las profecías*, known in English as the *Book of Prophecies*, which Columbus assembled in collaboration with Fray Gaspar Gorricio, consists of a large collection of quotes, most of which were taken from the Holy Scripture and from the texts devoted to exegesis. The second quote in the collection is a quadruplet from Jean Gerson's (1363–1429) *In Decretis*, which lists the four ways to interpret Holy Scripture, that is, literal, allegorical, moral, and anagogical: "Littera gesta docet; / quid credas, allegoria; / Moralis, quid agas; / quo tendas, anagogia." The quotation immediately following it is taken from *In Rationali divini offitii*, and it applies these principles to the interpretation of the place name *Jerusalem*: "The fourfold interpretation of Holy Scripture is clearly implicit in the word Jerusalem. In a historical sense, it is the earthly city to which pilgrims travel. Allegorically, it indicates the Church in the world. Tropologically, Jerusalem is the soul of every believer. Anagogically, the word means the Heavenly Jerusalem, the celestial fatherland and kingdom."[24] These two quotes were clearly important to Columbus as they inaugurate the collection and they suggest several things. First, they suggest that Columbus found the four principles used to interpret Holy Scripture useful for interpreting place names as well. Furthermore, they suggest that Columbus believed that a place name could contain more than one meaning and it could have both a practical use and a symbolic meaning. The same name could successfully be placed on a portolan chart and on a spiritual *mappa mundi*.

A name, therefore, could contain in it both information and symbolism and a single name was not limited to having only one meaning. Toponyms and proper names could contain in them rich meanings that needed to be deciphered. Precisely such was Columbus's signature or siglum and because of its mysterious nature historians are still unsure about its exact interpretation. Columbus frequently signed his letters with a siglum which consisted of seven letters distributed in a symmetrical fashion and the line Christ bearer, at the bottom:

.S.
.S.A.S.
X M Y
Xpo FERENS

Scholars have interpreted the last three letters as signifying Christ, Mary, and John the Baptist, and they have speculated that the three S's could symbolize the act of crossing oneself and the word "sanctum" repeated three times. Perhaps the most thorough examination of the design of his siglum is by Alain Milhou who interprets it in the light of Columbus's immersion in the Franciscan spirituality and scholasticism in fifteenth-century Spain. Milhou views the symbols used in Columbus's siglum as drawn from mysticism and humanism as well as from alchemy and kabbala. He also points to the evidence in some of Columbian place names (such as *Isla de la Trinidad* and those dedicated to the Virgin Mary) of his devotion to the Holy Trinity consisting, as is well known, of the Holy Father, the Virgin, and the Holy Spirit as well as Quaternity, which Milhou defines as "the Holy Trinity completed with the Virgin, wife of the Father, made fertile by the Holy Spirit and having become the mother of the Son").[25] It seems that Columbus intended for his siglum to contain complex and mysterious meanings encoded in the individual letters comprising it, not unlike the letters of Adam's name according to Augustine's interpretation.

For Las Casas, who also engaged in frequent interpretative exercises of place names (among them those invented by Columbus), a name was "right" if it encapsulated, as Aristotle had argued, the functions and properties of the thing or the place it identified ("propiedades y oficios de las cosas").[26] However, Las Casas's deliberation about the meanings of the names of two islands near the Strait of Gibraltar, *Islas Anegadas* (Sunken Isles) and *Islas Fortunadas* (Fortunate Isles), suggests that in his view, not a single property but a combination of several of them justified the individual meanings of each of the place names. Three properties motivated the name of *Islas Anegadas*, Las Casas claims: the first had to do with frequent storms and strong currents, because of which everything from the Mediterranean to the Strait of Gibraltar was deemed to be flooded by waters ("por estar todo anegado") (Las Casas does not specify what "everything" means, but presumably he refers to smaller islands covered by water); the second property affected the specific islands in the group known as *Islas Anegadas*, some of which were also hidden under water ("de la manera que ahora hallamos algunas islas o tierras anegadas en estas

Indias que están a las primeras tierras que topamos viniendo acá, y se llaman las *Anegadas*"); and the third property was based on the experience of the sailors in the vicinity of these islands, where many had drowned as their ships had sunk ("por las cuales aquel compás no se puede navegar, y ha acaecido perderse allí navíos").[27] Of the three properties that motivated the name, according to Las Casas's interpretation, two were related to the natural conditions of the place and its surroundings, while one was based on human experiences in that place or near it. As this example illustrates, historians of the time often had difficulty in pinpointing a single reason for the choice of a given place name. Instead, a combination of such reasons added specific aspects to the meaning of the name. Las Casas also applied the same principle to the interpretation of another name, *Islas Fortunadas*, which he believed was inspired both by the pleasant climate of the islands and the happiness of its inhabitants, "por la felicidad de la tierra," (because of the happiness of the lands).[28] In the case of all these place names, *Islas Fortunadas*, *Islas Anegadas*, *Cabo Verde*, and *Buenavista*, an interpretation based on only a single possible meaning would be limited and, ultimately, incorrect. This principle is important to keep in mind when considering the names that Columbus invented in the Caribbean, since they also exhibit a multiplicity of meanings.

For other historians, however, the "correctness" of a name lay not at all in its ability to faithfully describe the natural properties of the land or the mood it evoked. It also did not lie in the character of those living there or in the experiences of travellers. Instead, the name was deemed correct if it reflected a historical or political truth. This also meant that the correct interpretation of a true name could reveal such a historical truth. The pointed debate between Oviedo and Ferdinand Columbus about the meaning of the name of the Hesperides Islands demonstrates just how much weight both authors placed on the ability of a place name to aid in historical interpretation. Oviedo argued that the toponym *Hesperides* was derived from the name of the ancient ruler Hesperus, who once governed the lands now belonging to Spain; and since the historian identified the Hesperides Islands with the Americas, he consequently claimed that this interpretation of their name proved Spain's legal rights to their colonization. Deeply offended by such an affront to his father's achievement, Ferdinand rejected Oviedo's theory as "fábulas de poetas," and proceeded to prove him wrong by offering an entirely different interpretation of the place name in question. Quoting from Hyginus's compendium of classical myths titled *De poetica astronomia*, Ferdinand confidently concluded that the Hesperides were so named because of the planet Venus, "por la dicha estrella," another name of which was Hesperus.[29] What is striking in this debate, the actual meaning of Hesperides aside, is the complete faith with which both Oviedo and Columbus's son rely on the interpretation of a single place name to make such conclusive statements about Spain's legal rights to the colonization of the Americas or the originality of Columbus's idea. In cases such as this one, the authors did not view place names as descriptive, poetic, or symbolic; rather, they viewed them as verbal testaments of truths and used them in arguments of political, legal, and scientific nature, tracing them to specific prior textual sources.

Yet in the opinions of others, neither descriptive faithfulness nor historical accuracy played a role in determining the correctness of a place name. Instead, the name was considered to be correct if it was divinely inspired. Though not all divinely inspired names had to necessarily be religious, Columbus, a self-proclaimed messenger of God, viewed naming places with Christian names as part and parcel of spreading God's Word. In this regard, naming was an act of transferring a set of beliefs from one culture to another. Place names inspired by Christianity form the largest thematic group among the place names Columbus invented in the Americas, the most important function of which was the transferring of the Christian ideology from the Old World to the New. Christ's name itself was the metaphor of Christian faith, for which reason naming places after Christ or even saying his name in the New World was viewed as an act of spreading the Christian doctrine, an objective that is articulated in the *Relación del tercer viaje* ("divulgar *su sancto nombre y fe* a tantos pueblo").[30] Las Casas frequently commented upon Columbus's role as a divinely appointed messenger whose mission was to spread Christianity by making Christ's name known to the natives, "para publicar su nombre."[31] Ferdinand Columbus also exploited the idea that names could serve as vehicles for the transfer of ideas, or even of qualities, from one place to another and from one person to another. He suggested not only that Columbus's first and last names reflected, as if by a mysterious design ("misterioso designio") his deep religious faith, but that they predicted his role as divine messenger who would carry the Word to the peoples of the New World. This role, according to Ferdinand's interpretation, was encoded in his father's first name, in both its Italian and Latin forms, as *Colombo* in Italian means "dove," while *Cristóbal*, derived from *Christophorus*, alludes to Saint Cristopher (*San Cristóbal*), who had carried the Christ Child across the river.[32] Ferdinand further argued that his father's last name in its Latin form, *Colonus*, was a metaphor of his own function as a vehicle through which Christianity was transferred to the peoples of the Caribbean. Having first exploited the character traits of other "ilustres Colones" that were known to have lived, even if they had no relationship to his father whatsoever, and having suggested that his father shared some of the character traits with the former simply because they did share a name, Ferdinand applied the same argument to the indigenous inhabitants of the Caribbean islands. He stated that, as the latter became recipients of Christianity, they acquired his name as well and, since *Colón* in Greek meant "member," they became known as *Colones*, that is, members of Christianity.[33] Ferdinand's detailed dissection of his father's first and last names in three languages communicates just how significant he considered names, both proper names and place names, to be.[34]

Making Christ's name known to the natives was viewed as a metaphoric act of spreading the Christian doctrine among the inhabitants in the New World. Naming places with Christian names, marking them on navigational charts, and literally marking the landscape with Christian signs were acts of imposing the new ideology onto the landscape, literally and metaphorically. Following Columbus's instructions, signs of the Cross were placed in visible places and the names of the king and the queen were carved on the trunks of great trees:

> Item pues con el ayuda de Nuestro Señor avéis de andar mucha tierra, será bien e en todo caso, por doquiera que fuéredes, *por todos los caminos e sendas fazed poner algunas cruzes altas y mojones y asimismo cruzes en los árboles y cruzes en los logares que viéredes que son convenientes*, e do no se pueden así caher, porque allende qu'es razón que así se faga, pues, loado Dios, la tierra es de cristianos, aprovecharéis mucho por la perpetua memoria que d'ellas se avrá, e aun *faziendo poner en algunos árboles altos e grandes los nombres de Sus Altezas*.[35]

As he marked the foreign landscapes with both physical symbols and verbal signs of Christianity, Columbus was continuing the project of the reconquest that the king and queen had just finished on the Iberian Peninsula. Columbus viewed his own role as one of a vehicle for the transfer of the spiritual concepts to the native peoples, as a receptor of the divine inspiration, and as someone through whose lips divine truth was spoken.

The fervour with which Columbus and his contemporaries commented on the meanings of historical and mythical place names indicates that naming and the interpretation of names were approached as acts that had serious implications. They could be used as part of the legal proof about political ownership and claims to discovery as in the case of the *Hesperides*

Islands. Names were often not only powerful rhetorical constructs but imperialistic tools for bringing a new religion and ideology to the peoples being subjugated. Yet other names such as *Cabo Verde* appeared to have been assigned without such symbolic purposes in mind. The list of place names Columbus pronounced in the Caribbean included both kinds. If all of the place names could be located on a navigational chart, many of them could also be placed on a map that articulated the symbolic meaning of the landscape. Both Columbus and Las Casas took painstaking efforts to explain and justify many Columbian place names, whether based on a metaphoric or literal interpretation of their meanings. Columbus's names were filled with symbolic meaning and if they were not, they referred to some characteristic of the place: a shape, animal footsteps, the visual features of the landscape. Moreover, very often the physical features inspired the symbolic meanings that were in some ways associated with the former. There were no *cabos verdes* on Columbus's list.

2 Words and the World: The Known Corpus of Columbian Place Names

Columbus was one of the most prolific inventors of names in history. Reportedly, he pronounced as many as 700 toponyms during the first voyage alone and another 1700 during the second voyage.[1] While these numbers are almost certainly exaggerated, the list of Columbian place names in the *diarios* is nevertheless substantial: the *diarios* of the four voyages include 130 toponyms that Columbus invented in Castilian (including the additional pages Las Casas transcribed of the third voyage) and twenty-six toponyms of Taino and Island Carib origins. Other sources include additional toponyms.[2] Seventy new toponyms in Castilian are introduced in the *Diario del primer viaje*, while the *relaciones* of the subsequent voyages document significantly fewer new place names: twenty are mentioned for the first time in the *Relación del segundo viaje*, eight in the *Relación del tercer viaje*, and eight in the *Relación del cuarto viaje*. In addition, Las Casas included another thirty-four Castilian toponyms in the summary of the third voyage that he had not included in the *Relación*. The summary was a narrative Las Casas composed based on Columbus's original ship log, and he later used it to write his *Historia de las Indias*. He transcribed parts of it literally in his *Historia*; at other times, he provided additional commentaries to accompany the portions from the summary copied in *Historia*.[3]

Among the contemporary sources other than the *diarios*, Las Casas's *Historia*, not surprisingly, includes the most Castilian and Taino place names from the Caribbean Basin in addition to those listed in the *diarios*. Unfortunately, the authorship of many of the place names listed in the parts of *Historia* that deal with the four Columbian voyages but which were not included in the *diarios* is uncertain. For this reason, these toponyms have not been the focus of this study. Other contemporary sources, including Ferdinand Columbus's biography of his father, Peter Martyr's *Décadas*, Oviedo's *Historia Natural*, Oliva's *Historia de la invención de las Yndias*, and Las Casas's *Apologética Historia*, list only a handful of place names other than those that are mentioned in the *diarios*, which we could reasonably assume to have been assigned by Columbus. My study includes the place names from these contemporary sources but dedicates to them only marginal attention while focusing on the Castilian, Taino, and hybrid place names introduced in the *diarios*. In addition, Pané's *Relación acerca de las antigüedades de los indios* and Las Casas's *Historia* both provide valuable Taino place names as well as names of chieftains, deities, and mythical beings.

Given these textual circumstances, it is likely that the list of place names used as a basis for this study and provided in the appendix is partial. It is quite possible that, as Las Casas was preparing the *diarios*, he did not copy all of the Castilian and Taino place names that Columbus had recorded in his ship logs. The sections that the friar edited, condensed, and deleted must have included additional toponyms that were lost. The fact that omissions of place names occurred is apparent from the ways in which the *diarios* introduce some of the toponyms. In more than one instance, the place name is introduced for the first time accompanied by a qualifier such as *dicho*, *aquel*, or *este* ("the said," "that," or "this"), which implies that the place name had already been mentioned earlier, perhaps in a section that has been deleted. One example is the toponym *Puerto del Prínçipe* which is introduced on 18 November 1492 as "el dicho Puerto del Prínçipe" (the said Port of the Prince), though the *Diario del primer viaje* contains no earlier references to it. Another example is the toponym *Puerto de Mares* which is first introduced on 5 November as "aquel puerto de Mares" (that Port Mares), when the earlier pages of the *diarios* have not made any references to it.[4]

Another reason why the list provided here is probably incomplete is simply because it includes only the place names that were written down. We could think of naming as consisting of at least three steps. The first step occurred in the name-giver's mind, and it consisted of his conceptualizing the name and its relation to the place. The second step occurred when the name-giver pronounced the new name out loud in the presence of someone else such as a scribe or a larger audience, as during the ritual of taking possession. The final step occurred when the name was recorded in a document such as a ship log. One could also argue that an additional step occurred when the name became institutionalized as when it was included on a map and perhaps also became widely accepted as the name by which that place would be known, a fate that only a handful of the Columbian place names enjoyed. The only names that are available to us are those that Columbus wrote down and Las Casas transcribed. If, as some historians have argued, Columbus kept two ship logs (i.e., an official version and a secret version with notes, the true distances navigated and any other information not meant for the crew's eyes), the secret ship logs could have contained additional place names that were not transferred to the official version. Similarly, if Columbus drew any maps beyond the sketch of the coast of Hispaniola attributed to him, there is no way of knowing what place names he perhaps recorded on them. Any such maps were kept as strict state secrets and today they have been lost. To summarize, the selection of place names that has reached us is a partial list of the place names Columbus invented and wrote down in his ship logs and which Las Casas included in his transcription. The uncertainty of the completeness and the order of the place names included in the *diarios* also prevents us from identifying an accurate chronology of when places were named.[5]

A Quest for Order

Despite its incomplete nature, the list of Columbian toponyms that is available to us is valuable for gaining a deeper understanding of the processes that governed Columbus's acts of naming, the rhetoric they created, and the dynamic relationship between the words and the landscape. As was noted in chapter 1, the prologue to the *diarios* stated two different but overlapping functions of Columbian toponyms. One function was practical: naming places was a necessary step for preparing a navigational chart of the lands previously uncharted by the Europeans.[6] The other function was symbolic and it had to do with formulating a rhetoric of the new order of this part of the world. Columbus used various strategies to create a discourse that would exude a sense of order, control, natural harmony, and the potential for spiritual well-being. Much of this sense was related to the belief of early Christian and medieval thinkers that the divinely inspired world reflected the logic and the harmony of Creation. The references to hierarchy and structure also recreated familiar power and hierarchy patterns in the Caribbean landscape. Some of the discursive tools Columbus employed to create an impression of power and control through naming were toponymic clusters, principles of symmetry, progressive sequences based on hierarchies, arranging of subjects according to the chronology of Creation, and constructing a narrative sequence that mirrored those of the medieval epistolary genre and that of *relaciones*. The proliferation of toponymy originating from Taino and other indigenous languages and toponymies in the third and especially the fourth voyage together with the disappearance of toponymic clusters and sequences expressing symmetry and hierarchies indicate an overwhelming sense of chaos as an expression of Columbus's inability to subdue the unknown landscape through the ritual acts of naming.

Thematic Categories

The table below summarizes the thematic categories of the place names Columbus invented in Castilian and adopted from the Taino toponymy or language during the course of the four voyages. The toponyms listed in the second column are representative examples and they are not meant to provide an exhaustive list.

It is important to note that a number of the toponyms can be placed simultaneously in several categories: the physical world, philosophy, mythology, and spirituality. For example, Columbus had likely read in Marco Polo's *Travels* about the large quantities of pearls, gold, and precious stones found in Japan and China, and so *Golfo de las Perlas* could be considered a toponym tainted with Asian nostalgia. However, together with the toponyms *Isla Margarita* and *Boca del Drago*, it also evokes the legend of St Margaret of Antioch whose symbol was the pearl and who had been swallowed by Satan in the shape of a dragon. Columbian toponymy evokes several other well-known Christian and classical legends: for example, *Cabo de Sierpe* evokes the biblical stories associated with the serpent and *Cabo del Bezerro* evokes the legends about sea monsters or, alternatively, the golden calf in the Bible (since the primary meaning of the word *bezerro* is "calf").

It is also noteworthy that, in many cases, toponymy articulates different messages than those recorded in the narrative of the *diarios*, and the emphasis that the *diarios* place on certain subjects is not always repeated in the choice of place names. Given the importance that the *diarios* grant to Spain and the mercantilist nature of the voyages, one would expect to see a great number of places named related to these themes. This is not the case. In his toponymy, Columbus dedicated rather little attention to the royal family (four toponyms) although the letter to Santángel leads us to believe the contrary. The letter claims that the third, fourth, and fifth toponyms Columbus had pronounced were dedicated to King Ferdinand, Queen Isabel, and Prince Juan, whereas in the *Diario del primer viaje* they appear as the third, fourth, and twenty-sixth in the list, respectively. The only two other toponyms that belong to this category are the nineteenth toponym in

Thematic focus	Examples
Related to Native Cultures	
Taino and hybrid toponyms based on Taino, Island Carib and possibly other indigenous place names, words and fragments of speech	*Guanahaní, Monte Caribata, San Telmo de Xamaná*
Observations related to the native cultures:	
Dwellings	*Puerto de las Cabañas*
Weapons	*Golfo de las Flechas, Puerto de las Flechas, Cabo de las Flechas*
Spiritual	
Christ the Savior	*Isla San Salvador, Río y Puerto de San Salvador, Monte Cristo*
Virgin Mary and the Marian attributes	*Mar de Nuestra Señora, Isla de Santa María de la Concepción, Puerto María*
Christian saints and the liturgical calendar	*Puerto de Santa Catalina, Puerto de la Mar de Sancto Thomás, Cabo Sant Theramo, Puerto de San Nicolao, Isla Ioana, Puerto de la Navidad, Villa de la Navidad*
Sacred and the spiritual realms	*Valle del Paraíso, Río de Gracia, Cabo del Angel*
Referencing the Old World	
Dedicated to the Crown and the Royal functionaries	*Fernandina, Isabela, Juana, Puerto del Prínçipe, Cabo de Torres*
Spain	*Río Guadalquivir, Cabo de Campana, Islas de Arena, Punta del Arenal*
Portugal and Portuguese toponyms	*Valle del Paraíso, Río del Oro*
France	*Cabo Françés*
Scientific/philosophical	
Cosmography and geography	*Río del Poniente, Cabo Fin D'España, Alpha et Omega, Puerto del Retrete*
Cosmos	*Río de la Luna, Río de Mares, Puerto de Mares, Río del Sol*
Metals and stones	*Río del Oro, Monte de Plata, Punta del Hierro, Puerto de Plata, Golfo de las Perlas*
Visual	
Aesthetics	*Cabo Lindo, Cabo Hermoso, Cabo Belprado, Isla Belaforma, Belporto*

(*continued*)

Thematic focus	Examples
Landscape features	*Cabo de la Laguna, Cabo del Isleo, Cabo del Monte, Islas de Arena, Cabo de Palmas, Isla de las Pozas (or Isla de las Bocas), Punta de la Playa*
Shapes and sizes	*Isla Llana, Cabo del Pico, Punta Pierna, Punta Lançada, Punta Aguda, Cabo Redondo,*[7] *Cabo Tajado, Cabo Alto y Baxo, Punta Roxa, Cabo de Campana, Punta Llana, Puerto Gordo*
Physical senses	*Isla Buenavista, Cabo de Sabor, Cabo Rico*
Related to the Human World	
Kinships and emotions	*Peña de los Enamorados, Cabo del Enamorado, Isla Amiga, Cabo de Padre y Hijo, Los Dos Hermanos*
Currency	*Cabo de Cinquin*
Body parts	*Punta Pierna*
Related to the Natural World	
Flora	*Cabo de Palmas*
Fauna:	
Likely witnessed (monkeys)	*Puerto de Gatos*
Likely imagined	*Cabo del Elefante*
Marine life	*Cabo del Bezerro,*[8] *Cabo de Lapa, Isla de la Tortuga, Isla Delfín, Isla Caracol, Cabo de Conchas*
Aviary (mythical)	*Isla Martinet*

the sequence, *Puerto del Prínçipe*, possibly dedicated to Prince Juan, and the name of the town Columbus built during the second voyage, *Isabela*.[9] *Cabo de Torres* is a rare example of a place name possibly dedicated to a royal functionary, Antonio de Torres. Equal importance is given to the life and culture of the Taino people: four toponyms in this category invoke both a seemingly peaceful visit to a fishermen's village ("Hallaron ciertas casas de pescadores ... Púsole por nombre el Puerto de las Cabañas"),[10] while three more recall a violent encounter ("pelearon muy fuertemente, y fueron feridos tres personas de los nuestros con frechas" – hence the names *Golfo de las Flechas*, *Puerto de las Flechas*, and *Cabo de las Flechas*).[11] Other categories that receive similar attention to the royal family or Spain include landscape features (seven toponyms) and the cosmos (four toponyms).

Only one place name refers directly to Spain: *Española*. Its placement as the mere thirty-fourth toponym in the list of seventy assigned during the first voyage contrasts starkly with the central importance given to it in the letter to Santángel. Other references to the Iberian Peninsula were almost all inspired by places in Andalusia, and Columbus assigned almost all of those place names during the first voyage. Las Casas comments that at least two of these toponyms, *Río Guadalquivir* and *Cabo de Campana*, were inspired by physical resemblance: "Puso nombre ... al río Guadalquivir, porque diz que así viene tan grande como Guadalquivir por Córdoba" and "y le avía pareçido la tierra de Campana."[12] Echoes of other names of places in the vicinities of Seville, through which the Guadalquivir flowed – such as *Campana* and *Puerta del Arenal* – can be found in Columbian place names in the New World such as *Islas de Arena*, *Punta del Arenal*, and *Cabo de Campana*. Of the latter, *Islas de Arena* may also evoke a geographic feature of the landscape; as Las Casas suggests: "que llamó las islas de Arena, por el poco fondo que tenían de la parte del Sur hasta seis leguas."[13]

The narrative of the *diarios* also underscores the natural beauty of the Caribbean landscape, recreating the *locus amoenus* of the medieval tradition. In contrast, the Columbian toponymic discourse contains a surprisingly small number of toponyms that exalt the beauty of the Caribbean landscape. Only three such toponyms were assigned during the first voyage (*Cabo Lindo*, *Cabo Hermoso*, and *Cabo Belprado*) and just two more during the third and fourth voyages (*Isla Belaforma* and *Belporto*). This particular case may suggest that Columbus saw naming as an act that had political, ideological, and spiritual significance. In it, personal observations such as exclamations about beauty had little place. At the same time, the Columbian toponymic discourse formulated its own rhetoric, which in many cases differed from that of the narrative of the *diarios*, which were also mediated by Las Casas's pen. Other subjects such as alchemy or mythical animals, which are not discussed much or at all in the *diarios*, nevertheless yield various place names. In short, there is a clear disjunction between the themes emphasized in the narrative of the *diarios* and those that are salient in the Columbian toponymic discourse. The disjunction is significantly more jarring if one is to compare the Columbian toponymic discourse to the text of the letter to Santángel or the highly selected list of toponyms included in it. It is important to consider what this disjunction implies and the reasons why Columbian toponyms formulate a rhetoric that in some ways differs from the messages articulated in the *diarios*.

In contrast to the little emphasis placed on the relations with Portugal in the *diarios*, Portuguese toponymy left a visible trace in the Columbian toponymic discourse. *Valle del Paraíso*, the thirty-eighth toponym Columbus invented during the first voyage, may be a reference to *Vale do Paraiso* on the western coast of Portugal. Several Columbian toponyms recall toponyms pronounced by the Portuguese along the African coast. Many of the toponyms that the Portuguese assigned in the Atlantic and on the African coast over the course of the fifteenth century were recorded in the manuscript containing a list of *epístolas*, which was later published under the title of *Manuscrito de Valentim Fernandes*. Valentim Fernandes was a German printer and he divulged the geographic achievements of the Portuguese explorers. For example, the Columbian *Río del Oro* may have been inspired by, among other things, the Portuguese toponym *Rio do Ouro*.[14] In contrast, the solitary reference to France in the Columbian toponymic discourse (*Cabo Françés*) may be an allusion to the rivalry between the Spanish and the French Crowns in the matters of exploration and potential conquest of yet unclaimed (by Europeans) lands in the Atlantic. Furthermore, the fact that no Columbian names at all make a reference to Italy or Genoa is notable, especially given the prevalent theory about Columbus's birth in a village outside of Genoa. Given this long list of place names Columbus invented it would seem that he could have easily dedicated at least one place name to his birth town, wherever this town was. However, rather than proof that Columbus was not Genoese after all, this apparent omission is consistent with his overall reluctance to do homage in his naming to any places or people significant to him personally. This further suggests that Columbus saw the naming of places as an official enterprise, the implications of which were in the cosmographic, political, and spiritual spheres and in which personal biography had little if any relevance.

Christian toponyms comprise significant numbers in the Columbian toponymy: twenty-one out of seventy-three Castilian toponyms in the *Diario del primer viaje* are related to an aspect of Christianity. It is possible that Las Casas, who commented about religious toponyms frequently in the *diarios*, may have accentuated the religious theme in the Columbian toponymy by taking greater care when transcribing these names.[15] On the other hand, Las Casas frequently inserts secular names without commenting on them; for example, see the case of *Río de Mares* ("Vido otro río muy más grande que los otros, y así se lo dixeron por señas los indios ... llamó al río el río de Mares") and the case of *Isla Amiga* ("una ileta llana que en el medio ay, que le puso nombre la Amiga").[16] However, even accounting for the possibility of Las Casas's editing, the relative weight of religious toponymy in the Columbian toponymic discourse is significant. This suggests that Columbus saw Christian dogma as an important component in the formulation of the ideological rhetoric inscribed in the new toponymy of the lands he was surveying. This is also consistent with the tradition of the *mappa mundi* in which spiritually charged names were essential.

Other subjects salient in the Columbian toponymic discourse include celestial bodies (*Río de la Luna*, *Río del Sol*) as well as shapes and colours of the landscape (*Isla Llana*, *Cabo Lindo*, *Punta Pierna*, *Punta Aguda*, *Cabo Redondo*, *Cabo Tajado*). Land and sea animals also make an appearance (*Isla de la Tortuga*, *Cabo del Elefante*). Exotic names, words, and sounds, spoken by those who inhabited these lands and incorporated into hybrid Taino-Castilian and Island Carib-Castilian toponyms, are incorporated into the story as well (*Cabo de Cuba*, *Monte Caribata*, *San Telmo de Xamaná*).[17] Several toponyms encapsulate the idea of an ideal and prosperous landscape in which the earth engenders precious metals (*Río del Oro*, *Monte de Plata*). Human figures and expressions of human relationships are also notable (*Cabo de Padre y Hijo*, *Cabo del Enamorado*, *Peña de los Enamorados*). The first part of the naming endeavour ends with two names (*Golfo de las Flechas*, *Puerto de las Flechas*) that remind the reader, once again, of the local inhabitants of the lands and the increasingly conflictive relations with them.

In contrast to the naming of the river *Río del Oro*, as if foreseeing the meagre profit that the enterprise of the Indies would bring for him and his descendants, Columbus named a cape, *Cabo de Cinquin*. The *cinquin* was a coin of very low value and it was common in Castile and throughout the Mediterranean. This is the only toponym related to money. In his ship log, Columbus describes showing the natives the most valuable gold coin known as *excelente*, on which the image of the king and queen was imprinted: "Yo enbié por unas cuentas mías adonde por un señal tengo un exçelente de oro en que está[n] esculpido[s] Vuestras Altezas y se lo amostré, y le dixe otra vez como ayer que Vuestras Altezas mandavan y señoreavan todo lo mejor del mundo, y que no avía tan grandes prínçipes, y le mostré las vanderas reales y las otras de la Cruz, de que él tuvo en mucho, 'y qué grandes señores serían Vuestras Altezas!' dezía él contra sus consejeros."[18] However in his toponymy he chose to refer to *cinquin*, a coin that speaks neither of significant capital gains nor of successful imperial expansion.[19] Again, this contradicts the messages articulated in the narrative of the *diarios* where the riches of the Indies are underscored at every available opportunity.

Some categories that do not contain numerous toponyms are nevertheless present consistently in all four voyages. One example is the theme of cosmography. *Río del Poniente* (first voyage) formulates the cosmographic concept of sailing west to arrive east. *Cabo Fin D'España* (second voyage) refers to the great distance between the Indies and Spain and the resulting extension of the nascent Spanish empire. *Alfa et Omega* (third voyage) expresses the idea of the beginning and the end, the meeting of the two extremities of the world and of Columbus's eschatological mentality. *Puerto del Retrete* (fourth voyage), from *retirar* and *retirado*, encapsulates the sense of finding oneself in a place situated at a great distance from the familiar world. In contrast, the toponyms dedicated to the royal family, for example, were given only during the first voyage.

Furthermore, many of the place names in the Columbian toponymic discourse can be organized in toponymic clusters. I call a toponymic cluster a thematically, temporally, and geographically cohesive set of place names, which articulates a specific idea or scene. My definition and exploration of this concept begins in chapter 4 and continues in chapters 5 and 6.

The Old World Toponymy

In addition to the names Columbus assigned to places in the New World, the *diarios* mention places from the entire known world and makes references to geographical discoveries, imperial conflicts, spiritual destinations, and mercantilist routes. The *diarios* list dozens of known Old World toponyms, which refer to real places in Europe, Africa, Asia, and known islands in the Atlantic. Columbus compares the exotic places he sees to those that are familiar to him, looking for similarities and pointing out the differences in nature, kinds of fruits, trees, animals and fish, climate, people, dress, houses, customs and values, landscapes, smells, bird songs and other sounds, variations in temperature, and the position of stars. Other place names are based on travel accounts, navigational charts, and *mappae mundi*.

References to Europe are not limited to Castile, Andalusia, and Portugal, although these references are the most numerous. Columbus also speaks of places in the south of Europe, including Italy (Rome, Florence, Sicily, Pisa), France, Greece (Chios Island), and Corsica. In the north, he speaks of Flanders, Scotland, Ireland, and England. In his mercantilist discussions and geographic explanations, he refers to the islands of the Azores and of the Cape Verde colonized by the Portuguese in the Atlantic. When describing the indigenous inhabitants and bringing up the subject of slaves, he frequently remembers African territories, including Guinea and its

Malagueta coast, Ethiopia, Egypt, and Sierra Leone. The native inhabitants' ways of dressing and the spices they use remind Columbus of exotic places such as Egypt, Armenia, Syria, and Persia. He praises the plentiful rivers in the uncharted lands comparing them to Spain's three prides, the Guadalquivir, the Ebro, and the Tagus. He also compares them to the four greatest rivers in the world that, according to classical authorities, indicate the proximity of the Earthly Paradise: the Nile, the Ganges, the Euphrates, and the Tigris. Columbus also refers to the discoveries of earlier travellers and the descriptions of the world by ancient philosophers who provided information about Mesopotamia, Alexandria, and the Dead Sea. The reconquest of Jerusalem is one of Columbus's declared goals, and there are various references to Jerusalem in the *diarios*. He also expresses his desire to reach the Taprobane island depicted in the last of twelve maps Ptolemy dedicated to Asia in his *Geography*. Though these toponyms are not part of what I here call the Columbian toponymic discourse, they situate the Columbian place names in a geographic context of territories that had already been mapped and the names of which were familiar to Columbus.

Symmetry

Medieval humanists, mystics, and theologians viewed symmetry as an expression of divine order in such constructs as the Holy Trinity and Quaternity (consisting of the Holy Trinity completed by the Virgin made pregnant by the Holy Spirit with the Son),[20] and the Ave-Eva, in which symmetry fulfilled the function of a symbol. In painting and sculpture, symmetry was the single most important visual and symbolic tool for arranging images and shapes. Columbus was undoubtedly informed by these traditions, and the siglum that forms part of his signature is also built on the principle of symbolic symmetry.[21] In the Columbian toponymic discourse, symmetry is expressed either through pairs of synonymous place names (as in the case of the toponyms *Boca de la Sierpe* and *Boca del Drago*) or opposite ones (*Monte Cristo* and *Cabo de Sierpe*). In addition, some individual toponyms comprise two concepts that either mirror one another (*Los Dos Hermanos*) or that have the opposite meanings (*Cabo Alto y Baxo*, *Cabo de Padre y Hijo*, and *Cabo de Alpha et O*).

The toponym *Cabo de Alpha et O*, which Columbus assigned during the second voyage, illustrates the importance of symmetry in Columbian toponymy. It reflects the meanings of the letters *alpha* and *omega* used profusely in the iconography of Christian art and other Western cultural expressions. It expresses several opposing ideas: the beginning and the end, the east and the west, the rising and the setting of the sun.[22] In medieval Europe, churches were built oriented from the rising to the setting sun, so that the head of the church faced east. This custom, dating back to primitive Christian days, was so widespread that "from the eleventh to the sixteenth century it is difficult to find a badly oriented church."[23] The ship, an allegory of the church, was claimed to sail only eastward: "The Ship of the Church, like the Church as ship, always points east, for the journey is toward salvation."[24] The main portal of a church faced west where the sun set; it was the entrance for the faithful into the sacred territory of the church, a passage out of the earthly realm and into the sacred. The end marked by the setting sun was also the beginning marked by the entrance to the church. Conversely, the east, the land of the rising sun, was the beginning; it was also where the church finished, thus symbolic of an end. Columbus's *Cabo de Alpha et O* relates to all of these religious and cultural notions. Columbus sailed west to arrive east and when he did he greeted, like in a church, both the beginning (the rising sun) and the end (the setting sun). Spiritually, he believed he was moving towards the east and salvation; geographically, he was convinced he had reached the end of the known world and the beginning of the unknown, the end of the old Spanish empire and the beginning of a new one. In addition to the notion of symmetry, Columbus also employs that of centre, another archetypal symbol of the centre of the world, an *axis mundi* and "the meeting point of heaven, earth, and hell."[25] The notion of centre becomes apparent when toponymic clusters are considered, as in the case of the cluster inspired by metals and celestial bodies as well as the cluster that recreates a visual scene of the Crucifixion, which are examined in chapters 4 and 5, respectively.

Hierarchies

The most evident kind of hierarchical sequence is formulated in the letter to Santángel, which may or may not have been authored by Columbus. In the letter crafted to propagate the official version of "the Discovery" based, as Zamora has convincingly argued, on the 4 March letter, the five place names refer to God, the Crown, and Spain. This sequence is also present in the *Diario del primer viaje* but not in such a straightforward format since it is interrupted by other place names inserted among these five. Similarly, the *diarios* contain various other hierarchical sequences and patterns, but these are often obscured by "imperfect" ordering and the inclusion of other Castilian, Taino, or hybrid place names. Some hierarchies are based on the physical size and value of the object. In the *Diario del primer viaje*, *Golfo de la Ballena* is the first place name in the thematic category of marine wildlife inspired by the whale, the largest of sea animals. A list of other place names invented later refer to marine wildlife of smaller size: *Cabo de Lapa*, *Cabo Boto*, *Isla Caracol*, and *Cabo de Conchas*. The last place name in this sequence referring to marine wildlife, *Isla Delfín*, was inspired by a marine animal of medium size, and it is out of place in the sequence. Place names inspired by land animals are also arranged in a similarly visible sequence based on their size, although the order of the last two place names is reversed: *Cabo del Elefante* (6 December), *Cabo de Sierpe* (4 January), and *Cabo del Bezerro* (5 January). The same can be said about the place names referring to metals which are arranged in a decreasing order based on the perceived value of the metal: *Río del Oro* (8 January), *Monte de Plata* (11 January), *Punta del Hierro* (11 January), and *Puerto de Plata* (13 January). Once again, the final toponym upsets the order of this hierarchical sequence. Such "imperfect" sequences could be explained by the likelihood that not all Columbian toponyms were included in the *diarios*, or that they were not always recorded in the order in which they were assigned, or that Las Casas influenced their introduction through his transcription. These "imperfect" sequences could also be testimonies of the ways in which the preconceived order began to break down due to the inescapable influences that the New World exerted on Columbian naming. Certainly, the broken sequences could have resulted from the combination of all these factors.

Hierarchies in the Columbian toponymic discourse repeatedly recall the story of the Creation. According to Genesis, the greatest bodies and phenomena, such as the celestial bodies, the earth, the waters, and the dry land, were created first, followed by the smaller things and the "swarms of living creatures." Medieval glosses of the Creation story further elaborated the hierarchies. The scholastic poet and philosopher Bernardus Silvestris of Tours (1085?–1178?), who was closely connected with the School of Chartres, claimed that animals, including beasts, reptiles, winged creatures, and fish, were all created in an order that was based on their size. The largest animal, the elephant, was created first, and some of the smallest, the squirrel, the beaver, and the sable, came last. These references evoke the story of Creation as it was narrated in Genesis. The order in which things are evoked in Colombus's toponymy mirrors the order in which things were first created according to Genesis and medieval stories of Creation such as the one by Silvestris. In the *diarios*, the world emerging from the dark state of chaos is represented by the place names that recreate the celestial archetype on the landscape (*Río del Sol*, *Río de la Luna*)[26] as well as its shapes (*Isla Llana*, *Cabo del Pico*). The materialization of animals of various sizes (*Cabo del Elefante*, *Cabo de Sierpe*), humanity (*Peña de los Enamorados*, *Punta Pierna*), harmony (*Los Dos Hermanos*, *Cabo Alto y Baxo*, *Cabo Redondo*), and spirituality (*Río de Gracia*, *Cabo del Angel*) are narrated next. Only then do saints (*Isla de Sancto Thomás*, *Cabo Sant Theramo*) and various kinds of human figures, with their tools and innovations, populate the landscape (*Cabo Françés*, *Puerto de las Flechas*). Furthermore, the existing patterns of symmetry and hierarchies are expressions of acts of ordering and of trying to make sense of that which seems disorderly and unknown, symbolically repeating the act of Creation during which chaos is transformed into order. Ancient societies performed such acts of transformation by inhabiting or using territories.[27] The dramatic climax and the reversal in the process of Creation are reflected in the toponymy of the third and fourth voyages when Columbus assigned toponyms such *Boca del Drago* and *Boca de la Sierpe*. In addition to being expressions of Columbus's eschatological mindset and, as I will argue in the final chapter, of his fear of the proximity of Hell, these toponyms also articulated an overwhelming sense of the return of chaos rather than order.

Narrative Sequences: The Epistolary Genre and *relaciones*

Furthermore, the place names in the Columbian toponymic discourse mirror the structure of the medieval epistolary genre. Texts in this genre typically began with a salutation in the form of a prayer or of giving thanks, which was followed by the subject of the letter ranging from mundane to sublime. They ended with a farewell or a benediction. As in these epistolary texts, Columbian toponymic discourse is framed by a salutation in the beginning and a signature at the end. Columbus's first four toponyms are his salutation, with which he thanks first Christ and the Virgin Mary (*Isla de San Salvador* and *Isla de Santa María de la Concepción*) and then the temporal rulers of Castile and Aragon who funded the first voyage (*Isla Fernandina* and *Isla Isabela*). Also present in his toponymic discourse are elements from Columbus's signature which reproduces the act of signing a letter at the end: the word *sancto* inspired three – and only three – distinct place names (*Puerto Santo*, *Punta Sancta*, and *Cabo Sancto*), which imprinted the three S's from Columbus's siglum on the Caribbean landscape.[28]

The main body of the Columbian toponymic discourse addresses both secular (in particular, the geography and the features of the landscape) and religious subjects. Thus, the elements present in the rest of the Columbian toponymic corpus recall the general structure of the epistolary genre. They also foreshadow the main information to be included in *cartas relatorias*, which were written to inform the Crown about the lands being explored and conquered. *Cartas relatorias* emerge as a genre after Columbus's *diarios*, and Walter Mignolo defines the first stage in their creation as from 1505 to 1574.[29] Prior to these dates, the term *relación* is not yet used, and instead texts that fulfil some of the same functions are described as letters (*cartas*), books (*libros*), and writing (*escribir*).[30] An instruction signed by the queen and the secretary in 1533 during the reign of Charles V requests that all *relaciones* written about the exploration and conquest of lands in the New World include the following basic information: (1) the names of all the provinces, villages, etc.; (2) the names of their first (European) conquistadors; (3) the existence of provinces already populated by the Spanish; (4) places where mines of metals, precious stones, and pearl fishing are found.[31] The Columbian toponymic discourse, though created prior to the issuing of these official instructions, includes references to several of the categories, including names of provinces populated by the native inhabitants (*Cabo de Cuba*, *Monte Caribata*) and the mines of precious metals and pearls (*Golfo de las Perlas*). As they recreate elements of historical and literary genres, Columbian place names as a whole are infused with a sense of writing as well as of narrative and discursive purposes.

3 "Y saber dellos los secretos de la tierra": Taino Toponymy and Columbian Naming

In their letter of 16 August 1494 to Columbus, King Ferdinand and Queen Isabel requested that he provide them with the all the new place names he had assigned: "Of those islands you have named, what name has been given to each, because in your letters you give the names of some but not all of these." In addition, they wanted to know "what the Indians call them."[1] Implicit in this request are the Crown's two key messages. First, onomastics is viewed here as an important source of knowledge; because of this, the toponymic list must be recorded in its entirety so that no pieces are missing ("you give the names of some but not all of these"). Second, indigenous place names are equally important and likewise must be known ("what the Indians call them"). The king and queen say nothing about replacing Taino toponyms with the Castilian ones or about the rhetoric they desire to see expressed in the Columbian place names in Castilian. They simply request to know all the place names Columbus had assigned in Castilian as well as their corresponding "Indian" names. This chapter explores the Columbian toponymic discourse from the point of view of the two messages encoded in the Crown's request. The chapter comprises two parts. The first part deals with the "completeness" of the Columbian toponymic record as it considers the dramatically different treatment of the Taino and Castilian toponymies in the letter to Santángel and the *Diario del primer viaje*. The second part delves into the specifics of some of the ways in which the Taino influence was instrumental for the Columbian voyages and the significance it had for the Columbian naming project as a whole. Therefore, this chapter considers the impact that the Taino place names, the Taino language, and the information received from the native inhabitants had in shaping Columbus's experiences and views of the lands, which he consequently transferred into his toponymic discourse.

As briefly discussed in the introduction of this book, two texts announcing the discovery to different audiences – the letter to Santángel and the *Diario del primer viaje* – articulate the views of the lands Columbus had reached as well as of their native inhabitants in starkly contrasting ways. The first place name listed in the letter to Santángel is the first Castilian name Columbus assigned: *San Salvador*. It is followed by the Taino *Guanahaní*. In the *Diario del primer viaje*, the first toponym referring to the Caribbean lands is the name of the island that the Lucayo Tainos routinely used, *Guanahaní*. *San Salvador* appears for the first time many pages later, in the 14 October entry. "Carta a los Reyes anunciando el Descubrimiento," or the letter of 4 March 1493 to the sovereigns, which was most likely the model for the letter to Santángel as Zamora has argued, excludes the Taino *Guanahaní* altogether and presents only *San Salvador* together with some of the place names Columbus had invented in Castilian.[2] There are other differences between the letter to Santángel and *Diario del primer viaje*: the letter to Santángel presents a perfect toponymic sequence in contrast to a much longer and messier list of place names found in the *Diario del primer viaje*; it fictionalizes the centrality of the toponym *Española* while in the *Diario del primer viaje* it is just another toponym in a lengthy list; and Taino toponyms are almost completely absent from the letter to Santángel, while the *Diario del primer viaje* incorporates numerous Taino and hybrid toponyms. The following pages explore these differences in greater detail.

Without a doubt, the differences between the *Diario del primer viaje* and the letter to Santángel are in part reflections of the likely different authorship of the two texts as well as of the distinct circumstances under which each was written. As is well known, the *Diario del primer viaje* is Las Casas's transcription of Columbus's original ship logs. The letter to Santángel may have been crafted by Columbus under the supervision of the Crown or by someone else at court, possibly Santángel himself. The basis for the letter may have been the *Diario del primer viaje* or, more likely, the letter of 4 March to the sovereigns, as Zamora has argued.[3] Even though it is a transcription, Las Casas's text of the *Diario del primer viaje* renders some of the rhythm and detailed nature of the original ship log which was composed with events fresh in Columbus's mind. As discussed in the introduction, the letter to Santángel gauges events from a distance, after the appropriate strategic vision and intention have been formulated, which may or may not have been there from the beginning. Hence, the text of the letter is notably more organized, unified, and targeted, and each of the toponyms selected to be included in it serves a specific rhetorical function. In contrast, the *Diario del primer viaje* presents a much longer, more complete, and less organized list of place names. However, regardless of their authorship and the circumstances of composition, the textual differences in the letter to Santángel and the *Diario del primer viaje* reveal two radically different ways of presenting the Columbian project and the role of naming in it. Therefore, although a direct comparison of the two texts is not practical, a discussion of some of the differences between how toponymy is presented in the two texts will shed light on the portrayal of the discovery enterprise and the construction of a rhetoric through the toponymic discourse.

One of the ways in which the letter to Santángel manipulates the fibre of the Columbian naming discourse is by presenting the supposed sequence in which Columbus assigned the first five place names in Castilian. Written to announce the official version of the Spanish imperial expansion that was starting to take shape, it uses the rhetoric recorded in these five place names to project the message of a Christian, imperialistic ideology: "A la primera que yo fallé puse nonbre Sant Salvador a comemoración de su Alta Magestat, el cual maravillosamente todo esto a[n] dado; los indios la llaman Guanahaní. A la segunda puse nombre la isla de Santa María de Concepción; a la tercera, Ferrandina; a la cuarta la Isabela; a la quinta la isla Juana, e así a cada una nombre nuevo."[4] This sequence implies that the hierarchical value system and the rhetorical structure that reflected the main agents of power were to serve as the basis for the nascent empire. By presenting this highly formulated sequence of five place names, the letter to Santángel presents the acts of Columbian naming as forming a swift, strategic, and rhetorically unified sequence that resulted in the verbal and political conquest of the tropical islands. This version of the discovery and conquest creates an impression that strategic naming was continuous and uninterrupted ("e así a cada una nombre nuevo") and it deletes vacillation from the record, which is, in contrast, notable in the *Diario del primer viaje*.

Another way in which the letter to Santángel manipulates the presentation of the Columbian naming enterprise is by dedicating a substantial part of the description to the island Columbus had named *Española* (spelled as *Spañola* in the letter) and thus articulating its significance both as the symbolic centre of the Columbian enterprise and as the departure point for further expansion. The focus on the place name most explicitly related to Spain underlines the imperialistic objectives of the Columbian enterprise that started becoming more prominent after the first voyage had been completed. Due to such exclusive attention granted to *Española* in the letter to Santángel it became a common belief that it was the first place name Columbus had assigned in the Indies, a misconception that Ferdinand Columbus corrected in the second chapter of the biography where he pointed out that the first place his father had discovered was "Guanahaní, a la que el Almirante llamó San Salvador."[5] In contrast to the central place granted to *Española* in the letter, in the *Diario del primer viaje*, it is the mere thirty-fourth name in a long list. It is inserted between two other names in Castilian that have nothing imperialistic about them: the spiritual *Puerto de la Concepción* and the mundane *Punta Pierna*. It is not surprising that the letter omits altogether both of these toponyms that do not fit into the rhetorical model.

And yet another important way in which the letter to Santángel manipulates the fibre of the Columbian naming discourse is by diminishing the presence of Taino toponymy to the point of almost erasing it entirely. The Taino name of the island, *Guanahaní*, is mentioned in the letter to Santángel only briefly.[6] Besides *Guanahaní*, the letter mentions only two other toponyms of indigenous origin: the island of the flesh-eating *Caribes* and the *Matininó* island inhabited by women. Both of these are inserted not so much as references to conceivable geographic places on the map but rather as examples of the strange, quasi-monstrous peoples that the Spaniards encountered in the Indies: thus, they are sprinkled in moderation as if to add just enough exotic flavour to an otherwise tame text.

In contrast, toponymy is not projected in the *Diario del primer viaje* as an articulated discourse that fulfilled specific rhetorical objectives. Rather, it emerges as an evolving and messy organism. The *Diario del primer viaje* documents a lengthy list of Taino place names and thus it indicates Columbus's dependence on local knowledge. As mentioned earlier, the first toponym referring to the Caribbean lands introduced in the 11 October entry is the one that the Lucayo Tainos routinely used: *Guanahaní*. Even if this early introduction of *Guanahaní* is anachronistic as Zamora has argued, and was inserted by Las Casas during the transcription, even more striking is the three-day delay in introducing on 14 October *San Salvador*, the new rhetorically charged name in Castilian with which Columbus baptized the island.[7] The glaring absence of *San Salvador* is even more visible because the introduction of the Taino place name *Guanahaní* is followed immediately by the description of the ceremony of taking possession of the island, in which the Castilian toponym is inexplicably missing. Its absence from the description of the ritual of taking possession cannot be explained by a brevity of style, as the narrative is fluid and full of details, among which are the list of the individuals who participated, the mention of the royal flags that were raised, the summary of the speech that Columbus gave to the astounded locals who had gathered around to observe this performance, and the backdrop of the tropical climate against which all of this occurred. No apparent interruptions or omissions break the text, except for the absence of the new Castilian name of the island. Had Columbus pronounced *San Salvador* during the ritual of taking possession he performed on 11 October, there is little doubt that he would have recorded it in his ship log. Likewise, it would have been extremely unlikely for Las Casas not to incorporate in his transcription such a symbolic moment in the first act of taking possession.

Only two explanations are therefore plausible: either Columbus did not, in fact, invent and pronounce the new Castilian name during the first ritual of taking possession, or he intentionally omitted it from his ship log for some unknown reason. The second explanation can be discarded; given how much significance Columbus attributed to naming throughout his voyages and how zealously he wrote down the place names throughout the rest of the ship log, an intentional omission of the very first place name he assigned does not sound convincing. The only plausible explanation for this sizeable gap in the *diario* between the description of the ritual of possession and the first mention of the Castilian name of the island is that these two acts did not occur simultaneously as we think they did. Instead, we must admit the possibility that the new Castilian name of the island was not pronounced during the first act of taking possession but at a later date. The implications of this are significant for the way we think both about Columbus's naming and about his initial views and his subsequent response to the lands and the peoples he had encountered.

This initial focus on the Taino toponym *Guanahaní* and the failure to introduce the Castilian name of the island are both revealing of the textual shift that occurred in the way the contact and Columbus's verbal response to it were articulated in the description of the first three days of exploration. The three-day toponymic silence that extends between the first mention of the Taino name of the island, *Guanahaní*, and the Castilian one, *San Salvador*, severs the process of appropriation into two distinct, independent parts, inserting a gap between the verbal and the political. The textual silence between the two toponyms clearly documents Columbus's vacillation in his appraisal of the world he had reached. The evidence of the vacillation in his acts of naming as well as of his reliance on the information that the native inhabitants would provide is further documented in parallel naming, hybrid names, and new Castilian place names invented based on altering the pronunciation of difficult Taino names. These minute, yet undeniable, gaps between the new Castilian name introduced and the Taino name that continued to exist were sufficient to break open a crevice through which negotiation, translation, and manipulation keep on seeping through. Similar kinds of gaps are present even in the Crown's request to inform them of both the Castilian names of places and "what the Indians call them." The gaps reveal an undeniable awareness of another onomastic system or systems in existence. They also reveal a frustration that the space between the Castilian system and the native one(s) cannot be bridged completely, a frustration that would only grow during the subsequent voyages.

Finally, an important difference between the presentation of the Columbian naming enterprise in the *Diario del primer viaje* consists of the sequencing of the names in Castilian. Columbus did not name the five islands after Christ, the Virgin Mary, and three members of the royal family in the way in which the letter to Santángel suggests. Specifically, the letter presents *Isla Juana* as the fifth toponym Columbus invented, following suit after those inspired by the king and the queen. In the *Diario del primer viaje*, it is the twenty-sixth toponym in the chronological sequence, mentioned for the first time on 5 December. It is possible that Columbus had named it earlier, on or after 28 October, the date on which he entered the port in Cuba. However, even in that case he had already named at least *Islas de Arena* on 27 October, and three other places, *Cabo Hermoso*, *Cabo de la Laguna*, and *Cabo del Isleo*, on 19, 20, and 21 October respectively, all of which break the perfect rhetorical sequence as it is presented in the letter.[8] In the same vein, while the letter to Santángel implies that Columbus invented names inspired primarily by Christian figures, the Crown, and Spain, this is not the case in the *Diario del primer viaje*. The thematic scope of the place names recorded in the *Diario del primer viaje* is broad and the rhetorical impact of this list is far less targeted. While the list of toponyms in the *Diario del primer viaje* contains some rhetorical sequences and thematic groupings, the naming is not nearly as strategic as the letter to Santángel suggests.

To sum up, the letter to Santángel uses several strategies, including the use of the hierarchical sequence registered in the first five toponyms and the principle of centrality of the toponym *Española*, to articulate the politics of imperialistic expansion and spiritual influence. It (and the 4 March letter to the sovereigns) also diminishes the presence of Taino toponymy to the point of almost erasing it entirely to create a misleading impression that Columbus's acts of naming were decisively imperialistic from the very beginning. By doing so, it implies that the role of the native inhabitants in aiding or obstructing his exploration and appropriation of the local geography was minimal or non-existent. These messages contrast greatly with what we see in the *Diario del primer viaje* where the presence of the Taino toponymy is consistent and pervasive from the very first entry describing the initial encounter until the very end of the narrative of the first voyage, in which two of the final three place names in Castilian, *Golfo de las Flechas*, and *Puerto de las Flechas*, are reflections of the not-very-smooth encounters with the Tainos.

Different from what the letter presents, the presence of the Taino toponymy in the *diarios* is substantial. The *Diario del primer viaje* lists twenty-six toponyms, many of which likely have Taino origins: among them are *Samoet*, *Yamaye*, *Boriquen*, *Cuba*, *Jamaica*, *Cibao*, *Macaca*, and *Yanahica*.[9] In addition, *Caritaba*, *Caribo*, and *Mateninó* were borrowed by Tainos from the Island Carib language. Though no new Taino place names are recorded in the *Relación del segundo viaje*, this likely has to do with the incompleteness of this *relación*. The *relaciones* of the third and fourth voyages once again include a significant number of toponyms that are clearly Taino or that may have originated from another native language: five such new toponyms appear in the *Relación del tercer viaje* and nine more in the *Relación del cuarto viaje*. In addition to the specific Taino place names incorporated into the narrative of the *diarios*, allusions are made to much longer lists of Taino place names and information related to the local landscape. In the entry of 14 October in the *Diario del primer viaje* in which the Castilian place name *San Salvador* is first introduced, Columbus alludes to the great number of Taino names of islands that the locals had told him: "y vide tantas islas que yo no sabía determinarme a cuál iría primero. Y aquellos hombres que yo tenía toma[n]do me dezían por señas que eran tantas y tantas que no avía número y anombraron por su nombre más de ciento."[10] In many other instances, the *diarios* include comments about other toponyms that seem to be of indigenous origin of which Columbus and his crew were aware, as for example, the toponyms *Cami*, *Faba*, and "many other names": "y dixo el capitán de la Pinta que entendía ... quel rey de aquella tierra [Cuba] tenía guerra con el Gran Can, al cual ellos llamavan Cami, y a su tierra o ciudad, Faba y otros muchos nombres."[11]

The list of Taino place names in the *diarios* is complemented by additional place names registered in Las Casas's *Historia de las Indias*, some of which may have been borrowed directly from the now-lost original ship logs, as well as the additional names of places, people, and deities recorded by historian and missionary Fray Ramón Pané. Columbus had sent Pané to live with a local chieftain, learn his language, and find out about his people's customs and beliefs. The Catalan friar arrived at the island of Hispaniola on Columbus's second voyage and spent a little over a year in the province of Magdalena or Macorís, which was in the north of the island and was governed by the Indian chief or cacique named Mayobanex.[12] Following Columbus's orders, the friar subsequently transferred to the land of Guarionex with his local interpreter, Juan Mateo, with whom he developed a strong friendship. Guatícabanu, as he was called before becoming Christian, spoke both the local language of Magdalena and the more widely known language of the people of Guarionex. Named "the first ethnographer" of the Americas by the critic José Juan Arrom, Pané provided the earliest documentation of the beliefs, myths, and customs of the Tainos at the time of the European arrival. Some of the toponyms included in his *Relación acerca de las antigüedades de los indios* refer to smaller geographic bodies, such as mountains (such as *Cauta*), caves (*Cacibajagua* and *Amayaúna*), and provinces (*Caonao*), as well as names of the principal characters from creation myths that chart the mythical geography of the lands, and names of caciques, rulers of territories. Though many of the toponyms from Pané's account are not included in the list of the Columbian place names, Columbus must have been aware of them. The information encoded in some of them may have influenced his views of the resources, the peoples, and the geography of the area and it may have shaped some of his own acts of naming.

Before addressing in greater depth the presence of the Taino toponymy in the *Diario del primer viaje*, the following paragraphs sum up the languages spoken in the Caribbean at the time of Columbus's arrival.

The Taino culture developed in the Greater Antilles from the Saladoid culture after the latter had migrated from the Orinoco region of South America's northeast coast to the Caribbean islands between 500 and 250 BC.[13] The Saladoid culture obtained its name from their ceramics decorated with white and red painting found in the Venezuelan site of Saladero. *Taino* refers to the culture, language, and the ceramic tradition based on the archaeological record.[14] The word *taíno* itself is a derivative of *nitaíno*, which is not a proper name but the "adjective Taínos used to distinguish themselves from the Cariban people."[15] The Tainos also had names for other peoples living around them, including the *Ciguayo*, the *Caribe*, the *Caniba*, and the *Guanahatabey*.[16]

Coll y Toste, in his classic work entitled *Prehistoria de Puerto Rico*, claims that all islands in the Greater Antilles spoke the same language, which he calls Indo-Antillian, "indo-antillana."[17] In the introduction to another classic work, *Pequeño diccionario de palabras indo-antillanas* by Rodolfo Domingo Cambiaso, first published in 1916, Mariano Lebrón Saviñón points out that some call the language spoken by the Tainos of the Greater Antilles *Lucayo* while others call it *Taino*.[18] In more recent research, linguists and historians generally agree that the predominant language in the Greater Antilles was Taino, closely related forms of which were spoken in the Lucayos (Bahamas), eastern Cuba, Jamaica, Haiti (Española), and Boriquen (Puerto Rico).[19] The Taino language may have had dialects resulting from contacts with other languages: "even though the [Taino] language was intelligible over wide areas, it nevertheless had dialectal divisions, not only among the various islands but also within some of the larger islands as well."[20] To distinguish the language and culture from the Taino ceramics defined by the archaeological findings, the terms *Arawak*, *Island Arawak*, and *Lokono* are also used.[21] The Taino language belonged to the Arawakan or Arahuacan language family, which in addition to Taino also included Igneri and other Arawakan languages, and the roots of this language family can be traced to Proto-Maipuran.[22] I use the term *Taino* throughout the book to refer to the language of the native people Columbus met during his first and later voyages since it has been generally accepted and since it refers to the pre-Columbian peoples and their language, thus avoiding any confusion with the modern Arawakan languages spoken throughout South America.

Douglas Taylor distinguishes three major linguistic groups in this region: (1) Arawak or Lokono, (2) the Igneri, the Iñeri, or Island-Carib spoken by the Arawakan speakers in the Lesser Antilles, and (3) the Karina, Carib, Galibi, or Carinaco language from the Cariban linguistic family spoken by the people sometimes also called "True Carib."[23] The Igneri, also called the Island Karina, were an Arawakan-speaking people who lived in the smaller islands of the eastern Caribbean. The Igneri language was a result of linguistic interchanges between the men of Dominica who spoke Karina derived from the Cariban language and the women who spoke an Arawakan language.[24] Pre-Cariban Igneri and Taino were different languages from the same linguistic family, "much like French and Spanish."[25] The Arawakan languages were probably mutually unintelligible, due to centuries of living apart from one another.[26] Today, several Arawakan languages are spoken. In the south of Trinidad, Lokono, Jaoi, and Shebayo are spoken.[27] Lokono "is considered the closest surviving tongue to the sixteenth-century Taíno"; likewise, Karina (or Kalina) is a contemporary language derived from the sixteenth-century Cariban language.[28] The third major language spoken in the Caribbean region was that of the cultural group of Island Caribs who originated from the migration from South America of the Kalina or Karina also known as Kalinagos.[29] Originally, they spoke Galibi, a language related to the larger family of Cariban languages in South America.[30] Gradually, due to warrior practices and bride capture, Carib men adopted "a form of speech that soon came to be essential Arawakan, though embedded with numerous Cariban lexical survivals," the base of which was Igneri, Taino, and other Arawakan languages. The resulting language is called Island Carib and it was spoken in Guadeloupe, Dominica, and St Croix at the time of the second voyage of Columbus, in 1493.[31] Here, I am using the term "Island Carib" to refer to this form of speech in use by the Carib men at the time of Columbus's arrival.

Scholars have now abandoned the view of the Caribbean as having two kinds of people – Caribs and Tainos (Arawaks) – a view that emerged from the chroniclers' observations about the differences between the people of the Greater and Lesser Antilles. Instead, research shows that many different ethnic groups were spread out through the Lesser Antilles, Greater Antilles, and Bahamas.[32] A few other languages were "scattered through the islands of the Greater Antilles, adjacent to and among these Taino-speakers," as Tony Highfield points out, and "they were much older languages that had been forced into marginality by the growth of the Taino domain or they had only recently been established in the region and were therefore of minor status in their presence and influence."[33] The Guanahatabey of western Cuba "evidently spoke a language other than Taino."[34] The Ciguayo in northeast Haiti who inhabited the chiefdom (*cacicazgo*) of Macorix also spoke a language other than Taino (Arrom considers it to be a dialect of Taino). Very little is known about these languages.[35]

Columbus was aware that his not knowing the local language was one of the principal obstacles in achieving several objectives. Columbus's frustration about not knowing a local language is expressed repeatedly in the *diarios*: "y también no sé la lengua, y la gente d'estas tierras no me entienden."[36] The *diarios* and the letters Columbus sent to the Crown also document his thoughts about why knowing a local language would be extremely beneficial. In the April–May 1494 letter to the Crown ("Carta a los Reyes"), Columbus lamented that his lack of linguistic competence impeded his efforts to convert the locals to the Christian faith: "ansí lo torno a dezir y digo otra vez, que otra cosa no me falta para que sean todos christianos salvo *no se lo saver dezir ni predicar en su lengua*."[37] He pointed out that knowing their language would allow him to establish communication with the local inhabitants who would show him where gold and other riches were located: "Así que, demás de me faltar qu'esta gente toda no sean christianos, qu'e[s] *por no saver la lengua*, me falta muy mucha gran cantidad de oro y otras riquezas que ay en esta isla de espeçerías, qu'ellos cojerían para nosotros; [mas] *me falta la lengua para saverles hablar.*"[38] And finally, he complained that understanding the local language was the last missing ingredient before the native people could be made into vassals of the Spanish Crown: "otra cosa no falta salvo saber la lengua y mandarles, porque todo lo que se les mandare harán sin contradicçión alguna."[39] The Spanish interpreters, Luis de Torres, a converted Jew who knew Hebrew, Aramaic, and some Arabic, and Rodrigo de Xerez, who had visited an African king in Guinea and spoke his language, were not of much help. Pané, whom Columbus sent to live among the natives, learned Macorix, a language that the Taino speakers did not understand. Columbus also kidnapped several Taino men and women and took them back to Castile so they could learn "to speak" and thus would become his interpreters, but nearly all of them perished during the transatlantic voyage.[40] Columbus's efforts to establish transparent verbal communication with the local inhabitants were slow to bring any tangible results.

However, one part of speech served as a bridge for establishing a rudimentary kind of communication: nouns, and in particular, proper names and place names. Columbus soon learned a handful of nouns in the Taino language, such as *guanín* ("gold," "gold alloy," and jewellery made from it) and *cacique* ("chieftain"), among others, which gave him a way of asking the most essential questions. A significant portion of nouns Columbus acquired were place names, which were instrumental for asking questions about the local geography and for attempting to identify the places he had reached. Names of chieftains and names of peoples were useful for the same reasons.

Toponyms, names of people and deities, and nouns played an essential role in establishing a very basic kind of linguistic communication between the conquistadors and the natives. The vast majority of Taino lexicon recorded in the *diarios* are toponyms, proper names, and nouns. The great majority of words from the Taino lexicon that Spanish chroniclers recorded in their accounts were also nouns, while the other grammatical categories such as adjectives and verbs made up only a very small percentage.[41] Even today, the greatest portion of the surviving Taino lexicon in Cuba, Haiti, and Puerto Rico has been preserved "in the names of rivers, mountains, trees, fruits, toponyms, ports, capes, and so on."[42] The numerous surviving Taino toponyms testify to the Tainos' own naming practices: "That the Tainos traveled widely and readily in their waters is evident in the names they assigned to both nearby and distant islands and places."[43] Among the Taino toponyms that have reached us are their names of the islands in the Lucayos island group (*Guanahaní*, *Bahama*, *Caycos*, *Ciguateo*), the names of all the larger islands of the Greater Antilles (*Cuba*, *Jamaica*, *Haiti*, *Bohio*, *Boriquen*), as well as the smaller ones and cays lying off the larger islands (such as *Camito* off the northern coast of Haiti). The Tainos called the region of unlimited land, which lay far across the waters, "etched in their ancestral memory," *Caribana* or *Caribata*; the Spaniards would call it *Tierra Firma*. Toponyms that the Tainos appropriated from the Caribs included names of islands inhabited by Caribs to the east of the Taino domains called *Caloucaéra*, *Caribe*, and *Matininó*.[44] Surviving Taino names of places in the islands of Haiti, Boriquen, and eastern Cuba include names for valleys (*Hathathiei*), mountains (*Hybahaino*, *Macaya*), settlements (*Guanahibes*, "Gonaives," and *Hincha*, "Hinche" in Haiti), provinces (*Agueyabana*, *Baoruco*), regions (*Cibao*), and *cacicazgos* (*Xaraguá*, *Maguana*, *Higuay*, and *Marien* in Haiti).[45] Most of the rivers in the Dominican Republic today have retained their Taino names, including the *Agmina* and the *Jaina*.[46]

According to Arrom, the Tainos gave to places "very simple names" (nombres sumamente sencillos), which were precise and descriptive, and which reflected their natural view of the lands.[47] Thus, the Tainos called Trinidad *Caíri*, "Island," and Martinica *Iuonacaera* or *Iguana-caíri*, "Island of Iguanas." *Cay-cimú* meant "Beginning of an Island," and *Haiti*, "Mountain," *Job-abo*, "Hill of Cedar Trees," *Güir-abo*, "Place of *Güira* Fruit," and *Bara-coa* "There-the-Sea."[48] Such names also functioned as mnemonic resources for easier orientation. However, in their naming of themselves and of other peoples around them, the Tainos were anything but naive. *Taino*, the adjective they used to distinguish themselves from others, means "noble, wise."[49] Names of other peoples, on the other hand, including *Ciboney*, *Macorix*, and *Ciguayo*, all had derogative connotations in Taino. *Ciboney* was the name of the people who lived in a semi-nomadic state in the caverns in the more remote regions of the Antilles, and the name was composed of *ciba*, "stone," and *igneri* or *igney*, "man." *Macorix*, Las Casas informs us, means a strange, almost barbaric language. The only name for other people that the Tainos borrowed from others as far as we know was that of the *Carib* people.[50] In translating Taino proper and place names, Arrom found that the terms referring to visual images and especially light, such as "brilliant light," "shining," "brighter than gold," "as bright as brass [latón]," were frequently incorporated. Other words used to make up Taino proper names included *Starey*, "shining" (translated by some as "star"), and *Huiho*, "height."[51] Arrom finds this appropriate for the inhabitants of islands bathed with sunlight and he compares the repeated usage of these images to the Christian custom of using names such as José, Jesús, and María frequently to baptize newborns.

To sum up, the consistent and pervasive presence of Taino and other indigenous toponymy in the *diarios* is due to several factors. First of all, Columbus desired to obtain as much information from the local inhabitants as he could, including that which would help him know the waters for safer and faster navigation, and to be aware of settlements and their rulers as well as of the location of desired resources such as gold and spices. This necessity to learn practical information is recorded as one of the two key objectives in the prologue of the *Diario del primer viaje*, in which Columbus promises to situate places "in their proper places." One of the objectives was to compose a new map of lands previously uncharted by Europeans, and had to do with obtaining geographic information that would help understand the basic natural and sociopolitical features of the tropical landscape, which were needed for further exploration and conquest. Names of places and proper names also promised to be helpful in conveying to the natives messages about the Spanish Crown and the Christian faith. Finally, Columbus's interest in the local toponymy had to do with his questioning of whether he had reached the lands that were under direct rule of the Great Khan or whether these were islands in the margins of his kingdom. According to the then-current European law, the presence of inhabitants on the lands alone was not viewed as an obstacle to the usurpation and the renaming of both.[52] The papal bulls of 1455, 1456, and 1479 had legitimized taking possession of any lands that were not yet owned by a Christian ruler. Soon after Columbus's first voyage, on 4 May 1493, Alexander VI issued the bull *Inter caetera* to resolve the conflict of interest between Spain and Portugal in the New World. Even though the island quite clearly was not under the lordship of a Christian ruler, Columbus may have refrained from claiming it for the Spanish Crown if he believed that it belonged to the greatest emperor of Asia. And thus, the key question was not whether or not Columbus had reached Asia: his references to the local inhabitants as Indians (*los indios*), to the great emperor the Great Khan (*Gran Can*), to cannibals (*caníbales*), and to the generic place name of the Indies (*las Indias*) throughout the *diarios* speak to his conviction that he had, indeed, arrived at *a part* of Asia, an idea he did not abandon until his death. The more pertinent question for him at that point was whether the island he had reached was directly under the Great Khan's rule.

To determine the location of the lands he had reached relative to the territories of the Great Khan, Columbus not only looked for any signs of the wealthy cities he was hoping to reach but also listened for any names of places pronounced by the local inhabitants. The first name that reached Columbus's ears was the completely unrecognizable *Guanahaní*, one that bore little resemblance to words such as *Khan* or *Cipango*.[53] Few toponyms refer to Asian geography in the *diarios*. Columbus makes solitary references to other places in Asia, mentioning them no more than once or twice: the province called *Bafan* ruled by the Great Khan mentioned by Marco Polo (*Bafan* and *Faba*, perhaps different spelling variants referring to the same place), the province of *Cathay*, the cities *Zaitó* and *Quinsay* (also spelled as *Quisay*).[54] Several other toponyms that Columbus pronounced during the first voyage either refer clearly to Asia or they have an Asian flavour: *Cipango* (21 October) refers to Japan and *Quisay* to China (21 October). However, *Cipango* is the only place name referring to Asia that Columbus recalls consistently throughout his voyages (the variants of its name occur nineteen times in the *diarios*); he mentions it on 6 October, only a few days before reaching the islands and recording the first toponym referring to the New World, the Taino *Guanahaní*, on 11 October. *Cabo del Elefante* (6 December) may have been inspired by the image of Asian elephants and *Golfo de las Perlas* could be a reference to the abundance of pearls in that region described by European travellers to Asia. Aside from these examples, we do not find many more references to Asia. Judging from the scarcity of toponymic evidence relating to Asia it seems that Columbus concluded that the local people he had met were not the vassals of the Great Khan – they were too timid and too naked, and almost nothing they said sounded like the names of places in Asia. Since it looked as if his plans for engaging in mercantilist and diplomatic relationships with the great emperor had to be postponed, Columbus completed the ritual of taking possession he had begun three days earlier and pronounced the new name of the island in Castilian, *San Salvador*. His supposition would soon be confirmed as Columbus and the captain of the *Pinta* and the oldest of the Pinzón brothers, Martín Alonso Pinzón, deduced from what the locals were telling them that the chieftain of Cuba was at war with Great Khan: "y dixo el capitán de la Pinta que entendía ... quel rey de aquella tierra [Cuba] tenía guerra con el Gran Can, al cual ellos llamavan Cami."[55]

Due to this uncertainty about the place of his arrival in relation to the lands of the Great Khan, for Columbus there was also a lack of conceptual boundaries between the American and the Asian onomastics, which formed for him two overlapping categories. One example is the way Columbus used three toponyms: *Cipango*, *Cuba* (also spelled *Colba*), and *Cibao*. As Columbus vacillated among the three terms, the first of which was the Castilian word for Japan while the other two were Taino toponyms, he was attempting to reconcile his current location with where he hoped to be based on theoretical conjectures. *Cibao* sounded almost like *Cipango* and *Cuba* sounded almost like *Cibao*: "Çipango, al cual ellos llaman Çibao" (*Cipango*, which they called *Cibao*), and "después partir para otra isla grande mucho, que creo que deve ser Çipango, según las señas que me dan estos indios que yo traigo, a la cual ellos llaman Colba" (24 December and 21 October).[56] Columbus concluded he was very near Japan and the gold he was going to find there.[57] Thus, through the use of place names, he unwillingly invented a hybrid, transpacific space that was the product of a marriage between various language and onomastic systems. This is one of the reasons why Columbus's language of naming was not a rigid instrument with which a one-directional flow of power and single-handed appropriation of spaces was achieved. Rather, it was a verbal testament of the multidirectional linguistic, epistemological, and material exchanges that both enabled and complicated progress in Columbus's voyages and that subsequently altered the European vision of the American lands. The fact that the scarcity of Asian names is compensated for by the abundance of Taino names indicates that Columbus negotiated with the two verbal landscapes in an effort to fuse them into one. The textual landscape was composed of toponyms recorded in the textual sources he had consulted prior to embarking on his voyages and those he was hearing pronounced by the local inhabitants.

In addition to learning about the local geography, communicating with the locals was the only way to gain access to some of the secret information that could give him an advantage in his exploration efforts. In the context of rival relationships among the European powers, all information regarding the exploration of yet uncolonized lands was kept as a strict state secret. María M. Portuondo, in her recent book *Secret Science: Spanish Cosmography and the New World* (2009), has convincingly shown the strategic importance of secrecy in the gathering and safeguarding of scientific knowledge by Spanish cosmographers. Indeed, Philip II's policy of secrecy, established to protect the Spanish empire from foreign rivalry, delayed the publication of key cosmological works. Because of the concerns about foreign rivalry, any navigational charts or maps Columbus may have made would have remained unpublished as well. However, Columbus did not just view this information as something that needed to be kept secret from European rivals. He was also clearly aware that the locals possessed special, deep knowledge of their lands, much of which was connected to their religious beliefs and ritual practices and which was also guarded as secret and privileged.[58] Moved by the Crown's requests and by his own goals, Columbus gave instructions to his men to capture native inhabitants in order to learn from them "los secretos de la tierra."[59] Columbus was going to obtain the secrets of the lands that the locals guarded, if not peacefully, then by force: "Mandó el Almirante tomar algunos de aquellos indios, por fuerza, para llevar consigo y *saber dellos los secretos de la tierra.* Tomaron siete, no sin gran escándalo de todos los demás, y de los siete dos escogió que parecían los más honrados y principales; a los demás dejaron ir, dándoles algunas cosas de las de Castilla, dándoles a entender por señas que aquéllos tomaban por guías y después se los enviarían."[60] And again: "Tomaron dellas [de diez canoas con que se toparon] dos hombres que parecían ser dellos los más principales, *para, con los dos de Cariarí, saber los secretos de la tierra.*"[61] The emphasis on the secret knowledge in the hands of the native informants in Columbus's words signals his view of the natives as possessors of important cosmographical information and even as knowledgeable rivals.

Taino language, toponymy, and culture manifested itself in the Columbian toponymic discourse in various ways. Columbus recorded a number of hybrid toponyms consisting of Castilian and Taino elements, as in *Río Yuyuparí* and *Río Camarí.* Coll y Toste also points out that some of such hybrid toponyms exist to date, among which are *Sabána Grande* (which today is pronounced as *Sábana*) and *Xagua la Grande.*[62] These hybrid toponyms are important for understanding the extent of Columbus's reliance on local toponymy and the ways in which it began seeping through to warp his naming discourse. Also, toponyms such as *Costa de la Oreja* and *Puerto de las Cabañas* attest to aspects of local culture and customs that attracted Columbus's attention. Specifically, Columbus named *Costa de la Oreja* after witnessing the large holes in the ears of locals that had been purposely stretched out: "había otras gentes por aquella costa que tenían las orejas horadadas y tan grandes agujeros que cupiera un huevo de gallina bien por ellos, puso nombre a aquella ribera la costa de la Oreja."[63] Sometimes the invention of a toponym occurred because Columbus mistook a Taino word for a toponym: such were the cases of the Taino word *bohío* meaning "house," which Columbus appropriated and named the *Bohío* island, and of the Taino word *guanín*, meaning "alloy of gold and copper," which he applied to the region, naming it *Guanín.*

Even more intriguing are those place names in Castilian which Columbus moulded out of existing indigenous linguistic material, as in the cases of *Isla Caracol* and *Cabo de la Galera. Isla Caracol* is a fine Castilian name, which was perhaps even prompted, in part, by the physical features of the island.[64] *Cabo de la Galera*, pronounced during the third voyage, is another such Castilian toponym, which Morison attributed to a visual resemblance as well. However, the Taino toponyms by which the places were known at the time of Columbus's arrival shed new light on how they were renamed. *Isla Caracol*, the largest island located inside of *Boca del Drago*, was known locally as *Chacachacare*, while *Cabo de la Galera*, the southwestern tip of Trinidad, was known as *Guayaguayare*. Quite likely, when attempting to pronounce and remember them, Columbus and his men opted for a simpler solution and morphed the long foreign toponyms into shorter words in Castilian, based both on the affinities of sounds and on the visual aspect of the two places. Coll y Toste has also observed that many indigenous toponyms have been interpreted incorrectly by critics based on their spelling in Castilian, which has been adapted to an easier pronunciation by the conquistadors. From what he calls the Indo-Antillian lexicon, Coll y Toste points out the word *Caguas* was not derived from the Castilian "aguas" (waters), but rather it was derived from the name of a certain native from Hispaniola whose name was *Caguax*.[65] In an essay entitled "Proclaiming Place: Towards a Geography of Place Name Pronunciation," Robin Kearns and Lawrence Berg argue that "resistance to naming can occur on at least two levels: the creation and deployment of alternative names … and the use of alternative pronunciations for established names."[66] In my view, *Chacachacare* and *Guayaguayare* constitute another understated, yet powerful kind of resistance that leaves scars on the very discourse that made a futile attempt to invent an entirely new linguistic landscape. Columbus did not need to build his naming discourse in Castilian based on already existing names and words in Taino. The fact that he did so on various occasions indicates a silent dependence on the patterns and the signifiers on the landscape that he clearly recognized to be already marked. Therefore, place names like *Isla Caracol* and *Cabo de la Galera* are not examples of imperialistic naming that erased native onomastics and overwrote any existing toponyms with new, invented ones. On the contrary, these names are examples of a puzzled and anxious act of naming that attempted to make some kind of feasible connection among three components: the existing, though (to Columbus) opaque names of places in a native language, the shapes of the landscape, and the meanings of words in Castilian.

Because the Taino names of places contained important information necessary for future communication with the locals and for the continued deepening of Columbus's understanding of the local geography, Columbus sometimes recorded only the Taino names of places even after he had renamed them in Castilian, as in "la isla que llamavan los indios Bohío" (the island which the Indians called Bohio) and "aquella provinçia Caribata" (that province Caribata). More frequently, however, he recorded both the Taino toponym and the new Castilian toponym, presenting both in a parallel format, for example, when he said that they should "leave Cuba or Juana" (dexar Cuba o Juana).[67] Parallel structures composed of both the Taino and the Castilian place names Columbus used to identify a single place are frequent in the *diarios*: "esta Española, a que ellos llaman Caritaba" (this Española, which they call Caribata); "la Juana, a que ellos llaman Cuba" (Juana, which they call Cuba); "aquella isla Española, a quien llaman Bohío" (that island Española, which they call Bohio); "çipango, a que ellos llamavan çibao" (Cipango, which they called Cibao); and so on.[68] Columbus thus approached other linguistic categories as well, which he presented in his text using similar parallel structures, as in the case of names of rulers ("Gran Can, al cual ellos llamavan Cami" [Great Khan, whom they called Cami]), names of peoples ("los de Caniba, qu'ellos llaman caribes" [Caniba people, which they call caribes]), and names of things, in particular those that were not familiar to the Europeans ("almadías o canoas" [almadías or canoas]).[69] The frequent reliance on such parallel structures suggests that even when the place had been renamed in Castilian, Columbus still saw it as essential to remember and to document its local name.

Parallel structures are most abundant in the first half of the *Diario del primer viaje*. They become scarcer already in its second half and they make only an occasional appearance in the *Relación del segundo viaje*. While both Taino and Castilian toponyms are numerous in the *relaciones* of the third and fourth voyages, they are no longer paired up in parallel structures. The degree of clarity and control that was present with the use of such parallel structures is gradually lost, and place names are inserted haphazardly into the narrative in such a way that they are no longer directly embedded in the Columbian naming discourse.[70] In contrast, the presence of Taino toponymy is only stronger during the third and fourth voyages. It seems that while seeking to establish the supremacy of the Castilian language and of naming based on the European discursive rhetoric, Columbus was not able to erase the Taino toponymy altogether nor to integrate it smoothly into the toponymic discourse he was weaving.

Taino toponyms, homonyms, words, and syllables, rather than being silent markers, exerted substantial influence on Columbus's itinerary and even impacted his choice of place names in Castilian. Regarding this point, I would disagree with Highfield's view that "since such information [the Tainos' knowledge of the physical world and its working] would have been viewed by the chroniclers as nonproductive and unusable toward any specific end, it was neither solicited nor recorded. But certainly it must have existed. It is difficult to imagine, for example, that such intrepid seafarers had no knowledge of the secrets of the seas and the heavens so important in navigating those seas. Yet we know little of the intellectual content of their culture."[71] Highfield's point that the historical record is very incomplete is well taken; however, the Tainos actively provided Columbus with food, merchandise, and crucial information and thus shaped various aspects of the enterprise of exploration. The evidence in the *diarios* also shows that in some instances they deliberately manipulated the intruders. For example, Las Casas comments about Columbus's confusion regarding the proximity to the lands of the Great Khan, and he attributes a great part of this confusion to the false guidance that the natives offered him: "Lo cual todo, como se platicaba por señas, *o los indios de propósito se burlaban*, o él ninguna cosa dellos, sino lo que deseaba, entendía."[72] Furthermore, the Taino people not only served as interpreters but also participated in the undermining of the Columbian enterprise by serving as informants and even spies for rebellious Spaniards, as they did for Francisco Roldán: "Como Francisco Roldán entendió que ya no podía tardar en venir el Almirante, o por ventura luego que supo que era venido, porque él tenía amigos en esta villa que le avisavan de todo lo nuevo que sucedía, *o porque tenía sus espías de indios o de christianos*, y los indios buelan donde quiera que están con nuevas, acordóse acercar con buena parte de su gente a esta villa y así se vino hazia la provincia de Bonao."[73]

Elsewhere in the *Diario del primer viaje*, Columbus reveals how directly he is affected by the advice and the directions that the natives give him when he chooses to return to Samoet (which he had named *Isabela*) rather than to continue on to another island:

> Y después todos estos indios tornaron a dezir qu'esta isla era más pequeña que no la isla Samoet y que sería bien bolver atrás por ser en ella más presto … y así tomé la vuelta y navegué toda esta noche pasada al Leste Sueste, y esto para apartarme de la tierra, porque hazía muy gran çerrazón y el tiempo muy cargado; él era poco y no me dexó llegar a tierra a surgir … y nos, al cabo de la isla de la parte de Sueste, adonde espero surgir fasta que aclaresca, para ver las otras islas adonde tengo de ir.[74]

The natives' motivation to persuade Columbus to return to Samoet may have been due to various reasons, and these may have been benevolent or manipulative. The island to which they steered his caravel may indeed have been small and less worthy of exploration or, on the contrary, it may have been one of the rich islands that the natives wanted to protect. Either way, their explanation about the location of gold in Samoet was effective and Columbus turned his caravel around. These are a few of the many examples that demonstrate the active role the Taino people played in the process through which Columbus scouted their geography, chose his itineraries, searched for hidden treasures, and developed a verbal map of their territories.

Conclusion

Because of the multiple editions in Castilian, German, and Latin disseminated throughout Europe and because of its brevity and compelling style, the letter to Santángel had a much broader and more enduring impact than did the *Diario del primer viaje* on how Columbus's contact with the people and geography of the Caribbean was perceived. The six selected toponyms that Columbus invented (the "first" five and the "central" *Española*), listed in the letter, create the impression that the mapping of the newly discovered lands was carried out according to clearly conceived ideological paradigms. It suggests that Columbus's initial intention was one of immediate political appropriation and strategic imposition of spiritual, cultural, and linguistic hegemony and that he acted accordingly from the first moment his feet touched the ground of the Guanahaní island. It also suggests that the language of naming was an efficient and transparent tool for recording these acts. In its choice to convey to the readers only a fragment of the place names that Columbus invented during the first voyage and to exclude the Taino toponymy almost entirely, the letter to Santángel effectively silences the toponymic chatter of the Taino toponymy that does not serve its rhetorical purpose. The official version of the "discovery" in the letter to Santángel dismisses the entire onomastic systems of the Tainos and of any other groups of native inhabitants (with the exception of Guanahaní), and thus it denies them agency. However, the view that Columbus single-handedly imposed an entire verbal structure in Castilian onto the map of the Caribbean, without responding to Taino or other native elements, renders a limited understanding of language during the early stages of the conquest.

The *diarios*, on the other hand, provide evidence of the authority, influence, and subversion that the Tainos exerted on Columbus through their language, toponymy, maps, and directions. Indigenous toponyms – which were primarily Taino – were essential tools for composing the first sketch of a mental (and perhaps also a physical) map of the tropical islands that

Columbus was exploring. Although its form changed in the *diarios*, the pervasive presence of the Taino toponymy in Columbian discourse suggests a significant deviation from the original politics of verbal conquest articulated during the first three days of exploration of the island Columbus soon learned was called *Guanahaní*. Naming was not a result of a straightforward imposition of language produced by finite transfers of names from one continent to the islands and mainland of another. It did not turn out to be an orderly sequence of authoritative verbal acts suggested by the five toponyms listed at the beginning of the letter to Santángel. Rather, it consisted of circular attempts at approximation, translation, and negotiation with the prospect of locating the desired geographies based on the information acquired during the voyages and of inserting the new names onto the edges of the existing European navigational charts, something that required an equal amount of negotiation and adaptation. The effect of the impositions of names in Castilian and appropriation of others in Taino was not a succession of clean deletions and one-directional exertions of power. Instead, Columbian acts of naming resulted in a discourse that was messy, fragmented, and, to use Genette's terminology presented in the introduction of this book, contaminated.

The corpus of Columbian place names consisted of both those toponyms that Columbus invented in Castilian and the elements of Taino toponymy, language, and its fragments that he appropriated, translated, or repeated, even in those cases when he did not understand their meaning. In this new, hybrid onomastic system that emerged, Castilian names only appeared to create an imperialistic rhetoric while in reality they frequently translated, mirrored, and attempted to capture the naming practices of the local Taino people. Therefore, this system of "mutual contagion" registered an important subtext that undermined the strategic rhetoric of order and Western ideology that Columbus may have wanted to impose on the landscape of the Indies and that later would be propagated in the letter to Santángel. The parallel use of the Taino and Castilian versions of the place names as well as the exclusive use of Taino place names indicates that two parallel systems were being put into place: the Castilian place names were meant to take possession, baptize, and establish control; at the same time, the Taino toponymy persisted and became a sign of silent resistance, a countertext that warped the imperialistic discourse while at the same time providing it with a foundation.

4 Heavenly Bodies and Metallurgy in Columbian Toponymy

This chapter focuses on the toponymic cluster consisting of twelve place names invented during the first voyage: *Río de la Luna* (first mentioned in the *Diario* on 29 October 1492); *Río de Mares* (29 October); *Puerto de Mares* (5 November); *Río del Sol* (12 November); *Isla de Baveque* (or *Baneque* or *Babeque*; 12 November); *Río del Oro* (8 January 1493); *Monte de Plata* (11 January); *Puerto de Plata* (named between 11 and 18 January, included by Las Casas in the margins of the *Diario*); *Punta del Hierro* (11 January); *Isla de Goanin* (or *Guanín*; 13 January); *Cabo de Luna;* and *Río de la Fuente* (the dates of the naming of the last two toponyms are uncertain).[1] This toponymic cluster reveals Columbus's frustrating experience searching for the alchemical "source" of gold and his contentious relationship with the native inhabitants during his journeys, both of which were largely concealed in the narrative of the *Diario del primer viaje* and erased altogether from the letter to Santángel. The naming of places after metals and celestial bodies in Castilian and the integration of Taino toponyms into this cluster shows that Columbus was relying on two different systems of knowledge. On the one hand, he was relying on the theoretical understanding of how the cosmos worked that he had brought over from the Old World, including pseudoscientific traditions such as alchemy and astrology. Celestial mapping, which was on the rise in Europe after the importation of classical texts such as Ptolemy's *Almagest* and Islamic works such as Abū al-Ḥusayn ʿAbd al Raḥmān ibn ʿUmar al-Ṣūfī's constellation maps, also likely impacted Columbus's efforts to map the heavens on the landscape of the Indies.[2] He registered these Old World traditions in his orderly sequence of place names in Castilian inspired by celestial bodies and metals. At the same time, the knowledge of the lands that the Taino informants provided through language, gestures, and perhaps maps was also instrumental in determining Columbus's actions and discourse. My view is that though the Castilian toponyms related to metals and planets suggest that Columbus maintained control throughout his exploration and that he was able to implant Western ideological hierarchy onto the Caribbean landscape, his reliance on names borrowed from the Tainos implies that the information provided by the local inhabitants was equally essential in guiding him. The attempt to reconcile these two systems of knowledge was largely unsuccessful, in part because the natives did not only help but they also manipulated Columbus in ways that were convenient for them. Therefore, the first half of this chapter focuses on how the Old World traditions, in particular alchemy, shaped the Columbian naming discourse in Castilian, based on what he expected to find and the order he desired to project. The second half of the chapter addresses the influence and the manipulation that the native Taino inhabitants had on Columbus's actions and navigation, as reflected in the naming of places based on Taino words that he believed to be toponyms, *Baveque* and *Goanin*.

In the context of his theory of prediscovery – according to which an anonymous pilot told Columbus about unknown lands beyond the ocean seas – the historian Manzano Manzano speculated that Columbus knew about the native name of *Cipango / Cibao* and that he knew exactly where on it the gold mine was located. The historian argues that this is something that Columbus could not have simply guessed, as Las Casas had suggested ("parece que adivinando") nor could he have deduced it from the writings of ancients such as Toscanelli, D'Ailly, or Pius II. To support his argument, Manzano Manzano refers to the *Islario* by the humanist Alonso de Santa Cruz where the latter debates a statement made by Peter Martyr regarding the ancient names on Hispaniola.[3] Santa Cruz interprets *Cipango* as a Castilian derivative of the Taino name *Cibao*, with which the natives originally denominated the mountainous region under the rule of the cacique Maguana,[4] and which was later applied to the entire island of Hispaniola.[5] Manzano Manzano argues that Columbus adopted the name *Cipango* because he knew from the reports of earlier navigators, "por los protonautas," that on this island was the auriferous region he sought.[6]

However, in the *Diario del primer viaje* transcribed by Las Casas, the search for gold is not associated with finding the island of Cipango but rather with an island with the Taino name *Baveque*, a name Columbus believed to refer to a quasi-mythical place that contained marvellous amounts of the precious metal. Furthermore, although the sequence of place names inspired by metals and celestial bodies appears to be orderly, creating the impression that Columbus maintained control throughout the navigation, the circumstances surrounding his search for Baveque suggest otherwise. As it turns out, Columbus spent almost two months searching for this island because he believed, based on the information that the natives provided him, that it contained the "source" of gold in the region. The search was ultimately unsuccessful: Columbus never found the island named *Baveque* and large amounts of gold remained a theoretical possibility. If Baveque existed, a fact that is highly unlikely, it escaped baptism in Castilian and was never placed on Western maps.

As noted earlier, in the absence of specific commentaries about the circumstances of their naming, the meaning of most Columbian toponyms in the *diarios* can be interpreted in many ways. For example, the meaning of the toponym *Río del Oro* can be viewed as a descriptive name that refers, literally, to the pieces of the precious metal that Columbus spotted – or believed he spotted – in the river and on its banks or to the golden colour of the river. It can also be viewed as a toponym that was borrowed directly from Portuguese toponymy on the African coast, as Gil suggests: "En último término, sobre la toponimia indiana se proyectan nombres claramente africanos: Cabo do Monte, Cabo Verde, Cabo Roxo, Cabo das Palmas, Río do Ouro, Porto Santo, etc., entre otros tan portugueses como Valle del Paraíso."[7] Indeed, Columbus had spent years of his youth in Portugal and had sailed the African coast. These names were familiar to him, including the name of the river that the Portuguese explorer Alfonso Gonçalves Baldaya, who sailed under the orders of Prince Henry, discovered and named Rio do Ouro in 1436 on the western coast of Africa. *Río del Oro* could also be an allusion to the coveted lands of Asia which, according to the classical authority Pierre d'Ailly and, later, Marco Polo (both of whom Columbus had most likely read) contained vast quantities of this precious metal. Or it could be an expression of Columbus's desire to find precious metals and, more broadly, his mercantilistic goals.[8] Yet another possible connotation is a religious one: gold has important symbolic meanings in the Hebrew Bible as well as in medieval art and literature.[9] Since all of these possibilities are pertinent, and since the narrative provides only faint clues, the context of other toponyms Columbus invented in the vicinity is particularly useful for understanding more fully the connotations that *Río del Oro* has in the toponymic discourse.

To facilitate the analysis of the relationships among these place names, I will use the concept of a toponymic cluster introduced briefly in chapter 2. I consider a toponymic cluster to be a thematically, temporally, and geographically cohesive set of place names, all of which were inspired by a particular theme or concept. Place names in a toponymic cluster were usually, though not always, pronounced during a short period of time; in some cases, toponyms belonging to the same cluster were named months and even years apart. Usually, temporal cohesiveness resulted from Columbus's tendency to invent several place names related to a given theme and then to move on to a different one. Because of this, toponyms in a toponymic cluster also tend to denote places located in close geographic proximity or even places where one of them is located inside another, as when a smaller geographic body (a cape or a river) is located within a larger one (an island). For example, the fact that Columbus named *Río del Oro* on *Española* island implies a thematic connection between the two.

Though thematic unity is an important feature of a toponymic cluster, it alone is not sufficient for defining such a cluster. The fundamental characteristic that defines a toponymic cluster is a particular interdependence among the verbal units, that is to say, the individual toponyms in it. This interdependence clarifies the meaning of both the individual toponyms and the entire toponymic cluster. For example, some toponymic clusters are created based on the visual characteristics of the places they denote and as a whole they unite places that become symbolic markers on a single visual scene. For this reason, identifying and interpreting toponymic clusters is an essential step in deciphering the meanings of individual toponyms and in relating them to the ideas articulated in the toponymic discourse as a whole. Recognizing the toponymic clusters present in the Columbian toponymic discourse sheds light not only on the meaning articulated in the cluster but also on that of the individual toponyms in it.

Ten of the twelve toponyms discussed in this chapter were pronounced during the first voyage and during a comparatively short period of two and a half months, starting with the naming of *Río de la Luna* on 29 October 1492 and ending with the naming of *Isla de Goanin* on 13 January 1493. The temporal cohesiveness of the cluster is strengthened by the fact that two pairs, *Río de la Luna* and *Río de Mares* as well as *Monte de Plata* and *Punta del Hierro*, were probably named almost simultaneously since the names in each pair are introduced in the *Diario* on the same day (29 October and 11 January, respectively).[10] Four of the twelve toponyms in this group are related to metals (*Río del Oro*, *Monte de Plata*, *Puerto de Plata*, *Punta del Hierro*), while five are related to what were considered at the time to be "planets" (*Río de la Luna*, *Río de Mares*, *Puerto de Mares*, *Río del Sol*, and *Cabo de Luna*). The toponyms based on the Taino language, *Isla Baveque* and *Isla de Goanin,* were also related to the search for the precious metal, gold. While the thematic links among some of the toponyms in the cluster are immediately evident (e.g., *Río de la Luna* and *Río del Sol*, or *Río del Sol* and *Río del Oro)*, other conceptual relationships become clear only when the group as a whole is considered.

The different interpretations of the word "mares" in the toponyms *Río de Mares* and *Puerto de Mares* show how understanding of the toponymic cluster can facilitate the interpretation of individual toponyms in it. Neither of the two place names is discussed in the *diarios* or contemporary sources, and recent critics have provided two different interpretations of the meaning of "mares": Morison translated *Río de Mares* as the "River of Seas,"[11] while Varela and Gil later argued that "Mares" was a neologism and represented the popular spelling of the Latin word for the planet Mars, *marte*, which was introduced into the Castilian language in the thirteenth century.[12] What conclusion can we draw after taking into account their toponymic context? On 29 October, two places are mentioned: *Río de la Luna*, which was named around noon, and *Río de Mares*, named at the hour of vespers: "Andada otra legua, vido un río no tan grande de entrada, al cual puso nombre Río de la Luna. Anduvo hasta ora de bísperas. Vido otro río muy más grande que los otros, y así se lo dixeron por señas los indios; y açerca d'él vido buenas poblaciones de casas; llamó al río Río de Mares."[13] The geographic proximity of the two rivers and the temporal immediacy of their naming suggest that their meanings could be thematically related. It is possible, therefore, that the naming of *Río de Mares* was indeed inspired by a celestial body (the planet Mars) just as the naming of *Río de la Luna* was inspired by another celestial body (the moon). The context of the toponymic cluster begins to shed light on the meaning of individual toponyms; further consideration of these two toponyms and their relationships with the other toponyms in this cluster will continue to clarify their meanings.

Though the development of toponymic clusters is based primarily on Western cultural and ideological paradigms, a more careful consideration of the place names in a given toponymic cluster often reveals that the local experience had a significant role to play in their creation as well. Columbus routinely translated the physical features of the landscape into cultural symbols and signs, and he also incorporated into his toponymic discourse information that he acquired from native informants and place names, words, and fragments of speech he heard them pronounce. The phrase from Gérard Genette's *Mimologics* employed earlier in this book, "the mutual contagion of the name by the idea and the idea by the name," indicates here what the term "naming" does not: the porous nature of the Columbian "naming" and its anxious character as boundaries – geographic, linguistic, epistemological – were uncomfortably broken and previous definitions were dissolved, allowing organisms to travel. The incorporation into his toponymic discourse of the toponyms based on Taino words, *Baveque* and *Isla de Goanin*, and the enormous impact that the information related to these place names had on Columbus's actions, decisions, and acts of naming, shows that this mutual contagion was taking place starting with the first voyage.

Recognizing the toponymic cluster is useful in this case, as in many others, because the place names themselves are not clearly related to the narrative in the *diarios*. For example, references to metals in the *diarios* and the inventions of place names inspired by metals do not follow the same patterns at all. Columbus refers to gold ad nauseam as he describes the beaches and the rivers, the signs that the natives made about the locations of gold mines, the jewellery that the indigenous chieftains wore, the gifts that Columbus and his crew received, and the commodities that they bartered. He mentions silver much less often, perhaps because there is less of it and perhaps because of its lower value.[14] Finally, to convince the Crown that the Spanish conquest of the indigenous inhabitants would be swift and painless, Columbus repeatedly emphasizes the absence of iron and iron weapons in the West Indies: "Ellos no traen armas ni las cognosçen, porque les amostré espadas y las tomavan por el filo y se cortavan con ignorancia. No tienen algún fierro; sus azagayas son unas varas sin fierro y algunas d'ellas tienen al cabo un diente de peçe."[15] If place names inspired by metals were directly related to the narrative of the *Diario*, Columbus would have named numerous places after gold to emphasize its supposed abundance, a few places after silver to point out its relative scarcity, and none at all after iron to illustrate its absence (or perhaps he would have invented place names that otherwise emphasized the absence of iron, referring to rocks, wood, or fish bones that the natives used to make their weapons, for example). This is not the case. Columbus named only one place after gold (*Río del Oro*), two after silver (*Monte de Plata* and *Puerto de Plata*), and one after iron (*Punta del Hierro*). Furthermore, no connection seems to exist between when Columbus sighted the metal and when he named a place after it. The *Diario* records Columbus's seeing silver, *plata*, for the first time on 1 November 1492: "El Almirante no vido a alguno d'ellos oro, pero dize el Almirante que vido a uno d'ellos un pedaço de plata colgado a la nariz, que tuvo por señal que en la tierra avía plata."[16] However, the first name inspired by this metal, *Monte de Plata*, does not appear until 11 January 1493, more than two months later. Rather than merely mirroring the narrative in the *Diario*, Columbus's place names reveal hidden aspects of his outlook.

Let us consider a new pair of toponyms, *Monte de Plata* and *Río de la Luna*. *Diario del primer viaje* offers no explanation for Columbus's choice of the place name *Monte de Plata* nor is there any notable relationship between the naming of the place and Columbus's sighting of silver during the first voyage, or his use of the word silver, *plata*, in the narrative. There is a two-and-a-half-month gap between the first mention of the word *plata* in the *Diario del primer viaje* on 1 November 1492 and the first toponym containing this word, *Monte de Plata*, on 11 January 1493. However, the first mention of *Río de la Luna* occurs on 29 October 1492, only three days before the first mention of silver in the narrative. Did Columbus name *Río de la Luna* after sighting silver or after receiving information about it from the native inhabitants? If Gil's observations about "natural days" and "artificial days" are taken into account, the gap between the mention of silver and the naming of *Monte de Plata* becomes as small as two days or even one.

Gil shows that there is a visible pattern based on the calendar of when Columbus named places after "planets" – namely, *Río de la Luna*, *Río de Mares*, and *Río del Sol*:

> Se ve muy claro, ahora, que Colón va poniendo nombres a los ríos según el día de la semana en que esté, y que el Domingo no se acuerda del Señor sino del Sol, de acuerdo en todo con viejísimas concepciones astrológicas ... Ahora bien, cuando se repasa el *Diario*, el propio Colón, sus hijos o Las Casas tienen miedo de que este influjo astrológico quede demasiado en evidencia; así se camuflan los pasajes correspondientes, que quedan distribuidos según el siguiente cuadro:

Día	Río	*Diario*
Lunes	Luna	Lunes 30 oct.
Martes	Mares	Lunes 30 oct.
Domingo	Sol	Lunes 12 nov.[17]

Gil demonstrated that Columbus's choices of names for rivers are based on the days of the week on which he discovered them; this becomes evident when the sailors' habit of counting days from noon to noon is taken into consideration.[18] Both rivers, the Río de la Luna and the Río de Mares, were sighted on the same artificial day ("día artificial" or "giorno civile," counted from sunrise to sunset). However, since the first river was sighted in the morning and the second in the afternoon, they were sighted on two different natural days ("día natural" or "giorno astronomico," counted from noon to noon).[19] Similarly, Columbus probably invented *Río del Sol* on Sunday, 11 November, since, in Las Casas's words, it had been sighted the previous day, even though the name was recorded in the *Diario* on 12 November: "Toda aquella costa era poblada mayormente çerca del río, a quien puso nombre el río del Sol. Dixo qu'el Domingo antes, onze de Noviembre, le avía parecido que fuera bien tomar algunas personas de las de aquel río para llevar a los Reyes porque aprendieran nuestra lengua, para saber lo que ay en la tierra."[20] What is truly remarkable, however, is that the days on which Columbus invented place names based on Taino language also correspond to the calendar-based schedule for inventing place names in Castilian. Both place names based on Taino words, which he believed would lead him to gold, were introduced in the *diarios* on Sundays. Thus, Columbus first mentioned *Isla de Baveque*, the island he believed to contain immense quantities of gold, on Sunday, 12 November 1492. Likewise, he first mentioned the *Isla de Goanin*, which was derived from the Taino word *goanin*, on Sunday, 13 January 1493. Though in the Taino language the word actually referred to an alloy of gold and copper, Columbus believed that *goanin* referred to pure gold. The fact that both names of Taino origin were assigned on Sundays is significant for two reasons. First, this serves as further confirmation that Columbus gave names of places he associated with gold on Sundays, regardless of when he actually sighted the place. Furthermore, this suggests that Columbus relied on local knowledge as much as he did on Western paradigms when designing his toponymic discourse.

Returning to the toponyms *Monte de Plata* and *Río de la Luna*, in the context of a seven-and-a-half-month journey, the gap of one or two days between the mention of silver and the naming of *Monte de Plata* is very modest. Its existence can further be explained by the fact that either Columbus himself waited for a day or two before writing about the samplings of silver he saw or Las Casas omitted the initial reference to silver in the entry of 29 October and mentioned it only in the lengthy entry of 1 November, in the description of the items the natives had brought to exchange with the crew on the Río de Mares. The discussion of silver and the naming of *Río de la Luna* occur closely enough in the text of the *Diario* that the meaning of the toponym can be seen as inspired by the sighting of silver. The moon, the celestial body believed to influence the metal silver according to the alchemist tradition, is the appropriate choice for naming a place where silver has been found. Based on this relationship, *Río de la Luna* and *Monte de Plata* are toponyms with closely related meanings. When alchemical principles are considered, three well-known pairs emerge from the group of toponyms being studied here: gold and sun (*Río del Oro*, *Río del Sol*); silver and moon (*Monte de Plata*, *Puerto de Plata*, *Río de la Luna*, *Cabo de Luna*); and iron and Mars (*Punta del Hierro*, *Río de Mares*, *Puerto de Mares*).

The alchemical notion that the growth of each metal was affected by a particular celestial body originated in ancient Egypt and Mesopotamia and it was still popular in Europe at the end of the fifteenth century (it persisted in isolated cases until much later). Alchemists believed that all life on earth was affected by the movements of the "planets," and that each planet influenced the gestation and maturation of a particular metal in the womb of the earth: the sun influenced gold; the moon, silver; and Mars, iron. In the sixteenth century, the argument that stars and planets influence the health of human beings and the climate and fertility of lands, as well as the formation of metals, was still debated with passion. In 1555, the Italian humanist Girolamo Cardano argued that the sun produced gold and precious stones, while Joseph Justus Scaliger presented a counterargument to this theory in 1557. Various others used climate to discuss nature, species, and race in America, including the Spanish chronicler Oviedo, the Jesuit José de Acosta, the Franciscan Diego Valdés, and the Spanish physician Juan de Cárdenas, among others.[21] As late as the eighteenth century, the Spanish alchemist D. Torres Villaroel still called the study of metals and stones "inferior astronomy": "la astronomía superior trata de las estrellas verdaderas, fijas y errantes y de sus movimientos, en tanto que la astronomía inferior trata de las 'piedras fixas,' que también se llaman *estrellas* en el vocabulario de los alchemistas, son el Sol, Luna, Marte, Saturno, Júpiter, Venus, nitro, carbunclo, esmeralda y las demás piedras que no huyen del fuego."[22] Works of such diverse nature as philosophical and religious treatises, fairy tales, classical mythology, medieval and Renaissance poetry, prose, and the visual arts include references to pairs consisting of a celestial body and a metal influenced by it. In the *Canon's Yeoman's Tale* (1343? –1400), Chaucer lists seven such pairs:

The bodies seven, eek, lo heer anon.
Sol gold is, and Luna silver we declare;
Mars yron, Mercurie is quyksilver;
Saturnus leed, and Jubitur is tyn,
And Venus coper, by my fathers kyn.[23]

Las Casas also shared this interest in alchemy and in the ways that cosmography, geography, and philosophy dealt with the order of the cosmos and the relationships between the sky and the earth. Inspired by *De coelo et mundo*, where Aristotle reasoned that all life on earth was affected by the motions of the heavens around the earth, Las Casas argued in his *Apologética Historia* that one must read signs in the sky in order to understand the life on earth. The friar discussed the influence of the stars on the climate, on the soil, and on the character and health of the inhabitants of a place: "De todas las cosas referidas desta isla se puede bien colegir su salubridad y templanza, así por su sitio por respecto del aspecto y figura del cielo como por la figura y disposición de la misma tierra."[24] He continued to argue that in order to assess the small changes occurring in the body or anywhere on the earth, in geography as in medicine, one must regard the movements of the stars:

> así como los médicos dicen que para cognoscer la naturaleza y disposición del cuerpo humano es necesario considerar no sólo la raíz o la causa superior y universal (conviene a saber: el cielo o cuerpos celestiales y su disposición y movimiento), pero también debe el médico de tener consideración de la raíz o causa inferior (y ésta es la complexión y disposición de la persona), por esta misma manera es en el propósito, conviene a saber, que para haber noticia de las tierras si son aptas y dispuestas para la habitación humana, si son templadas o destempladas, sanas o enfermas, si son pobladas o frecuentadas mucho o poco de los hombres, se requiere que tengamos noticia y cognoscimiento de la causa universal que es el cielo ... y también de las causas particulares o especiales por respecto de la tierra y disposición della.[25]

Columbus's inversion of the meanings of the place names, and thus the naming of a "higher" place (*Monte de Plata*) after a metal and of a "lower" place (*Río de la Luna*) after the celestial body reinforces the implied connection between the two.

According to the alchemist tradition, metals and "planets" were arranged in a well-known hierarchy, in which gold occupied the central place. The alchemical treatise *Summa perfectionis magisterii*, written by Geber, a celebrated alchemist whose Arabic name was Jabir ibn Hayyan and who lived around 800 AD, was translated into Latin in the thirteenth century and was popular in the Iberian Peninsula and beyond, prior to Columbus's transatlantic voyages. We do not know whether Columbus had read this work; however, the basic principles explained in this work were common knowledge at the time. In it, Geber argued that, if given the right conditions and enough time, all metals could be transmuted into gold. The amount of time that a metal required until it would become gold determined the perfection and excellence of that metal. Because of the lengthy process through which *mars* (iron) had to go before it becomes gold, Geber considered it to be the least perfect metal in this hierarchy: "Mars has the least perfection of all the bodies in transmutation, also being of very difficult treatment and of the longest labor."[26] In a chapter titled "Sermo particularis de sole" (Particular Discourse on Sol), Geber set forth a hierarchical sequence of seven metals in which gold was the most perfect of all metals, silver was next, and iron was the least perfect:

> It [gold] is broken very easily with mercury, and it is triturated with odor of lead. There is none *in actu* which agrees with it more in substance than jupiter and luna. There is none which agrees more in weight, muteness, and putrefiability than saturn; none more in color than venus; none more *in potentia* than venus, then luna, then jupiter, then saturn, and finally mars; this is one of the secrets of nature.[27]

As in the alchemical sequence, Columbus placed the toponyms inspired by gold and the sun in the middle of his string of placements dealing with metals and celestial bodies, thus granting them central importance. Furthermore, he arranged the remaining toponyms first in the order of their increasing and then of decreasing value. The toponyms in the cluster are first introduced in the *Diario* in the following order: silver / moon (*Río de la Luna*), iron / Mars (*Río de Mares*), iron / Mars (*Puerto de Mares*), gold / sun (*Río del Sol*), gold / sun (*Isla de Baveque*, as I will argue later), gold / sun (*Río del Oro*), silver / moon (*Monte de Plata*), silver / moon (*Puerto de Plata*), iron / Mars (*Punta del Hierro*). Three more toponyms that belong to this toponymic cluster cannot be placed easily into the hierarchical sequence. *Isla de Goanin*, a toponym based on a Taino word that refers to an alloy of copper and gold, is out of place as the last toponym in the sequence.[28] The dates when *Cabo de Luna* and *Río de la Fuente* were named are unknown, making their placement in the sequence uncertain.[29] Aside from the last three toponyms, the first half of the sequence expresses the hierarchy imperfectly since the order of *Río de la Luna* and *Río de Mares* is reversed. The imperfect order of this sequence may be explained by the implied parallel between silver and iron. In the 25 November description of a river on the island Columbus named *Isla Llana*, silver and iron are so alike that one could be mistaken for the other: "Vido por la playa muchas otras piedras de *color de hierro*, y otras que dezían *algunos que eran minas de plata*, todas las cuales trae el río."[30] The place names in the second half of the sequence are arranged exactly in the order of their decreasing value: gold / sun (three times), silver / moon (twice), and iron /

Mars (once). Gold and the sun occupy the middle place between the two halves of the sequence.

Columbus's belief that gold, because of its perfect status, occupied a privileged place among all metals and was a symbolic centre of the things in the universe, was consistent not only with the alchemist tradition but with other schools of thought as well, including Christian philosophy. In scholastic philosophy, gold embodied perfection, the sun, and also Christ. In alchemy, gold, a materialization of *sol* or the sun, in its most perfect stage, became Christ. Both in alchemy and in Christian religion, gold, the sun, and Christ were perceived to be central figures and symbols: the sun was viewed as the ruler of "planets" and of the maturation of gold on earth; gold was believed to be the most perfect of all metals; and Christ, God's son, was revered as the saviour of humankind. Therefore, the evidence of the patterns of alchemical thinking in Columbus's naming does not detract from his (or Las Casas's, for that matter) character as a devout Christian but rather reveals another layer of his mentality – a passionate zeal to understand how the cosmos works and how its secrets could be uncovered. Nevertheless, this belief in alchemical principles or the correspondences between the sky and the earth was mostly obscured in the pages of the *diarios*. In this regard, Gil has noted that the interest in astrology was hidden in the texts about Columbus's voyages: "cuando se repasa el *Diario*, el propio Colón, sus hijos o Las Casas tienen miedo de que este influjo astrológico quede demasiado en evidencia; así se camuflan los pasajes correspondientes."[31] Place names thus record principles that were otherwise largely edited out of the narrative of the *diarios* but that reveal important aspects about Columbus's views.

The limits of a particular toponymic cluster are also defined by the absence of other toponyms related to its theme. Beyond the twelve place names listed at the beginning of this chapter, Columbus named no other places after either "planets" or metals during the rest of the four voyages. This particularly calls for attention given that the narrative of the *diarios* makes frequent mentions of other metals, such as copper. It also refers rather frequently to heavenly bodies and celestial mapping, as it mentions other planets (Mercury and Jupiter), constellations, and the signs of the zodiac (Libra and Aries). This suggests that the choices for which heavenly bodies and metals should be included in the toponymic discourse are intentional.

Two other names could potentially be included in the toponymic cluster of place names related to celestial bodies and metals: *Cabo del Estrella* (6 December 1492) and *Golfo de las Perlas* (*Relación del tercer viaje*: "A este golpho puso nombre 'golpho de las Perlas'").[32] *Cabo del Estrella* (used with the masculine article) differs from the other place names that evoke celestial bodies in that it was named after a star and not a "planet." During Columbus's time, the sun, the moon, and Mars were all considered to be planets (and not satellites or stars). In *Cosmographia*, the scholastic philosopher Bernard Silvestris listed "the seven planets" according to their distance from the earth: the moon, Venus, the sun ("in the central position"), Mars, Jove, and Saturn (78–9). Columbus's names are inspired by the first three "planets": the moon, the sun, and Mars (with the exception of Venus). While it could also be a tribute to Columbus's skills in celestial navigation, *Cabo del Estrella* also has an important religious meaning. Columbus dedicated a series of place names during the four voyages to the Virgin Mary, and during the first voyage, on two consecutive days, he pronounced three names related to this theme: *Puerto María* (6 December), *Cabo del Estrella* (6 December), and *Puerto de la Conçepción* (7 December). In medieval and Renaissance written texts and in visual imagery, the Virgin Mary was portrayed as wearing a blue cloak decorated with stars and standing on the moon. In the book of Revelation the woman was also associated with the stars, the sun, and the moon ("A great portent appeared in heaven: a woman clothed with the sun, with the moon under her feet, and on her head a crown of twelve stars" [Rev. 12:1]) as is also the great beast whose "tail swept down a third of the stars of heaven and threw them down to the earth" (Rev. 12:4). My view is that *Cabo del Estrella* evokes the spiritual image of the Virgin Mary as well as the star that showed the way to Columbus's flagship *Santa María*, but that it is not related to the pairings of "planets" and metals based on alchemical principles.

The toponymic cluster built on Western alchemical concepts and formulated as a sequence based on symmetry and hierarchies sends a message of control and harmony. In reality, however, Columbus's search depended largely on the willingness of the local people to provide guidance via verbal, gestural, or material signs. Columbus undertook a lengthy voyage to an island where he believed large quantities of gold existed, and during his search (which took two months) he relied on the directions of the local inhabitants when he mentioned the name *Baveque*. It almost seems as if Columbus hoped that the name itself would serve him as a vehicle through which local knowledge would be channelled. However, during those two months he became the target of manipulation and he was sent into a maze of trajectories at the end of which he found neither Baveque nor gold. The second half of this chapter explores the ways in which the Taino inhabitants manipulated Columbus into navigating fruitlessly in search of an island and the source of gold on it, neither of which existed. It also explores the ways in which Columbus attempted to integrate the information he was getting from the local informants into the system of knowledge he had brought with him from the Old World as he named two more places, *Isla Baveque* and *Isla de Goanin*, based on the same alchemical and astrological principles as in the case of the place names inspired by metals and planets in Castilian.

According to Coll y Toste's philological commentary, the place the Tainos called *Baveque* may not have existed. Coll y Toste informs us that *Baveque* was not a Taino toponym but a combination of Taino words which Columbus interpreted as a toponym. Columbus had done the same in other cases such as *Bohío* and *Guanín.* In the Lucayo Taino language, prefixes applied to the beginnings of words were used as pronouns. The word *aneque* meant "why," therefore *b-aneque* meant "why you?" When Columbus inquired of the natives about places where gold could be found, they pointed to the horizon and exclaimed "baneque, baneque," that is, "and you, who are you? Who are you?"[33] If Coll y Toste's interpretation of the etymology of this word is correct and the place did not exist, then the natives' response, based on a phrase that did not refer to any known place, becomes a form of manipulation and derision.

The name of *Baveque* appears in the *Diario del primer viaje* for the first time on 12 November 1492, and it is mentioned for the last time on Sunday, 6 January 1493, never to be brought up again. The first and the last mention of *Baveque* coincide with the first mention of *Río del Sol* on 12 November and the first mention of *Río del Oro* on 4 January. Columbus clearly identified *Baveque* with gold. For two months, Columbus's goal was to reach *Baveque*, and the *Diario del primer viaje* includes numerous references to the place names. According to Morison, *Baveque* refers to what we know today as Great Inagua Island, which is located to the north of the canal that separates Haiti from Cuba.[34] However, some critics have interpreted *Baveque* as referring to Santo Domingo, others as *tierra firme* or other islands, and yet others do not believe that it referred to any place in particular.[35] Columbus had understood from his native informants that Baveque island was a quasi-mythical place where the locals gathered gold on the beaches at night, by candlelight: "Partió del Puerto y río de Mares al render del cuarto de alva, para ir a una isla que mucho affirmavan los indios que traia que se llamava Baveque, adonde, según dizen por señas, que la gente d'ella coge el oro con candelas de noche en la playa y después con martillo diz ue hazían vergas d'ello" (12 November).[36] Enthused by the news, Columbus departed in search of the island right away, and he sailed in such a hurry that he did not even stop to explore two magnificent rivers on the way because "weather and wind were fair for going in search of the said island of *Babeque*" (el tiempo y viento era bueno para ir en demanda de la dicha isla de Babeque).[37] From his ship, he named one of the two rivers *Río del Sol*,[38] which was "very copious and bigger than any of the others that had been discovered" (muy caudaloso y mayor que ninguno de los otros que avía hallado).[39] The nearly two-month voyage seeking Baveque was a difficult one, and Columbus's quest was undermined not only by the disobedient captain of the *Pinta*, Martín Alonso Pinzón, and contrary winds but also (why not?) by Satan himself ("las malas obras de Sathanás, aue deseava impeder aquel viaje, como hasta entonçes havía hecho," 6 January).[40] On 6 January Columbus finally reunited with the rebellious captain of the *Pinta*, who had departed to sail in search of gold, leaving his admiral behind, and had reached Baveque alone, or at least so he claimed. During their conversation, Columbus discovered that, alas, Pinzón had found no gold there at all. Most likely, Pinzón did not reach Baveque either and so Columbus felt a relief that he could finally put the search for Baveque to rest by documenting in his ship log, which in some shape or form was going to reach the Crown's eyes, that it was Pinzón who found Baveque but no gold on it. At least Columbus did not have to bear the blame for this one.

After aborting the search for Baveque, Columbus made an interesting linguistic manoeuvre as he continued naming places. Rather than admitting his failure, his acts of naming imply that he had gained adequate understanding of the location of metals in the region. His narrative also claims that he did find gold after all, but it shifts the location of this gold from Baveque to Bohío, which Columbus named *Española*. Everything in the narrative is presented as divine intervention that favoured his finding gold. Triumphant Columbus concludes that he miraculously found Española / Bohío instead of Baveque: "Así que, Señores Príncipes, que yo cognozco que milagrosamente mandó quedar allí aquella nao Nuestro Señor, porqu'es el mejor lugar de toda la isla para hazer al assiento y más açerca de las minas del oro."[41] Even the shipwreck of his flagship *Santa María* was interpreted as an intervention by Divine Providence to build a settlement which would then lead him to the discovery of gold. From this point on in the *Diario*, descriptions of finding gold are even more frequent. Columbus continued on to the island he had named *Española*. There, with the help of the native informants of the chieftain Guacanagarí, he claims to have found large pieces of the desired metal: "Y dize aquí el Almirante que resgató la caravela mucho oro, que por un cabo de agujeta le divan vuenos pedaços de oro del tamaño de dos dedos y a veces como la mano" (6 January).[42] Afterwards, they went to a river where the explorer was once again amazed to find sand shining with gold: "y halló que el arena de la boca del río, el cual es muy grande y hondo, era diz que toda llena de oro, y en tanto grado que era maravilla, puesto que era muy menudo" (8 January).[43] Columbus proceeded to guide a smaller boat into the marvellous river of both salt and fresh water and discovered, or at least so he tells us, abundant quantities of gold: "hallavan metidos por los aros de los barriles pedaçitos de oro, y lo mismo en los aros de la pipa."[44] Much of it was actually *magasita*, fool's gold, as Las Casas remarked in the margins of the *Diario*, while some of it may have been real gold, as even today some gold is found in the valley of the Yaque.[45] On 8 January 1493, to mark the supposedly successful end of his odyssey in search of the island of Baveque, Columbus named the river on Española *Río del Oro*: "Puso por nombre el Almirante al río el Río del Oro."[46] The reality, however, was that he found no gold in Río del Oro. After 6 January 1493 Columbus never mentioned Baveque again (a single exception occurs in the *Relación del tercer viaje*).[47] During the next few days, he named three other places after two other metals in the order of decreasing value and thus swiftly completed the alchemical sequence: *Monte de Plata* (11 January), *Puerto de Plata* (named between 11 and 18 January), and *Punta del Hierro* (11 January). On 16 January 1493 Columbus departed from the gulf he called *Golfo de las Flechas*, homeward.

What is of particular interest here is the change in the language that Columbus used (and Las Casas maintained it in enough instances for us to see its significance) when he referred to his search for gold and for the island of Baveque over the course of nearly two months. The change in the language begins in the passages that deal with Columbus's act of capturing several native men in the vicinity of the Río del Sol, from whom he learned about Baveque. He states that his desire to take them back to Spain and to teach them Castilian was related to his objective to find out where *in* the earth gold was hidden: "Dixo qu'el domingo antes, onze de Noviembre, le avía parecido que fuera bien tomar algunas personas de las de aquel río [Río del Sol] para llevar a los Reyes porque aprendieran nuestra lengua, *para saber lo que ay en la tierra*" (12 November).[48]

Columbus was no longer satisfied with finding samplings of gold, such as small pieces in the water of the rivers or gold dust scattered on the sand on the beaches. Rather, he began insisting on finding larger quantities of gold buried *in* the earth: "Porque sin duda *es en estas tierras* grandíssima suma de oro, que no sin causa dizen estos indios que yo traigo que ha en estas islas lugares *adonde cavan el oro* y lo traen al pescueço, y a las orejas y a los braços e a las piernas, y son manillas muy gruessas, y también ha piedras y ha perlas preciosas y infinita especería."[49] This is consistent with how contemporary alchemical treatises insisted that metals were not inert, lifeless objects, but rather dynamic substances that were "born" in the womb of the earth. Apparently influenced by this way of thinking, Columbus used alchemical terminology, specifically the words "nasce" or "nasçe" (born) and "fuente" (source) when referring to Baveque: "Después de comido, un escudero traía un cinto ... y dos pedaços de oro labrados que eran muy delgados, que creo que aquí alcanzan poco d'él, puesto que tengo qu'están muy vezinos de *donde naçe y ay mucho*" (18 December);[50] and again, on the same day, Las Casas retains Columbus's alchemical language when he transcribes the explorer's interpretation of the information that a local inhabitant provided about gold: "En este día se resgató diz que poco oro, pero supo el Almirante de un hombre viejo que avía muchas islas comarcanas a cient leguas y más, según pudo entender, en las cuales *nasçe mucho oro*, hasta decirle que avía isla que era toda oro, y en las otras que ay tanta cantidad que lo cogen y ciernen como con çedaço y lo funden y hazen vergas y mill labores" (18 December).[51] This idea of "growing" metals was consistent with Aristotelian physics. Incidentally, before finding out about Baveque, Columbus had used the word *naçe* (or *nace*) mostly in the general sense to refer to plants, grasses, and trees: "y otra yerva que naçe en tierra" (11 October) (and other plants that grow [or literally, are "born"] from the earth); "Aquí naçe [algodón] en esta isla, mas por el poco tiempo no pude dar así del todo fe. Y también aquí naçe el oro" (13 October) (Here [cotton] grows [or literally, is "born,"] although because of the lack of time I am not entirely certain of this. Also, gold is "born" here); "y nace por los montes árboles grandes" (4 November) (and in that land great trees grow [or literally, are "born"]). Only occasionally did Columbus use the word in the alchemical sense at that point: "no puedo errar con el ayuda de Nuestro Señor que yo no le falle adonde naçe [el oro]" (15 October) (I cannot be mistaken with the help of Our Lord and fail to find where [gold] is "born").[52]

When speaking about Baveque, however, Columbus used the word *naçe* exclusively in the alchemical sense. For him, the location of gold could be determined based on a harmonious interpretation of the alchemical principles and the local knowledge of the Tainos that gold was "born" in its "source," Baveque: "dixo el Almirante que no creía que en aquella isla Española ni en la Tortuga oviese minas de oro, sino que *lo traían de Baneque*, y que traen poco, porque no tiene[n] aquellos qué dar por ello ...

Y creía el Almirante *qu'estava muy cerca de la fuente* y que Nuestro Señor le avía de mostrar *dónde nasce el oro*" (17 December).[53] In contrast, the location of gold was a simple question of geography for members of his crew. They claimed that the proximity of Baveque and Isla de la Tortuga accounted for the fact that more gold was found on Tortuga, in contrast to the more distant Hispaniola: "y dixeron al Almirante, después de ida, que en la Tortuga avía más oro que en la isla Española, porque es más cerca de Baneque" (17 December).[54] The different views that Columbus and his crew held about the nature of gold on the island of Baveque show their distinct philosophical approaches to navigation. While the interests of the crew were strictly practical, Columbus also had larger questions in mind. His use of alchemical language in his narrative and toponymy is another testament to his efforts to perform acts of ideological mapping, rather than of simply naming by resemblance. His integration into the sequence of hybrid toponyms based on Taino language is another testament to his reliance on the local epistemology and ongoing efforts to integrate the Western and the native systems of knowledge, languages, and onomastics. Prior to learning about Baveque from his native informants, Columbus's commitment to the alchemical principle in his naming was a tentative one (which may also explain the imperfect order of the toponyms related to silver and then to iron given before any news was received about the "source" of gold in Baveque). Having learned about Baveque, however, the explorer became convinced that he would find the place where gold was "born" and expressed this conviction as he chose the place name *Río del Sol*. As soon as he learned that no gold was found on Baveque, he quickly shifted his focus, named *Río del Oro*, and then named the remaining places right away, finishing the alchemical hierarchy of metals in the correct order: *Monte de Plata* (11 January), *Puerto de Plata* (named between 11 and 18 January), and *Punta del Hierro* (11 January).

Likely, the reliance on the alchemical principles also explains his choice for the name of another river on Hispaniola, *Río de la Fuente*, which Columbus probably assigned during the first voyage. Like the toponym *Río del Oro* on this island, it expresses his belief that the "source" of gold was somewhere near.[55] Alchemical principles explain his decision to name *Río del Sol*, the name inspired by the celestial body that influences the birth of gold, immediately after learning the news about the desired "source," and they justify Columbus's beginning the voyage towards it. They also explain his decision to make *Río del Oro*, the name inspired by the imagined finding of the metal itself, mark the end of this voyage. Columbus's choice to name both *Río del Oro* and *Río de la Fuente* on the island he had named *Española* is significant in itself. As Columbus chose to name places after the most excellent of all metals, he associated the idea of centre and of superiority with *Española*, which also became the administrative centre of Spanish colonial power in the Indies during the early stages of conquest and colonization. Its name rhetorically proclaimed the superiority of Spain, the mercantilist and spiritual potential of the voyages, and Spain's imperial domain in the Indies. The letter to Santángel later reinforced this idea of the centrality of Spanish power and of the symbolic centrality of Hispaniola by framing this toponym at the centre of its narrative.

The toponymic cluster based on metals and celestial bodies brings to light Columbus's attempt to create a symbolic order based on Western cultural sources and Taino intervention in altering his itinerary. Columbus's choices of place names, in which he recreated planet / metal pairs and emphasized the supremacy of gold by placing it in the middle of the sequence, reflects his abiding interest in alchemy and astrology. Columbus's hunt for gold challenged the symbolic order he desired to create in his toponymy, and yet it also reflects how the uncertainty he felt was still largely edited out of the toponymy in order to retain and project an impression of control and calm. When naming places, Columbus used all sources of information available to him – human, natural, and spiritual – to create, through language, a new ideological map of uncharted territories. Columbus invented names inspired by metals and planets to assure the Catholic monarchs that their desires would be fulfilled: precious metals were abundant, the inhabitants were ready to convert to Christianity, and the lands were filled with riches. His place names also articulate Columbus's philosophical view of the universe and his idea of harmony and symmetry in the world created by God. In reality, however, they only projected a desirable theory onto the landscape. The proverbial wisdom, "Not all that glitters is fit to hold, not all that shines will be pure gold," became bitter truth when the stream of golden grains sifting through Columbus's fingers became mere sand. The suggestion of the interminable "source" of gold in the Indies through the creation of a hierarchical sequence based on metals and celestial bodies was but a rhetorical falsification. It seems that even Columbus himself may have realized the extent to which it was false and he may have wanted to erase some of the rhetorical statements connected to it. During the next voyage, Columbus renamed *Río del Oro* as *Río de las Cañas*. Though Las Casas believes that this was an oversight on the part of Columbus ("al cual llamó el Almirante el río de las Cañas, no se acordando que en el primer viaje lo nombró Río del Oro" (by which the admiral named *Río de las Cañas*, forgetting that during the first voyage he had named it *Río del Oro*), changing the name of a river that clearly had nothing to do with finding the precious metal was a step toward correcting a previous rhetorical fiction built on ideal toponymic sequences and hierarchies.[56] Likewise, during the third voyage Columbus was near Jamaica, which was perhaps the island he had named *Baveque* during the first voyage, though we do not know for sure. However, he never mentioned the name *Baveque* again, something that Las Casas noted: "afirmando que había mucho oro (y creo, cierto, que es la que llamaban el viaje primero Baneque, que tantas veces la nombraban, pues que no veo que aquí el Almirante haga mención de Baneque)."[57] It seems that it was useful to erase the verbal marks left by the unsuccessful search for gold during the first voyage, the excessive reliance on the directions of the natives, and the idealistic way of naming places inspired by alchemical sequences of metals and celestial bodies that had nothing to do with the reality found.

As the search for Baveque and gold on it suggests, we should think of place names not only as projections of a theoretical certainty or as mirages of desire but also as products of negotiation, translation, manipulation, and subversion. It appears that neither *Isla Baveque* nor *Isla de Goanin* existed in reality, and the abundance of gold as well as the orderly arrangement of the cosmos was just an illusion that Columbus's toponymic discourse strived so hard to affirm. Ordinary words in Taino, such as *bohío* (house) and *goanin* (alloy of copper and gold), used as toponyms to refer to places that did not exist attest to the difficult communication between Columbus and the local inhabitants, something that the narrative of the *Diario del primer viaje* largely conceals. Columbus remained entirely silent about the fact that he did not find the island named *Baveque* nor the "source" of gold on it or anywhere else. He also did not dwell on his frustrating communication with the locals who sent him on a futile search for the island of Baveque. Perhaps he hoped that after receiving funding from the Crown for the second voyage, he would be able to find the "source" of gold based on better linguistic communication with the local people. To improve his chances, he took several Taino men to Spain so they would learn Castilian and serve as interpreters. This, however, also never bore fruit. The Taino men suffered diseases and perished during the return voyage. During the later voyages, as it became increasingly clear that he would never find gold, Columbus shifted his focus from the precious metal to finding the Earthly Paradise, as his toponymic discourse also attests.

Columbus's quest to find the Baveque island failed, in part, because it implicitly contained two clashing objectives. On the one hand, Columbus needed to understand the world he was exploring so that he could discover the secrets hidden in its lands ("para ... saber dellos los secretos de la tierra"); this crucial geographical and social information would enable him to find the gold he was seeking and help him shape the itineraries of his voyages. On the other hand, Columbus had hopes of instituting, through the verbal acts of naming, the ideology – spiritual, political, and cultural – of the nascent empire whose interests he was serving. He also hoped to appropriate on behalf of the king and queen of Spain the "uncharted" lands through the performative function of naming. To achieve this second set of objectives, Columbus relied on the instruments and rituals of the imperial institution – the plume, the parchment, and the formal ritual of taking possession – as well as on theoretical knowledge based on Western science in its current state, which he had acquired from treatises and maps. In contrast, the quickest way to achieve the first objective was with the help of information acquired from the local inhabitants. Columbian toponymy reflects these two conflicting goals which involved imposing and inquiring, erasing and translating, taking possession and becoming a subject at the mercy of the natives, who were willing to help as much as they intentionally manipulated and derided him.

5 Iguana and Christ

This chapter addresses the shifting visions documented in *Cabo de Sierpe*, a toponym Columbus invented during the second half of his first voyage, as well as in the toponyms *Villa de la Navidad*, *Cabo Sancto*, *Monte Cristo*, and *Punta Roxa*, which he assigned to nearby places.[1] According to my earlier definition, these toponyms form a toponymic cluster: they were named during a brief period of time and the places they denominate are located in geographic proximity. Furthermore, as I will argue in this chapter, they form a cohesive visual scene which incorporates elements of the physical and cultural realms originating from both sides of the Atlantic. Rather than thinking in terms of imposition of power of the European discourse onto a landscape that Columbus presumably saw as bare, or of the resistance of American natives only as a subsequent response to this imposition, this chapter instead focuses on the silent dialogues between landscapes, minds, and discourses, during which presences and memories both contaminated one another. It addresses Columbus's role as a conduit through which these dialogues occurred and it focuses his shifting mode of seeing that moved across the Atlantic from the Caribbean to Andalusia and back again, and the inevitable juxtaposition, negotiation, and translation of real (Caribbean) and imaginary (Andalusian) images. Therefore, it is concerned with the fragmentation and desecration of the existing spaces and the subsequent creation of new hybrid landscapes and, through them, of grotesque, monstrous landscapes.

The passage in which the toponym *Cabo de Sierpe* appears does not include any comments about its naming:

> Saliendo el sol, lebantó las anclas con poco viento … para ir por delante de la Villa de la Navidad … segund aquellas restringas eran grandes, que duran

> desde el Cabo Sancto *hasta el Cabo de Sierpe*, que son más de seis leguas, y fuera en la mar bien tres … Navegó así al Leste camino de un monte muy alto … el cual tiene forma de un alfaneque muy hermoso, al cual puso nombre Monte Cristo, el cual está justamente al Leste de el Cabo Sancto.[2]

Judging from its introduction in the *Diario del primer viaje* on 4 January 1493, Columbus most likely named *Cabo de Sierpe* during the second half of the first voyage. While we could assume that Las Casas omitted any comments regarding its naming during the process of transcription, it is more plausible that Columbus himself chose not to say anything about the matter in the ship log. As we shall see, given the Christian overtones of the place name *Cabo de Sierpe*, had Columbus offered any such explanations of its meaning, Las Casas surely would have included them in his transcription. Columbus's choice, as it seems, to remain silent on this subject speaks to the likelihood that the naming occurred under tenuous, anxious circumstances during which the Caribbean and the Andalusian landscapes were juxtaposed in the search for parallelisms that resulted in necessary adjustments and in the moulding of the contours of both landscapes to fit the other.

"La más asquerosa cosa que hombres vieron"

In Spanish medieval bestiaries, the term "serpent" did not refer to a single species; rather it was an umbrella term, like the terms "beast," "bird," "fish," and "stone," and it encompassed various lizards, snakes, and reptiles. Furthermore, the distinctions between "serpents" and other categories such as "birds" or "beasts" were not definite, and "serpents" were described in a variety of fashions: some of them were believed to have one or two pairs of legs while others were believed to be legless; some were depicted as having wings while others were wingless; and some, just to make matters even more confusing, were depicted with a pair of curly horns. Amphisbaena, basilisk, dragon, hydrus, cerastes, asp, and even frog were all listed as varieties of serpent. Early European chroniclers who wrote about the New World, among whom were Oviedo and Oliva, exploited this vague definition of the term "serpent" (*sierpe* or *serpiente* in Spanish) to describe the various kinds of creatures they had seen or had heard about: *culebras* were great in size but they were not venomous or malicious; the American crocodiles, just like the ones known to reside in the Nile, could devour men; the length of some *sierpes* or *serpientes* reached as many as eight feet, but despite their frightening appearance most of them were not aggressive nor did they have the ability to sting, as they were "serpientes sin ponzoña." Snakes in the modern sense of the word also inhabited the Caribbean islands, and some were even brought back to Europe as curiosities.[3] Given the flexibility of the terms "sierpe" and "serpiente" as they were used by European writers both prior to and after Columbus's first voyage across the Atlantic, Columbus could have invented the toponym *Cabo de Sierpe* as a reference to a whole host of real and mythical animals. In the *diarios*, however, the words "sierpe" and "serpiente" refer to a single species, one that had left on him a lasting impression as documented in his letter of 26 February 1495: "Allí mui çerca bi en muchos lugares presos, al pie de los árboles muchos serpientes, la mas asquerosa cosa que hombres vieron; todas tenían cosidos las bocas, salvo algunas que no tenían dientes" (the spelling variants and the grammatical mistakes are part of the original).[4] Hundreds of these "serpientes" roamed the beaches of the Caribbean islands and were hunted and consumed as food by the native inhabitants. They were iguanas.

It is easy to imagine Columbus sighting a statuesque iguana, or perhaps a swarm of them, on the tip of the cape he then named *Cabo de Sierpe*, wich we could translate as "Cape of the Iguana." For anyone who has visited any of the less populated islands in the Caribbean, the sight is familiar. The impression that this creature, one of the larger animals on the islands, left on the early explorers was truly unforgettable. Not surprisingly, contemporary chronicles dedicated a fair amount of attention to the iguana.[5] The uncertain location of the iguana as one suspended between European literary and visual traditions, on the one hand, and the emerging discourses dealing with what soon would be known as the New World, on the other, is expressed in Las Casas's binomial definition of iguanas as "propias sierpes" and as "las que llamaron *iuanas*."[6] The friar provides a lengthy description of an iguana which, on the one hand, follows the tradition of medieval bestiaries in which some commentary about the animals was needed to explain their complex, monstrous, or miraculous nature; and which, on the other hand, is part of the nascent European discourses about the New World that attempt to define its unfamiliar environment through description and comparison, given that appropriate vocabulary to denote them in European languages was lacking:

Es tan grande como perrillo de halda, de la hechura de un lagarto, pintada como él, pero no de color verde las pinturas o azafranadas sino pardas, que la afean más. Tiene un cerro de espinas desde la cabeza por el lomo hasta lo postrero de la cola, que la hace más horrible y espantable. Cuando la iban a

> tomar los indios hacía y hace un papo como las lagartijas, más grande o tanto como una vejiga de una gran ternera, y abre la boca y muestra los dientes como una fiera sierpe (como lo es, al parecer), pero no hace mal y fácilmente la prenden y atan y traen.[7]

It was just a ghastly thing. It was a lap-dog ("perrillo de halda"), a lizard ("lagarto"), a wall lizard ("lagartija"), a calf ("gran ternera"), and a ferocious serpent ("una fiera sierpe"), all mingled into one. The brownish-grey colour and the heap of thorns on the spine ("cerro de espinas") made it appear even more horrendous and frightening ("que la hace más horrible y espantable"). Moreover, while the monstrous physical appearance of the iguana left an indelible imprint in the visual memories of the European conquistadors, the Tainos' demonstration of how it could be converted into a cultural product played a decisive role in the Spaniards' opinions of this creature and the fostering of communication between the two groups. The iguana may have been the first to silently greet Columbus in the Caribbean, but it was served as a welcome meal to his brother Bartolomé by the cacique Cahonaboa and his sister Anacaucoa. Throughout the first and later voyages, Columbus and his men witnessed the production of local culture, in Levi-Straussian terms, as they saw iguanas being hunted, their flesh being prepared for storage by drying, and raw meat being cooked and eventually consumed as part of a meal.

The *Diario del primer viaje* documents Columbus's awareness of Taino and Carib cultural spaces and his quest to learn the place names that denote them, even if this quest was self-interested and even if such awareness remained fragmented. As chapter 4 argued, the Tainos provided Columbus not only with food and desired material objects, but also with what he needed the most: information about the local geography. Despite the fact that Columbus chastised his men for stealing the material belongings of the local inhabitants, he himself kidnapped indigenous men with the purpose of acquiring information about the local lands and social networks. Furthermore, he used local toponymy as another source that could provide him with desired insights.

Columbus's creation of hybrid toponyms, which consisted of linguistic elements in Taino and Castilian, shows how he absorbed information available to him through local names of places. These hybrid toponyms are composed of an element in Castilian, usually the geographic term, and the indigenous word or name of the place, resulting in compound place names, such as *Isla de Goanin* (*Guanín*), *Golfo de Samana* (*Xamaná*), and

Monte Caribata. Hybrid toponyms, Taino toponyms, and names of chieftains are interspersed throughout the *Diario del primer viaje*: mentions of territories in which the caciques Guarionex, Macorix, Mayonic, Fuma, and Coroay were in charge appear in the entry of 29 December; *Isla Yamaye* and *Río Yaqui* are mentioned on 6 and 8 January, respectively; and after a longer absence of Taino toponymy, nearly all of the toponyms introduced during the final week of the first voyage are based on Taino toponymy or vocabulary: *Isla de Matininó*, *Isla de Goanin*, *Isla de Carib*, and *Higuay*,[8] all of which are introduced on 13 January; *Golfo de Samana*, *Río Yuma*, and *Río Tamo*, which appear in the margin of 16 January; and *Golfo de las Flechas* and *Puerto de las Flechas*, which are introduced on 16 January. Therefore, *Cabo de Sierpe*, introduced in the *Diario del primer viaje* on 4 January 1493, appears in the larger context of a string of place names derived from the Taino toponymy or dealing with encounters with the local inhabitants, recorded in Columbus's ship log during the last twenty days of his first voyage.[9] This string of Taino toponymy and hybrid place names provides a context within which *Cabo de Sierpe* should not be considered a straightforward Castilian toponym, but rather one that is probably concerned with features of the Caribbean landscape and aspects of the local cultures, such as hunting, cooking, and consuming an iguana, all of which Columbus witnessed.

Seen through Columbus's eyes, the iguana can be thought of as a symbol of the transformation of the physical landscape into the cultural. It can also be thought of as an expression of Columbus's own gradual immersion into the local culture, despite his initial distance from it and even revulsion of it. Contemporary historians document the disgust that the Europeans experienced upon witnessing the natives consume iguana meat for food: "vianda muy espantosa a los nuestros y entre ellos [los pescadores] muy preciada."[10] However, during the meeting between Bartolomé and the cacique Cahonaboa, who was accompanied by his sister Anacaucoa, the cooked flesh of an iguana became the connecting medium that drew the two parties into a ritual of a diplomatic encounter: "Allí en la mesa de Anacaucoa pusieron al Adelantado de las serpientes que el Almirante había visto en el primer puerto de Cuba, aborrecimiento de las cuales le quitó una hermana de Anacaucoa que con mucha gracia a ellas le convidaba."[11]

Perhaps it was no *Cabo de Sabor* (Cape Taste) or *Cabo Rico* (Cape Rich or Cape Delicious), but *Cabo de Sierpe* fostered the start of a relationship with at least a façade of amicability on one side and hospitality on the other. It is another matter that these peaceful attitudes were short-lived. The parallel between the violent victories over the native people and the hunting of the iguana described by Las Casas is hard to ignore ("fácilmente la prenden y atan y traen") as it was suggestive of the quickly spreading Western attitude towards the local peoples who could be easily captured. Soon enough, the conquistadors' greed and extreme cruelties provoked Cahonaboa's equally violent response, which was to slaughter all of Columbus's crew from the first voyage who had stayed at the fort of La Navidad, on Hispaniola, after the Genovese *almirante* had headed back to Castile. The fate of Bartolomé's hosts was tragic as well: Cahonaboa was sent to Castile in shackles and died in a shipwreck, while the governor Nicolás de Ovando ordered Anacaucoa's public hanging in 1504. Fittingly, two of the last three Columbian toponyms recorded in the *Diario del primer viaje* – *Golfo de las Flechas* and *Puerto de las Flechas*, both introduced on 16 January – record some of the violence on both sides and the justifiable warlike response that the native peoples had towards the intruders.

As the example of the iguana illustrates, it would be futile to attempt to separate the natural landscape from the sociocultural one, or the European visions of the physical shapes of the tropical landscape from the development of intangible but instrumental, decisive, and usually annihilating relationships. By the same token, regarding all social, cultural, and even natural agents in the tropical landscape solely as passive objects (in the colonial view) would result in a partial understanding of the processes that shaped the creation of the hybrid American landscapes. And by extension, considering only the European sources that informed Columbian naming would result in an impoverished understanding of it.

Columbus's *diarios*, as well as contemporary chronicles and histories, contain various records about Columbus and his men seeing iguanas, being disgusted by them, and, after overcoming the initial shock, tasting their cooked meat. And yet the paragraph in the *Diario del primer viaje* says nothing about a close encounter with "la más asquerosa cosa que hombres vieron" (the most disgusting thing that the men have seen) on *Cabo de Sierpe*. It does not even suggest that the cape was explored on foot. On the contrary, the sweeping gaze documented in the paragraph featuring *Cabo de Sierpe* implies that Columbus viewed and named most important landmarks from afar, as all the distances and shapes mentioned in it are large. Aside from the mention in the paragraph in question, *Cabo de Sierpe* is never brought up again in the entire text of all four *diarios*. This suggests that Columbus quickly understood that the cape he had named *Cabo de Sierpe* did not present lucrative possibilities: it did not host a human settlement nor did it offer any easily identifiable natural resources. Columbus saw the cape, named it *Cabo de Sierpe* from afar, and continued sailing.[12] He never returned to it again.

As the *Santa María* passed *Cabo Sancto* and *Cabo de Sierpe* and as Columbus's memory brought to his eyes recent visions of iguanas, he may have identified similar shapes in the landscape such as the extended shape of the cape reminiscent of an iguana's body. The serpentine canals that penetrated *Cabo Sancto* and perhaps *Cabo de Sierpe* also easily brought to mind the shape of the iguana. Columbian place names commonly focus on shapes, and throughout history shapes have served for geographers, map makers, and artists as tools for assimilating and representing a landscape. Landscape painting, for example, has always been "concerned with the morphology of these places, their shapefulness."[13] Even the word "landscape" itself in various European languages contains one of the suffixes connoting shape: the Dutch *-schap*, the German *-shaft*, and the English *-ship*, *-skip* and *-scape*. Columbus's focus on geometric and geographic shapes and objects is expressed in toponyms such as *Isla Alto Velo*, *Punta del Aguja*, and *Isla Belaforma*, among various others.

The possibility that the place name *Cabo de Sierpe* was initially prompted by the shapes of the landscape does not mean that Columbus did not see a lonely iguana perched on the tip of that cape. It is entirely likely that Columbus did see an iguana there and that it – that particular iguana – provided the initial impulse for the name *Cabo de Sierpe*. But it is also possible that it was only an image in a collection of images in Columbus's recent memory, a product of a mental process through which the Caribbean landscape was becoming a mirage of remembrances in his mind, just like the Genovese, the Portuguese, and the Andalusian landscapes had become. Regardless of whether a live iguana on the cape or the serpentine canals that reminded Columbus of one evoked the naming of *Cabo de Sierpe*, to stop the interpretation here would only scratch the surface of the complex connections that tied two distinct worlds in a process of a mutual contagion of which Columbus was the conduit. My claim, therefore, is not that the first interpretation, which focuses on the meaning of the word "sierpe" as an "iguana," should, or should not, be favoured over the next one that is presented in the pages that follow. Rather, my argument is that Columbian place names are expressions of all these different visions that were layered on top of one another and prompted one another, thus creating a meaningful, though phantasmagoric, chain of reflections, all of which contaminated one another. Columbus's gaze was characterized by shifts: from a small object or shape to vast spaces; from the Caribbean landscape to the Mediterranean; and from visions of physical places to mirages of places remembered. All these shifts resulted in new place names, which then became testaments of the creation of a new, complex, monstrous, and hybrid landscape. No longer faithful to either of the original landscapes, Columbus's was a virtual, invented landscape located not on either side of the Atlantic but in the fissures that cracked open in-between their fractured pieces. But, if Columbus indeed looked at larger shapes – how do we know whether they were the shapes of an unfamiliar landscape or those of a familiar city that he saw?

"Estrecha y retorcida": A Street in Seville

The central street in Seville, the heart of Andalucia from which Columbus departed and to which he returned, was called *Calle de la Sierpe* and it is still known as *Calle Sierpes* today.[14] It was a multifaceted street: vivid and turbulent on most days, crowded by forgers, locksmiths, and printers who worked on artefacts right on the street and sometimes received fines for obstructing transit; festive, decorated with triumphant arches, the pavement of the street covered with decorative carpeting for the procession of the Corpus Christi in the summer; ill-smelling during the time of day when fetid waters ran down freely towards La Campana; triumphant and jubilant when Columbus, upon his return from the first voyage, paraded along the street with his crew and native people from the islands he visited who carried exotic birds as well as golden and silver artefacts promising greater riches yet to come and who walked not only to be seen, but also to see.

The name of the street has inspired a range of explanations. According to the oldest known explanation, found in the sixteenth-century *Historia de Sevilla* by L. Pereza, the street owes its name to a snake's bare jaws hanging on the wall of a tavern on the street: "llamáronla así por una quijada, que dicen ser de sierpe, que está colgada en un mesón que está en medio desta calle, el cual, por la quijada, llaman de la Sierpe."[15] In the nineteenth century, the historian and novelist Próspero Merimée proposed that the name was inspired by the twisting shape of the street which itself resembled a serpent; this version was popular among the nineteenth-century writers and poets, including the Nicaraguan poet Rubén Darío who described the street as "estrecha y retorcida" (narrow and twisted) and the Spanish novelist Pío Barroja who saw it as "estrecha y tortuosa" (narrow and winding).[16] According to another nineteenth-century interpretation, the street was named after a certain gentleman named Gil de Sierpe. This now-forgotten character is only briefly mentioned in the *Diccionario histórico de las calles de Sevilla* and, although no further details are available, he must have played a role in the local history.[17]

In addition to these interpretations, all of which say something about the character and history of *Calle de Sierpe*, the street has a unique geological feature: it runs along what, in ancient times, used to be a branch of Spain's greatest river, the Guadalquivir. In the fifteenth century, Seville still witnessed flood seasons during which the river would rise and recover its old course, inundating the street. Temporarily inaccessible to transit, the street would turn once again into a river branch that snaked through the city. Could the water canals of *Cabo de Sierpe* and *Cabo Sancto* have reminded Columbus of the street in Seville when it was filled with water? This allusion to the Andalusian landscape is certainly possible given the other references to it in Columbian naming during the first voyage. For example, *Cabo de Campana*, which Columbus had named a month earlier in the vicinity of *Cabo de Sierpe*, was inspired by the *Amor de Dios y Campana* in Andalusia: "Y le avía pareçido la tierra de Campana."[18] And thus, the various versions of the meaning of the street name *Calle de la Sierpe* – its physical shape, the presence of a motionless jaw bone or perhaps of a dull old skin, the street flooded and turned into a branch of the Guadalquivir – form the whole of this toponym and evoke meanings similar to the Columbian toponym *Cabo de Sierpe* – a vision of the silhouette of an iguana, the shape of the cape itself, or the veins of the winding canals in it. In Columbus's eyes, the cape that he named *Cabo de Sierpe* was populated with images of the street in Seville: crowded even when empty, triumphant even when serene, and a witness to Christ's rebirth before the advent of Christianity in the Americas.

At the Foot of the Mountain, beneath Christ's Bleeding Feet

Now that several possible meanings of the place names themselves have been considered in isolation, it is necessary to direct our attention to the toponymic context that they form as a group, which will deepen our understanding of the formulation, and the simultaneous rupturing, of an authoritative rhetoric. The religious meanings of all of the toponyms immediately surrounding *Cabo de Sierpe* in the *Diario del primer viaje* must be taken into consideration in continuing the analysis of the meaning of this place name. A thematic context is immediately apparent in the three toponyms, *Villa de la Navidad*, *Cabo Sancto*, and *Monte Cristo*, two of which evoke Christ. While the meaning of *Villa de la Navidad* is transparent as it refers to the birth of the Christ Child and it was named sometime around Christmas, *Monte Cristo* could evoke more than one biblical event.

The fact that *Monte Cristo* is a religious toponym is not accidental. The associations between physical features of the place and the literal as well as symbolic meanings of its name are an underlying characteristic of the Columbian toponymic discourse. In the lengthy list of Columbian toponyms, two features of the landscape are consistently associated with Christianity: high mountains and wide, expansive waters, usually of a sea or a bay. For example, the following religious toponyms all denote bays: *Puerto de Santa Catalina* (24 November), *Puerto Santo* (1 December), *Puerto María* (6 December), *Puerto de la Concepción* (7 December), *Mar de Sancto Thomás* (21 December), *Puerto Sacro* (12 January), *Puerto de la Navidad* (third voyage); and *Puerto Belén* (fourth voyage).[19] Zamora argues in *Reading Columbus* that Columbus's later writing increasingly reflects "the medieval tendency to favor ideological geography over empirical geographical experience" (150–1). This is clearly noticeable in the way Columbus's toponyms show the relations between the natural and the spiritual. For example, on 14 November 1492, Columbus chose a religious name, *Mar de Nuestra Señora*, both because of the expansive size of the bay and because of the height of the mountains on the islands around it: "Maravillóse en gran manera ver tantas islas y *tan altas* y çertifica a los Reyes que desde las montañas que desde antier a visto por estas costas y las d'estas islas, que le pareçe que *no las ay más altas en el mundo* ni tan hermosas y claras" and "Púsoles nombre la mar de Nuestra Señora ... algunas d'ellas que pareçía que llegan al çielo y hechas como puntas de diamantes; otras que sobre su gran altura tienen ençima como una mesa, y al pie d'ellas fondo grandíssimo, que podrá llegar a ellas una grandíssima carraca, todas llenas de arboledas y sin peñas."[20] The toponym Columbus pronounced on 21 December, *Puerto de la Mar de Sancto Thomás*, unites the liturgical calendar and the physical character of the place in the name: "Púsole nombre el Puerto de la mar de Sancto Thomás, porque era oy su día; díxole mar por su grandeza."[21] Conversely, names of non-mountainous capes, islands, promontories, and rivers are largely not religious (the notable exceptions are the entire list of islands Columbus named after saints during the second voyage).

As Columbus's gaze undergoes another transatlantic shift, it brings into focus the biblical textual tradition, according to which three important events in Christ's life either occurred on a mountain or were otherwise connected to one. First, the mountain symbolizes Christ's rejection of Satan's temptation: "Again, the devil took him to a very high mountain and showed him all the kingdoms of the world and their splendor" (Matthew 4:8). Second, Christ, together with his disciples, stood on the holy mountain when they heard the voice of God from above announcing that Christ was his Son: "For he received honor and glory from God the Father when that voice was conveyed to him by the Majestic Glory, saying, 'This is my Son, my Beloved, with whom I am well pleased.' We ourselves heard this voice come from heaven, while we were with him on the holy mountain" (2Pe: 17, 18). And third, the event of the Transfiguration occurred on a "high mountain," where Christ took Peter, James, and his brother John six days after revealing to his disciples the secret of his upcoming death and resurrection. This last scene has been frequently depicted in medieval and Renaissance art and the work of Fra Angelico (1387–1455), a celebrated artist of the Early Italian Renaissance who dedicated his life to painting religious subjects and events, provides several examples. In a well-known fresco in the monastery of San Marco, Florence (created between 1437 and 1445), Fra Angelico depicted Christ standing on a stylized mountain, his face and body shining with the sun, the folds of his garment mirroring the ridges of the mountain, and the mountain becoming the foundation out of which the divine figure of Christ rises, even almost becoming one (figure 5.1).

Yet another image by Fra Angelico suggests a different interpretation. In this fresco, in which the defining liturgical event for Christianity, the Crucifixion, is portrayed, the Cross on which Christ has been crucified is shown erected on a stylized mountain (figure 5.2). This interpretation is not unique to Fra Angelico and the view that the Crucifixion occurred in the place known as Calvary or Golgotha, located on a hill or a mountain, has been explored extensively in art and literature. Columbus frequently used the principle of symmetry in his toponymy by either inventing names that contain two terms of opposite meaning such as *Cabo Alto y Baxo* and *Cabo Alpha et Omega* or by composing pairs of toponyms that have synonymous or opposite meanings. In this toponymic cluster, *Villa de la Navidad* marks the birth of the Christ Child while *Monte Cristo* could easily refer to Christ's physical death and spiritual rebirth, that is, the Crucifixion, in which these two place names would form an oppositional pair. However, if that were the case, what then could be the meaning of the place name *Cabo de Sierpe*?

The Serpent and Christ in Scripture and in Medieval Art

As the shapes of the Caribbean landscape morphed in his eyes to form a well-known Christian visual scene, it came to occupy a permanent place in Columbus's mind. The final formation of this scene was due to yet another shift to the Western textual and visual traditions. As a result of this shift, the iguana was transformed into another creature, known in Castilian by the same names, *sierpe* or *serpiente*, and which was, and is, one of the oldest and most complex Christian symbols: the serpent.[22]

5.1. *The Transfiguration*. Fra Angelico (1387–1455). Fresco. Florence, Convent of San Marco, Italy (1437–45). Courtesy of Gianni Dagli Orti/The Art Archive at Art Resource, NY.

5.2. *Crucifixion with the Virgin, Saint Dominic and Angels.* Fra Angelico (1387–1455). Fresco. Museo di San Marco, Florence, Italy. Courtesy of Scala / Ministero per i Beni e le Attività culturali / Art Resource, NY.

The serpent manifests itself in other ways in the Columbian discourse. Critics have noted the possible presence of the serpent in the three S's of Columbus's siglum, which could be interpreted either as abbreviations of the triple *sanctum*, *sanctum*, *sanctum*, or, according to a different theory, as S (*Sîn*), a symbol of *Naschassch* (serpent), and God, the Saviour of the World.[23] Columbus used the word *sancto* in just three toponyms: *Puerto Santo*, *Punta Sancta*, and *Cabo Sancto*. As discussed in chapter 2, this appears to be a metaphorical act of inscribing his signature onto the New World landscape as in the act of signing a letter with the siglum containing the same symbol repeated three times. Columbus also invented the place name *Boca de la Sierpe* during the third voyage, although its meaning needs to be interpreted in a different context, as will become apparent in the final chapter of this book. The presence of the serpent is also consistent with the cosmographic belief at the time that the south, generally associated with Africa, was uninhabitable because of heat and serpents.[24] This land was also envisioned to be red, "presumably to signify the burning heat which one must suffer there."[25]

In the Bible, the serpent makes an appearance during three important moments: the cunning serpent appears in the Garden of Eden to cause the Fall of Man; Moses elevates the serpent on a pedestal for veneration; and finally, in the Revelation, the serpent symbolizes Satan.[26] In medieval and Renaissance art, the serpent is sometimes associated with the Virgin Mary, who is frequently shown standing on the moon and trampling a serpent, representing her victory over original sin. Less commonly, the serpent is associated with the figure of Christ and is done so in one specific context: that of the Crucifixion. In these depictions of the Crucifixion, Christ, shown trampling the serpent that coils around the base of the cross or raised above it, triumphs in his victory over death. In some cases, a skull replaces the serpent at the bottom of the Cross, also representing death. Golgotha, the name of the place of Christ's crucifixion at Calvary, means "the place of the skull" in Hebrew. This last meaning of the serpent as a symbol of death suggests a religious scene emerging from the toponyms *Cabo de Sierpe*, *Monte Cristo*, and others Columbus assigned in their vicinity.

In comparison to the numbers and variations of depictions of the Virgin Mary trampling the serpent, depictions of Christ elevated above the serpent are fewer. However, in the context of Columbian place names, the latter images are particularly suggestive. The manuscript copy of the Sacramentary of Bishop Drogo, written in the middle of the ninth century in Paris (figure 5.3), contains an illumination with a scene that helps us to understand the meaning of the toponymic cluster as one that evokes a visual scene. In the image contained inside the capital letter O, the letter

5.3. Initial O with Crucifixion. Sacramentary of Bishop Drogo (c. 830). MS Latin 9428, folio 43v. Courtesy of the National Library of France, Paris, France.

with which the text begins, a cross is erected on crumbled earth. Christ is crucified on it and the serpent, at the bottom of the cross, raises its mortally wounded head. Christ's victory over death is also symbolized by the wreath that adorns Christ's head, between two angels and the personified sun and moon at the top. This image was reproduced with considerable consistency throughout Europe, and other examples can be found as well. A similar image is carved in the ivory relief on the book cover of the Pericopes of Heinrich II (figure 5.4). The Crucifixion provides the only context in which Christ, the mountain, and the serpent are all linked together in a unified scene. It seems as though the shapes of the landscape fulfil assigned functions in the spectacle representing the Crucifixion. Christ, in triumph due to his victorious spiritual rebirth, represented by *Monte Cristo*, is elevated above the serpent represented by *Cabo de Sierpe*.

One final toponym that Columbus pronounced in the vicinity brings the entire scene together. In the visual depictions of the Crucifixion in which a serpent appears, its head consistently appears with a red mark, which represents the blood dripping on it from Christ's wounds. It is a representation of the biblical prophecy, "It shall bruise thy head, and

5.4. The Crucifixion. Visit of the Holy Women to the Sepulchre, and Resurrection of the Saints. Ivory on book cover of the Pericopes of Heinrich II (Munich, c. 820–30). MS Clm. 4452. Courtesy of the Bavarian State Library, Munich, Germany.

thou shalt bruise his heel" (Gen. 3:15). In the Columbian toponymic discourse, the toponym *Punta Roxa* represents this feature in the visual depictions of the Crucifixion. *Punta Roxa* is mentioned in the *Diario* for the first time on 9 January, and the promontory is located in the vicinity of the *Monte Cristo* and *Cabo de Sierpe*. *Punta Roxa* is one of only two toponyms that Columbus invented using names of colours (the other being *Río Verde*), and its presence here completes the visual scene emerging from the landscape.

Columbus's sources for learning included not only maps and cosmographic treatises but also, as for any devout Christian, church sermons and visual illustrations of biblical stories in various art forms. These ranged from small and portable items such as illustrated psalters and manuscript illuminations to large and immovable ones such as stone reliefs on church tympanums and trumeaus. Columbus certainly saw some of these depictions in various kinds of religious art in cities, towns, and monasteries in Andalusia and across the Mediterranean. Various examples in which the serpent is shown wrapped around the bottom of the Cross, below the crucified Christ's feet, can be found in minor and major artwork, including images engraved on gold crosses, painted in manuscript illuminations and on church walls, carved in miniature ivory reliefs and on large wooden crosses, and even engraved on rock crystals. Italian, French, German, and English artists repeated the motif with considerable consistency, as was usually the case with other themes of didactic and symbolic nature in medieval art as well.

The reliance on visual imagery was particularly amenable to Columbus who, as the majority of critics today agree, was writing in a language that was not his native tongue. Furthermore, given this linguistic impediment of not being a native speaker of the language in which he wrote the ship logs and official correspondence, religious references provided Columbus with a safe harbour for expressing his thoughts in a way that would be understood by others of the same cultural and religious background.

Mount Christ Rises above Cape of the Serpent

From the way the toponyms are inserted in the narrative of the *Diario*, we can reconstruct the vision that Columbus saw emerging from the landscape he was facing. Christ, standing tall and beautiful on a high mountain (*Monte Cristo*), which could be seen from the cape Columbus thought of as being sacred space on one side (*Cabo Sancto*), was trampling the serpent in triumph, represented by the cape on the other side (*Cabo de Sierpe*). Just as the dying serpent coils below the bleeding feet of Christ, *Cabo de Sierpe* was located – appropriately – at the foot of the mountain named *Monte Cristo*. Columbian toponyms and their distribution in the New World landscape conformed to the same rules and patterns as those observed in medieval religious art and, specifically, in representations of the Crucifixion. Thus, the sacred realm was placed in the higher plane of the representation, while evil occupied the lower plane, similar to how in medieval religious paintings the serpent, a symbol of death and of the diabolic forces, was shown subdued by the victorious figure of the Saviour. As this vision emerged in Columbus's mind, the New World landscape conformed to a well-known Christian scene, and the Christian scene itself conformed to the landscape as it was stretched and deformed in places according to the location of points that could be named appropriately. The scene represented on that particular landscape was altered beyond the point of return into a new, phantasmagoric one as the traditional serpent was replaced by the exotic iguana.

Conclusion

Cabo de Sierpe provides a different way of viewing Columbian naming in the Caribbean than does the toponymic cluster inspired by metal and celestial body pairs explored in the previous chapter. *Baveque* is a symbol of an unchanging but ever-so-slightly out-of-reach goal which was based on a conjectural idea of the existence of gold and the possibility of finding it with the guidance of cosmographical clues as well as verbal and gestural directions provided by the Taino informants. In this case, Columbus's idea of his desired destination remained constant, while the presumed location of *Baveque* constantly shifted based on the changing information that he received from the locals. In contrast, *Cabo de Sierpe* was a stable physical presence but its visual perception underwent significant transformations. It is an example of the mediation to which both the scene on the landscape and Columbus's gaze were subjected. The silhouette of the iguana, the shapes of the canals or the capes, the twisting shape and the name of a familiar street in Seville, and the Christian visual depiction of the Crucifixion are all interlacing facets of a single scene that formed before Columbus's eyes as his gaze moved from a small shape to the landscape on a large scale, and from concrete physical features to an abstract visual scene. The formation of this scene represents the transatlantic shifts of his gaze and the resulting mediation of the physical and the cultural realities which Columbus witnessed in the Caribbean, on the one hand, and the remembered expressions of the Old World culture, episteme, and nomenclature, on the other. The word *sierpe* itself is an example of a plurisign: it was used in the Columbian toponymic discourse with more than one meaning simultaneously.[27] Based on verbal and visual signs, Columbus's mind created a scene in which the physical features of the landscape, such as its shapes, the distribution of the high and low points, and its colours, comprised its literal meanings. At the same time, the symbolic was constructed through the reflections of the worlds on both sides of the Atlantic that the multiple meanings of a word projected.

Multiple shifts of Columbus's gaze, both across the Atlantic and along the line separating the literal and the symbolic, created new realities that were no longer faithful to either the Caribbean landscape immediately present or the Andalusian one vividly preserved in his memory. Instead, familiar creatures and visible scenes were transformed into new, hybrid, monstrous ones. As a result of the vision that quickly shifted across the Atlantic, from an imaginary serpent of medieval bestiaries to a live and very impressive ("horrible y espantable") creature of the Indies, a hybrid creature emerged that was neither one nor the other but a conjectural product of both. One part of this imagined creature was a projection of the customs and culture of the local inhabitants; another, of the European book culture (medieval bestiaries). Yet in another way, one part of it reflected the grid of an Andalusian city and the other, the shapes of the Caribbean coastal landscape. This imposition of the Castilian "sierpe" onto a New World species altered not so much the understanding of this species but more the umbrella concept of "sierpe." As historians like Las Casas described iguanas, they added to the descriptions of serpents in medieval bestiaries and, as a result, they altered their collective definition of "sierpe" during a process which Mignolo described as "this dual process of inventing the Americas and redefining Europe."[28]

Columbus's gaze not only transformed the visible landscape before him into a Christian scene, but it also transformed the existing Christian scene into a new, phantasmagorical one that was mediated and altered as it suggested the possibility of substituting the Western serpent with the New World iguana. Centuries later, indigenous and *mestizo* artists would do so intentionally, as they replaced certain details in Christian visual scenes with others taken from the New World, as the indigenous Andean painter Marcos Zapata (c. 1710/20 – c. 1773) did in his painting for the Cathedral of Cuzco entitled *The Last Supper with Platter of Cuy* (1753). In it, Christ and the apostles gather around the table, in the centre of which stands a dish with roasted guinea pig, and in the glasses standing on the table, instead of traditional red wine, is the Inca beer called *chicha*. Indigenous, *mestizo*, and white *criollo* artists created these hybrid images intentionally to reveal society's hybrid culture and the underpinning indigenous base on which the Christian ideology had been built. Centuries earlier, Columbus's gaze fused the New World iguana and the Old World serpent, not in a conscious effort to affirm the local identity but in an effort to recognize unfamiliar shapes and to give them familiar names. As a result, Columbus himself became the conduit through which the dialogue between the two worlds began to take place. The scene of the Crucifixion in which an exotic iguana crouches underneath Christ's feet not only transformed the local landscape, but it also bent the familiar paradigms of Western culture.

6 Infernal Imagery: Spirituality and Cosmology in the Final Two Voyages

The larger portions of the cosmographic discussions in the *Relación del tercer viaje* and *Relación del cuarto viaje* – that is, the narratives of the third and fourth voyages transcribed by Las Casas – are dedicated to the location of the Earthly Paradise, *El Paraíso Terrenal*. The discussion of the navigation and the experiences during the last two voyages focus on the physical and spiritual dangers that Columbus and his crew experienced, the fear resulting from these dangers, and the conflicts that Columbus had with Spaniards and the native inhabitants alike. The lengthiest description of extremely exhausting and risky navigation is in the *Relación del tercer viaje*. The situation occurred near a series of straits which Columbus named *Boca de la Sierpe* and *Boca del Drago* (also spelled as *Boca del Dragón* in the *diarios*). Both straits are still known by these names today, and the former is also known as Columbus Channel. This chapter addresses the conflicting paradisiacal and infernal imagery in the toponymy and the narrative of the third and fourth voyages, related in particular to the experiences near these two *bocas*. Through the analysis of the toponymic discourse of the last two voyages, the chapter aims to provide a better understanding of the discourse of despair that permeates the narratives of these final voyages, which contrasts sharply with the expressions of hope for salvation and the theory about the proximity of the Earthly Paradise. I argue that the imagery of danger and suffering does not just stand in opposition to the ideas of spiritual salvation and the proximity of the Earthly Paradise, but rather that the impact of the former on the rhetoric in the two *relaciones* is even stronger and that it taints the message of salvation otherwise articulated in those narratives. In addition, I consider the proliferation of toponymy of indigenous origins, the demonization of the native peoples, the infernalization of the Caribbean landscape, and the notable absence of orderly sequences and hierarchies in the toponymy as signs of the chaos that characterized the second half of the Columbian toponymic discourse. These can be considered as representative of Columbus's failure to order the landscape by a symbolic act of creation through naming and to inscribe himself on the map.

At first glance, the role of the place names *Boca de la Sierpe* and *Boca del Drago* in the *diarios* appears marginal: in the *Relación del tercer viaje*, the summary that Las Casas made from the original ship log, *Boca de la Sierpe* is mentioned only once, and *Boca del Drago* twice.[1] Both toponyms are introduced in the same sentence which appears late in the *relación* and lacks any further explanation of why they were chosen: "En esta boca del austro, *a que yo llamé de la Sierpe*, hallé que, anocheçiendo, que yo tenía la estrella del norte alta caso çinco grados, y en aquella otra del setentrión, *a que yo llamé del Drago*, heran casi siete."[2] However, a closer reading of the *Relación del tercer viaje* reveals that the narrative makes many references to the *bocas* as "una boca," "esta boca," and "estas dos bocas." In fact, most of the *Relación del tercer viaje* centres around the circumstances of navigating through the two *bocas*, the physical dangers Columbus and his crew experienced there, and their psychological and spiritual responses. The descriptions of these phenomena in the *Relación del tercer viaje* are convoluted and repetitive. This repetition could be due in part to the fact that Columbus sailed through Boca de la Sierpe and approached Boca del Drago several times. Some of the omissions of the toponyms may also be due to Las Casas's editing. However, the overall lack of clarity in the narrative suggests that other causes were also at play, and my view is that it had to do with the underlying concerns, obsessions, and deep fears Columbus had about the destination he had reached.

The fact that both *Boca del Drago* and *Boca de la Sierpe* are still found on maps today attests to the impact of these two place names; the same is true for only a small handful of the place names Columbus invented. The locations of the actual series of straits Columbus named *Boca del Drago* and *Boca de la Sierpe* are well known, which is also not frequently the case with Columbian toponyms; they both lead by way of water into the present Gulf of Paria (which Columbus named *Golfo de la Ballena*) and they separate the island of Trinidad (which Columbus so named, *Isla de la Trinidad*) from the coast of present-day Venezuela. Ferdinand Columbus describes their location accurately as flanking Trinidad on either side, opposite each another: "Ambas estaban formadas por las dos puntas occidentales de Trinidad junto con otras dos de tierra firme, encontrándose casi en orientación norte-sur una con la otra."[3] Boca del Drago is the northern mouth that separates Trinidad from the Paria Peninsula. The southern mouth, Boca de la Sierpe, is located between the southern tip of the island (Columbus named it *Punta del Arenal* and it is known today as Icacos Point) and the continent of South America just to the east of the mouth of the Orinoco River.[4]

Visually, Boca de la Sierpe is a narrow passage that resembles the body of a snake or, alternatively, a thin passage through which one might slither. Boca del Drago, in contrast, is a wide passage with protruding dramatic rocks reminiscent of the huge teeth in a monster's jaws.[5] Previous critics have frequently pointed out that resemblance motivated much of Columbian naming, and this principle can be applied to various toponyms from the third and fourth voyages. The gulf, marked by the two *bocas* on opposite sides, which Columbus named *Golfo de la Ballena* (also referred to as *Golpho de la Vallena*), is large, round, and visually like the belly of an enormous whale.[6] Named soon after, *Punta del Arenal* is, not too surprisingly, sandy. As Morison noted, based on his experience during which he retraced Columbus's trajectory on a ship, the resemblance of *Cabo de la Galera* to "a many-masted galley under sail was striking. In addition to the bright-peaked cliffs which resemble lateen sails, there are diagonal marks on the rocks that look like a bank of oars."[7] Similarly, the visual appearance of the two *bocas* and their other physical characteristics, including their audible and other features, appear to have triggered their naming. However, while physical features may have initially prompted the choice for these names, their meanings understood in a more comprehensive context reveal significantly larger concerns Columbus had about the cosmography and the spiritual landscape in which he found himself immersed.

Cultural Origins of the Dragon as a Symbol

When one thinks of cultural associations of the dragon and the serpent, Asia immediately comes to mind. Enrique Gandía has previously suggested that *Boca del Drago* refers to Asia.[8] This seems logical since until the end of his days Columbus believed that Cuba was part of mainland Asia. As with other literate Europeans, he was familiar with aspects of Asian life and culture from tales from travellers who had returned from the Orient as well as from the objects of art and practical items they brought back. However, an examination of such texts and items reveals that the Asian dragon or serpent probably did not captivate the minds of Western readers much more than various other Asian figures, images, and symbols did.

Marco Polo's *De consuetudinibus et conditionibus orientalium regionum*, known in English as *Travels*, describes the Venetian traveller's impressions of various parts of Asia. Though it is still debated whether or not Columbus had read Polo's account prior to his first voyage, it is generally accepted that he was acquainted with it and that by 1497 – that is, by Columbus's third voyage – he had made annotations in the margins of his printed copy of Marco Polo's account.[9] Columbus also may have read other accounts of travels in Asia, such as the accounts by two fifteenth-century Spanish travellers, Ruy González Clavijo and Pero Tafur, which circulated widely in Europe prior to his first transatlantic crossing. Clavijo (?–1412) travelled to the Middle East on behalf of King Enrique III of Castile to establish diplomatic relations with the Mongol emperor Tamerlan. Sometime around 1406, he wrote an account titled *Vida y hazañas del Gran Tamorlán*. Tafur (1410? – between 1453 and 1457) travelled across Europe and Asia between the fall of 1437 and the spring of 1439 and left a detailed account entitled *Andanças e viajes de Pero Tafur por diversas partes del mundo avidos (1435–1439)*. Although Tafur's account did not appear in print until 1874, it circulated in manuscript form for centuries. The accounts by both travellers depict the nature and the cities of the East, ways of life and customs observed there, gifts and merchandise, and animals and plants. Tafur, for example, vividly describes living creatures from the natural world, including monkeys ("gatos"), parrots, elephants, and crocodiles; he also writes about the array of gifts and merchandise that he purchased or received. Clavijo's tome portrays churches and monasteries, the sports arena built by Theodosius the Great and the Church of Saint Sophia in Constantinople, as well as the mountainous landscape, small villages of Armenia, and the city of Sultania in Persia. He also describes various objects he saw in the market of Sultania, including cotton and silk cloths, pearls, and precious stones.[10] Marco Polo's extensive account details the wealth, customs, and curiosities of the various regions of Asia, including Cathay (China). Neither account, however, contains any mention of mythical dragons, myths in which they figured, or of their use in carnivals and celebrations. This omission suggests that European readers did not necessarily conceive of the dragon as the emblem of Asia. As for Columbus, nowhere does he make an explicit connection between the dragon and Asia. Ginger and cinnamon, silk and gold were all higher on his list.[11]

By around the fourteenth century, European map makers and artists were consistently using animals to represent the known continents, a tradition that continued well into the nineteenth century. In cartography, the animal chosen most frequently to represent Asia was the elephant. It was featured in Asian scenes in European works of art, including paintings and engravings, from the medieval and Renaissance periods. Examples are numerous, and many of them depict one, two, or more elephants roaming through Asian territories, as in the scene of Ceylon in a painting in the *Livro de Lisuarte de Abreu* or in the scene of Calcutta in an engraving in the Netherlandish collection of town atlases, *Civitatis Orbis Terrarum* (*Atlas of Cities of the World*), by Georgius Braun and Franz Hogenberg.[12] Other animals and birds that artists chose to represent Asia include the rhinoceros, the lion, the camel, and the parrot. *Atlas nautique du Monde, dit atlas Miller* by Lopo Homem-Reineis includes all of these in a scene from India.[13] The dragon is decidedly absent from all these works.

It would seem sensible that at least some of the Asian artefacts and merchandise which travellers and traders brought back to Europe would have featured the mythical creature that was, after all, a commonly used symbol in Asian myths, rituals, and celebrations. The world art exhibition of 1992 in Seville displayed various collections of Asian art and artefacts such as drawings, aquarelles, metal objects, and porcelain plates representative of those which circulated in Europe around the time of Columbus's first voyage.[14] And indeed, some of them did feature the dragon. However, the collection of hundreds of items includes only three such artefacts: specifically, two items from the Chinese Ming Dynasty (1368–1644, a gold relief with precious stones and a golden dragon on a white porcelain plate) and one item from Vietnam (a ceramic figure of a dragon with white and blue porcelain paint). Numerous other objects present a variety of themes and motifs, among them scenes of fighting warriors depicted in paintings from Iran, landscapes painted in watercolour on silk from China, and floral motifs shown on ornamented carpets and tapestries from Asia Minor. Other objects representing various aspects of Asian culture and life include porcelain plates with hieroglyphs from the Ming Dynasty, book covers, drawings, and colourful items of clothing.

Gandía notes that the dragon was also a central mythical figure in several South American indigenous cultures.[15] But while in many cases indigenous cultures do provide significant clues to understanding the Columbian naming process, in this case the *diarios* make no statements to relate the dragon to a specific object or image from the local culture. The *Relación del tercer viaje* does not include any references to Taino or other indigenous artwork featuring these creatures or the food prepared from them (in contrast, memorable is Peter Martyr's description of two iguanas hanging on two wooden statues which Columbus saw during the first voyage).[16]

Furthermore, the distinction between the "Asian dragon" and the "South American one" is only theoretical since in Columbus's mind the two areas were part of the same larger region.[17] The idea that Asia and South America were parts of the same large continent was entertained by some cosmographers following Columbus's voyages and perhaps even before. In a treatise titled *Tratado de los descubrimientos antiguos y modernos* published in Lisbon in 1563, Antonio Galvão refers to the South American continent as "Dragon's Tail" ("la Cola del Dragón"), using the term for the first time. Galvão refers to another source (he does not state its author) that describes a *mappa mundi* which Dom Pedro, the son of the king of Portugal, brought from a distant land as a gift for his brother Dom Enrique. Produced in about 1408, this *mappa mundi* depicted the entire known surface of the earth. It included the Cape of Good Hope labelled as Fronteira de Africa as well as a strait today named after Magellan, both of which were situated at the end of the land mass, or "en *la Cola do Dragam*."[18] Historians from the first half of the last century have explored the antecedents of these so-called dragon maps in which South America constituted the tail of the dragon and their relevance to the subsequent voyages of exploration and conquest.[19]

This conflation of two parts of the world into one is particularly notable in those toponyms that Columbus invented based on words he heard in the New World but that reminded him of Asian names of places or people. The name of the Caribs is a fitting example: Columbus heard, in the Taino name for the warlike *Cariba* peoples, the name of the vassals of the Chinese emperor, the Great Khan: *caniba*. According to Las Casas, he attempted to rationalize the different pronunciation of these words in different areas: "Dize más el Almirante, que en la islas passadas estavan con gran temor de Carib, y en algunas le llamavan Caniba, pero en la Española Carib ... que los indios que consigo traía [no?] entendían más, puesto que fallava differençia de lenguas por la gran distancia de la tierras."[20] The place names *Monte Caribata* and *Cabo de Caribata* that Columbus had assigned during the first voyage (19 and 20 December, respectively) were most probably also products of a similar conflation. The Asian toponym of the province of Mango named after Kublai Khan's brother, the Great Khan, and the Columbian toponym *Tierra de Magón* in the western part of Cuba based on a Taino toponym or word also suggests an identification of this territory with Asia.[21] *Cabo de Cuba* and *San Telmo de Xamaná* are examples of culturally and linguistically hybrid toponyms that Columbus invented by incorporating into a single place name components from two or even three languages. *San Telmo de Xamaná* incorporates both Taino and Castilian vocabulary: *Xamaná* was the name of a place in Taino and

Columbus named it after a Christian saint, Saint Telmo, forming a hybrid Taino-Castilian toponym. *Cabo de Cuba* incorporates all three geographies: American since the word *cuba* is based on a Taino word Columbus heard from the locals; Asian, since in his mind, Cuba was part of the Asian mainland; and Mediterranean since the toponym includes the Castilian geographic term *cabo*.

It is not necessary to discard the possibility that Columbus associated the dragon or the serpent with Asia (as well as with the region he had reached). Asian scenes were familiar to Columbus from oral accounts, written texts, and maps. These images, contaminated by the reality he found in the Americas, may have crossed his mind as he was naming *Boca del Drago* and *Boca de la Sierpe*. However, the imaginary dragon of Asia and the harmless Caribbean iguana had morphed into a frightening, enormous monster that was threatening his physical and spiritual safety. This textual transformation occurred due to its symbolism associated with the serpent and the dragon in the region of the world with which Columbus was most familiar: the Western hemisphere, and in particular, its classical and Judaeo-Christian traditions.

A Two-Headed Monster

The dragon and the serpent were deeply rooted as symbols in a variety of European cultures and traditions, and they are frequently featured in textual and visual sources spanning the classical, Byzantine, medieval, and Renaissance periods. Both the dragon and the serpent were commonly associated with negative notions, in particular, sin and temptation, Hell and the devil, evil and eternity. These ideas are present in the Bible, alchemical and cabbalistic treatises, maps and *mappae mundi*, and works of art.[22] Until quite late, most of these sources made no clear distinction between the dragon and the serpent. The perception that the dragon and the serpent may really be a variant of a single creature is embedded in the roots *draco* and δρακων, which mean "serpent" in Latin and Greek respectively. The Roman author Gaius Suetonius Tranquillus (70?–130?) speaks of a kind of a snake he calls *serpens draco*, and Egyptian snakes in Latin were called *dracunculi*. Pliny the Elder, in his work encompassing the entire field of ancient knowledge about nature titled *Historia Naturalis* and published c. 77–9 AD, makes no clear distinction between the serpent and the dragon; neither does *Physiologus*, the highly influential encyclopaedic bestiary that deals with the physical and moral characteristics of the animal world. During the era of the early conquest of the Americas zoological science in Europe was still in its cradle stages, and medieval bestiaries incorporated empirical knowledge along with spiritual guidance and moral advice. Most medieval bestiaries that followed were based on one of the two aforementioned models, and thus they defined the dragon and the serpent in a similarly ambiguous fashion. There was not even a consensus about whether serpents and dragons should be considered beasts or birds as they were believed to possess qualities of both. Thus, some sources described them as limbless while others as having one or two pairs of legs; some showed them wingless while others as having a pair of wings. And yet some others, as if to confuse the reader even further, embellished the head of the serpent or the dragon with two curly horns.[23]

Later, Renaissance historians writing about the flora and fauna of the New World applied these ambiguous definitions to the whole array of snakes and lizards that the European explorers testified spotting there, claiming that some of them looked more like mythical creatures than like any of the Old World species. For example, in his *Sumario de la natural historia de las Indias*, Oviedo dedicates a whole chapter to New World lizards which he titles, with exemplary ambiguity, "Lagartos o dragones" (Lizards or Dragons). Oviedo engages in a discussion about whether caymans (*caimanes*), a particular kind of New World lizard, should be compared to dragons (*dragones*) or to basilisks (*cocatrices*). He reaches the conclusion that they should most appropriately be called dragons: "Finalmente, que estos lagartos son muy espantosos dragones en la vista: quieren algunos decir que son cocatrices, pero no es así."[24] Just as for him the distinction between a lizard and a dragon was ambiguous enough, the distinction between New World reality and Old World myths was also hazy, and the "dragons" Columbus faced were probably the fruit of both.

Furthermore, it is significant that Columbus named two places after creatures that were believed to be either related or variants of a single one. The synonymous nature of the place names echoes the physical similarity of the two *bocas* and the similarity of the experiences near them. According to Ferdinand Columbus, this similarity was such that his father invented the two names so he could later distinguish between the two *bocas* more easily: "Después de tomar la que necesitaban, el Almirante decidió pasar a otra boca … a la que luego daría el nombre de Boca del Dragón, *para distinguirla* de aquella donde en ese momento se hallaba, que era la Boca de Sierpe."[25] Hence, *Boca de la Sierpe* and *Boca del Drago* form what I have earlier called a toponymic double, which consists of two place names of closely related meanings that are either synonymous or sometimes antonymic, and which were typically, though not always, invented during a brief time period and assigned to places that are located in close proximity. As seen in earlier chapters, toponymic doubles are common in the list of Columbian place names and they were usually invented to emphasize a particular idea or image. However, here the use of the toponymic double creates a deeper and more specific meaning.

In literary and artistic traditions of classical antiquity and the Middle Ages, a pair of dragons and a pair of serpents as a unit were each associated with specific allegorical meanings. Some of these were positive: in ancient Greece and Rome, the caduceus of two copulating serpents signified healing power, as it still does today; and two asps depicted in a misericord at Chichester as stopping their ears to resist the voice of the charmers symbolized that the faithful were able to resist earthly temptations.[26] However, more commonly a pair of serpents was associated with evil; since one serpent was an important symbol of evil, sin, and temptation, two serpents embodied all of those things multiplied. Two venomous snakes caused the death of Cleopatra, queen of Egypt. According to the well-known classical myth, Hera, jealous of Zeus's sexual union with Alcmene, sent two snakes to kill their child Hercules; the child, however, strangled them with his bare hands. In medieval bestiaries, two vipers were an icon of the abominable sin of unnatural sex, that is, copulation through the mouth, which was punished by the death of both participants as the female viper bit off the male's head at the height of its sexual orgasm. Medieval bestiaries also portrayed the amphisbaena, which was depicted as a serpent with two heads, one on each end, and which Pliny considered to be so evil that it needed two heads to be able to discharge all its venom.[27] Two dragons together also had specific meanings, which were also usually negative. They were frequently featured in medieval and Renaissance art, architecture, and cartography. Commonly, a pair of dragons symbolized the underworld, especially in opposition to Christ and Paradise. For example, in two English psalter maps reproduced here, Christ tramples two dragons facing one another at the bottom of the globe, symbolizing the victory of Christianity over paganism and of good over evil (figures 6.1 and 6.2).[28]

Danger and Fear as Sea Monsters

Imaginary sea monsters such as sea dragons, sea serpents, and whales commonly appear in Western ancient, medieval, and Renaissance maps and *mappae mundi* at the edges of the known world. These monsters symbolize both the spiritual perils and the physical dangers, such as high waves, powerful currents, and uncontrollable winds, faced by sailors who dared

6.1. Psalter world map. BL Add. MS 28681, folio 9 (English, c. 1265). Courtesy of the British Library Board, London, United Kingdom.

6.2. Psalter world map. BL Add. MS 28681, folio 9 verso (English, c. 1265). Courtesy of the British Library Board, London, United Kingdom.

to venture out beyond the limits of the known world. The illustration in *Sucesso de Segundo Cerco de Diu* by Jerónimo Corte Real is a fitting example: lightning is striking the waters of a stormy sea and frightening sea monsters surround sinking ships.[29] As the limits of the regions explored by European navigators shifted outwards, the location of the sea monsters portrayed on maps also moved: from the vicinities of the African coast to the Atlantic near the New World coast in the fifteenth century. Finally, after the contours of the Americas had been drawn, sea dragons and monstrous whales moved further out in the Pacific. For example, Sebastian Münster's *Typus Cosmographicus Universalis* (Basel 1537, figure 6.3) features two prominent sea beasts, one quite clearly a dragon, the other resembling a great fish or a whale, swimming in the Oceanus Australis under Africa. In a *mappa mundi* printed three decades later, Ortelius's *Africae Tabula Nova* (Antwerp, 1570?), in addition to two sea monsters swimming in the Atlantic Ocean, a whale is portrayed near the African shore and a dragon near the South American shore.

Consistent with this tradition in maps where sea dragons, whales, and other kinds of sea monsters represent the physical dangers of exploring regions beyond the limits of the known world is the emphasis the *diarios* place on the dangerous navigation near the two *bocas*. Descriptions of danger, largely absent from the narratives and the toponymy of the first and second voyages, dominate the description of navigating near and through the two *bocas* in the *Relación del tercer viaje*. The sensation of danger also permeates most of the descriptions of the navigation during the third and fourth voyages. The descriptions of the dangers are accompanied by descriptions of fear in all shades (*temor*, *miedo*, *espanto*, and *angustia*) that Columbus and his crew felt. Columbus emphasized the sensation of fear (*miedo*) in his comment about his experience near Boca de la Sierpe when he almost experienced a shipwreck because an incredibly high wave nearly sank the caravels: "oy día traigo el miedo en el cuerpo que no me trabucase la nao cuando llegase debajo d'ella ('una loma [de agua] tan alta como una nao')."[30] Other historians, such as Oliva and Peter Martyr, also speak of the fear that haunted Columbus near the *bocas*: "do sintió el Almirante, según dijo después, el mayor miedo que hubo de las aguas de la mar"[31] and "Ibi se, ex quo navigare a teneris coepit, nusquam tantum formidasse fatetur."[32] According to Ferdinand Columbus, fear determined the name of *Boca de la Sierpe*: "El nombre que le dieron [a la Boca de la Sierpe] se debe precisamente al miedo que allí experimentaron."[33] Las Casas believed that the danger experienced near the two *bocas* resulted in Columbus's choice of both names: "Porque este gran peligro puso a esta

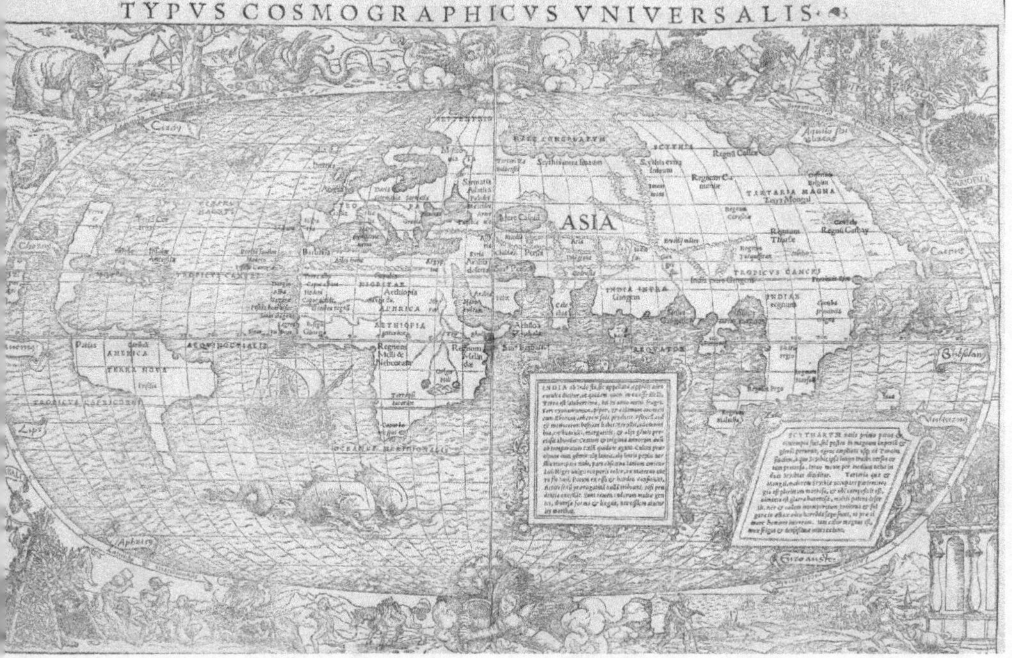

6.3. *Typus Cosmographicus Universalis*, Sebastian Münster. BL MS G.7034 (Basel, 1537). Courtesy of the British Library Board, London, United Kingdom.

boca nombre la Boca de la Sierpe" and "la boca que llamó del Drago por la siguiente causa y peligro [en] que allí se vido."[34] Peter Martyr states that both danger and anxiety, translated in Spanish as "peligro y angustia," characterized the navigators' experience near the *bocas*.[35] While the *diarios* provide no explicit comments about the meaning of the names of either of the *bocas*, contemporary historians consistently attribute their naming to the fear and the danger experienced near them.

Boca as the Entrance to Hell

On maps, dragons and serpents were almost always located in tempestuous waters near the ends of the earth. However, a well-known medieval spiritual map brings up yet another aspect of the meanings of the dragon and the serpent. In the Hereford Cathedral map by Richard of Haldingham

6.4. Richard of Haldingham or Sleaford. Hereford Cathedral map. (Lincoln, England, c. 1285). Courtesy of the Mappa Mundi Trust and Dean and Chapter of Hereford Cathedral, Hereford, United Kingdom.

or Sleaford (Lincoln, England, c. 1285; figure 6.4), two dragons face one another, their heads intertwined, positioned close to the entrance to the Earthly Paradise.[36] In this map, the two dragons represent the Fall of Man, and in the right corner of the map, an angel with a flaming sword is driving Eve and Adam away from the Garden of Eden. However, it is not the mere presence of the dragons or of the Earthly Paradise but rather the ideologically charged juxtaposition of the two that is most significant in this map. Likewise, in the Columbian toponymy, there is a striking tension between the parts of the narratives of the third and fourth voyages that speak about spiritual salvation and those of great dangers, thus creating a new level of meaning.

Significant portions of the *Relación del tercer viaje* and *Relación del cuarto viaje* are dedicated to discussing the location of the Earthly Paradise. Based on the information in ancient and medieval authorities as well as in visual and cartographic sources, Columbus claimed that the Earthly Paradise was close, at arm's reach.[37] For signs of the proximity of the Earthly Paradise, Columbus refers to the unusual natural phenomena he and his crew experienced, including the gentle climate ("temperançia suavísima") as well as speculations about the Tree of Life and the stream that gives origin to the four great rivers, Ganges, Tigris, Euphrates, and Nile. These observations culminate with the proposition about the pear-like shape of the earth and the location of the Earthly Paradise on its very top, on the "nipple" of the pear ("salvo qu'él sea en el colmo, allí adonde dixe la figura del pezón de la pera").[38] The idea that the lands Columbus was exploring were blessed and that he was coming ever closer to the most sacred destination is registered in some of the toponyms he invented during the third voyage, namely, *Tierra de Gracia*, *Isla Sancta*, and *Isla de la Trinidad*.[39]

The Earthly Paradise can be frequently found represented on maps and *mappae mundi*, and frequently it was located in Asia. Scafi, in his *Mapping Paradise*, tells us that ancient thinkers considered Eden to be a region of Asia, and that Isidore argued thus in his *Etymologiae* (c. 653): "Asia includes many provinces and regions. I shall briefly list their names and locations, starting with Paradise. Paradise is a place in the east, whose name translated from Greek into Latin is *hortus* [garden]. Moreover, in Hebrew it is called *Eden*, which means in our language *deliciae* [delights]."[40] Scafi also interprets the following excerpt from the *Relación del tercer viaje* as evidence that although Columbus believed that the Earthly Paradise existed, at no point did he think that the Earthly Paradise was accessible to men: "no porque yo crea que allí, donde es la altura del estremo, sea nabegable ni agua en que se pueda sober allá, porque allí creo que sea el Paraíso Terrenal, adonde no puede llegar nadie salvo por voluntad divina."[41] Zamora, as she urges us to consider the ideological as well as the empirical context of the paradigmatic cartographic discourse, argues that "in the textual cartography of the third voyage, the Indies is not only on the figurative way to Jerusalem, it is also in the vicinity of Paradise."[42] Therefore, some medieval cartographic sources place the Earthly Paradise in the vicinity of Jerusalem; others place it in the eastern part of the world, in Asia.

However, the proximity of the Earthly Paradise could hardly have caused in Columbus the overwhelming fear and anxiety that permeate the narrative of the *Relación del tercer viaje*. The toponyms of the last two voyages suggest that these emotions were caused by an understandable angst: according to spiritual maps, some of the natural signs that indicate the proximity of the Earthly Paradise are also attributed to proximity to the gates of Hell. According to my reading, the conflicting infernal and paradisiacal imagery in the third and fourth voyages reveals Columbus's vacillation about the destination to which he had arrived. This vacillation is summarized in the toponyms *Alpha et omega* and *Costa de los Contrastes* as well as in the juxtaposition of toponyms of contrasting meanings, such as *Boca del Drago* and *Boca de la Sierpe*, on the one hand, and *Isla de la Trinidad* and *Tierra de Gracia*, on the other.[43] Columbus's fear was consistent with the theory that Hell was located in the southern hemisphere: "The idea that hell might be located in the southern hemisphere was not unknown to the Latin West, although a subterranean site was a more common idea."[44] His fear of having come near the place forbidden to humans, where those who came faced great physical and spiritual trials, may also have been founded on speculations about the location of Mount Purgatory in the South Atlantic, as Dante had written in the Canto 26 of the *Inferno*.[45] Likewise, it could have been related to the idea that both the underworld and the South Pole were located below our feet.[46] Given our deeper understanding of Columbus's geographic "southing" as both a practical and an ideological concern, convincingly explained in Wey Gómez's *The Tropics of Empire* (2008), the infernal and purgatorial imagery that was associated with the tropics also should not be ignored. As much as medieval and early modern cosmographers were curious about the location of the Earthly Paradise, they were also interested in the location of Purgatory and of Hell. Instructions for making a medieval *mappa mundi* (which Woodward describes as "a blending of history and geography") by Hugh of St Victor include conjectures about the spiritual *and* geographic location of the Last Judgment to the west and of Hell in the northern corner of the apex.[47]

The depiction of Hell on medieval and early modern *mappae mundi* was done in cosmographic, philosophical, and satirical contexts. Instructions on where to draw Hell were based on Dante's fiction and Ptolemaic cartographic science, which located it in the Antipodes, directly beneath Jerusalem.[48] Given these traditions, Columbus's fear of locating Hell and his obsession with finding the Earthly Paradise are compatible. Furthermore, the sensations he described experiencing in the vicinity of the two *bocas* – the scorching heat, the roaring noise, and the sensation of being swallowed – were what unhappy sinners were believed to experience when caught in a Hell Mouth. In the *Relación del tercer viaje* as he approaches the two *bocas*, Columbus speaks of the seas turned to blood, the sensation of burning as if in a cauldron in a great fire ("mal fecha sangre, ferviendo como caldera por gran fuego"). He also speaks of the burning sky: "El çielo jamás fue visto tan espantoso: un día y una noche ardió como forno, y ansí hechava la llama con los rayos."[49] Other signs are those of chaos and include storms, rain, thunder, and lightning: "no entré en porto ni pude, ni me dexó tormenta, agua del çielo, trombones y relanpagos de continuo, que pareçía el fin del mundo."[50] Ferdinand Columbus describes the "mountain" of a wave that crushed his father and the crew: "Aquella montaña [de agua] se dirigió hacia los barcos ante el espanto de todos, que temieron verse ser arrollados."[51]

Furthermore, according to the *Relación del tercer viaje*, when they came close to the *bocas* Columbus and his crew were particularly overwhelmed by the sensation of being swallowed. Peter Martyr's reference to Boca del Drago as "throats," translated into Spanish as "dichas gargantas," underscores the sensation of being swallowed.[52] Las Casas even states that the fear of being swallowed was the main reason why the names of the *bocas* remained unchanged: "Dizen que dixo aquí el Almirante, aunque no lo hallé en escripto de su mano como hallé lo susodicho, que si de allí se escapavan podia hazer cuenta que se escapavan de la boca del drago. Y por esto se le quedó este nombre y con razón."[53] Other Columbian place names also document the fear of being swallowed. *Golfo de la Ballena*, "Gulf of the Whale," located between the southern border of the South American continent and the island of Trinidad, known today as the Gulf of Paria, is connected to the Atlantic Ocean by the two *bocas* on both sides. The gaping throat of the whale was also frequently used in Christian iconography to portray a Hell Mouth. And though the gulf was large, Las Casas's description implies that Columbus experienced in it the sensation of being entrapped and had a desire to escape, as if he had been caught in the belly of a great beast: "Deseando salir ya deste Golpho de la Vallena, donde andava cercado de tierra firme y de La Trinidad."[54] In addition to *Boca del Drago*, *Boca de la Sierpe*, and *Golfo de la Ballena*, another toponym that Columbus invented during the fourth voyage records his anxiety of being swallowed: *Isla de las Bocas*, "Island of Mouths" in Varela's 1989 edition (spelled as *Isla de las Pozas*, "Island of Water Streams," in Varela and Gil's 2003 edition). *Isla de las Pozas* refers to water streaming out of sand, as Ferdinand Columbus explains in his *Historia*; but *Isla de las Bocas*, as the handwriting in the manuscript may be interpreted, evokes a powerful image of multiple mouths gaping around frightened navigators. Terrified that not only he and his crew but also his caravels and even entire areas of land were at risk of being swallowed by the voracious seas, Columbus developed a theory that explained the formation of the islands in the region: "Y por esto *se a comido* [el agua] tanta parte de la tierra, porque por eso son acá tantas islas, y ellas mismas fazen d'ello testimonio."[55] His extraordinary conclusion that the lands had been literally "eaten" or "devoured" by the seas once again underscores the capacity of the *bocas* and of water to swallow.

The association between the two *bocas* and the act of swallowing is related to the word *boca*, which in Castilian literally means "mouth." In geography, the term signifies an entrance in the sea or the ocean between two bodies of land. It also describes an enclosed and typically narrow space. Based on this latter meaning, the word has deeply rooted metaphoric and allegorical meanings which, as in the case of the serpent and the dragon, are primarily negative. According to Genesis, the mouth is the origin of the downfall of mankind: from the mouth of the snake in the Garden of Eden came the fateful words that motivated Eve to give the apple to Adam who ate it with his mouth. While Christian saints and the Virgin protected the navigators in the open waters of the sea, mouths and gulfs were perceived to be diabolic nests of evil because they were hidden from God's sight. The serpent's mouth in medieval religious philosophy was believed to be the place where unnatural sex took place, the result of which was the immediate or eventual death of both participants.[56] In medieval Christian iconography, the gaping throat of a dragon or of a serpent were two of the most common ways of representing the entrance to Hell, known as Hell Mouth (also sometimes referred to as Hell's Mouth or the Mouth of Hell). It was sometimes also portrayed as the throat of a whale, lion, or leviathan. Double, triple, and quadruple Hell Mouths were also depicted (figures 6.5 and 6.6).[57] Hell Mouths were depicted in various kinds of visual art across Europe, including paintings, stained glass windows, illuminated manuscripts, and carvings, the image reaching the apogee of its popularity in the

6.5. The Beast and the False Prophet in the Fire (La Bête et le faux prophète dans le feu) (beginning of the thirteenth century). MS French 403, folio 40. Courtesy of the Bibliothèque nationale, Paris, France.

Middle Ages. Textual references to Hell Mouth can already be found in Scripture and later in visionary and exhortatory texts. Theatre employed the allegory of Hell Mouth as well and stage props representing Hell Mouth were featured in mystery cycle plays.

The Hell Mouth was perceived to be a place where the condemned suffered excruciating physical and spiritual pain. It was believed that, caught inside, doomed sinners experienced the swallowing force of the Hell Mouth, frightening confinement, deafening noise, and scorching heat.[58] The description of their navigation through the *bocas* focuses on the exact phenomena that Columbus and his crew witnessed. The first such phenomenon was the extraordinary heat, which they felt early during the third voyage, soon after leaving the islands of Cape Verde as several sources state: "entré en tan grande ardor, que creí que se me quemavan los navíos

6.6. The Fall of the Rebel Angels (La chute des anges rebelles). The Psalter of Blanche of Castille (1223–30). MS 1186, folio 9v. Courtesy of Bibliothéque de l'Arsenal, Paris, France.

y gente"; "fallé tan grande ardor y los rayos del sol tan calientes, que pensava de quemarme"; and "temían no se encendiesen los navíos"; and "navigia ihi incenderentur."[59] The second phenomenon was the great roaring noise produced by the currents of water rushing through the *bocas*: "avía unos fileros de corriente que atravesavan aquella boca y traían un rugir muy grande."[60] The third unusual phenomenon was the battle between streams of fresh and salty waters and the resulting pulling towards the inside of the *bocas* that they experienced when they came near them: "que era pelea del agua dulze con la salada: la dulze empujava a la otra porque no entrase, y la salada porque ésta otra no saliese."[61] Finally, Columbus described witnessing extremely high waves that threatened to bury the caravels under water.

The desperation that permeates the Columbian toponymic discourse of the third and fourth voyages is not surprising given both the difficult navigation and the troublesome relationships Columbus had with Spaniards and natives alike. When Columbus landed at Santo Domingo on 31 August 1498, his experiences there were as troubled as the ocean he had been sailing: Francisco Roldán had begun a rebellion and a large number of Columbus's men had deserted. Naming was also no longer a privilege that was only Columbus's: other conquistadors were quick to claim territories and name them as they saw fit. One of those names was *Venezuela*, "Little Venice" (today the Gulf of Maracaibo), assigned by Alonso de Hojeda who sailed on an exploratory voyage with Amerigo Vespucci without Columbus's permission. Another was America, printed on a new *mappa mundi* in multiple editions published by Waldsemüller in 1507, a permanent record of Vespucci's superior skills, not necessarily in exploration and not even in diplomacy but surely in his capability to inscribe his name on the map. Because of their failure as administrators, at the beginning of October 1500 Columbus and his brother Diego were sent back to Spain in chains, a humiliation from which Columbus would never recover. Similarly, the wearisome events of the fourth and final voyage, lasting from 9 May 1502 until 7 November 1504, could be summed up as a constant battle with hostile nature and enemies. The narrative in the *Diario* attests to Columbus's growing physical and emotional discomfort, which undoubtedly contributed to his death two years after his return to Spain, on 20 May 1506 at the age of fifty-four. When the governor of Hispaniola, Nicolás de Ovando, denied Columbus permission to enter the harbour during a storm, it was yet another insult and the disillusioned explorer later wrote in his ship log that he had been turned away from the very territories he had won for Spain (of course, he says nothing of the local inhabitants' rights to those lands).

Since the events of the third and fourth voyages have been abundantly described by others, I will describe here only those that directly shaped the process of Columbian naming.[62] As he departed on 30 May 1498 from the port of Sanlúcar de Barrameda aboard a ship, *la nao*, the name of which he never mentions (alongside five caravels), Columbus announced that he was doing so "en nombre de la Santa Trinidad," in the name of the Holy Trinity.[63] He named a land mass *Isla de la Trinidad* as soon as he saw three hills that appeared in his view like a sign from God.[64] In all likelihood, this is the first toponym Columbus pronounced during the third voyage. After naming *Cabo de la Galera*, which is, in fact, the first new toponym mentioned in the *Relación del tercer viaje* (and which is now called Galeota Point), Columbus sailed through Boca de la Sierpe into the gulf which he named *Golfo de la Ballena* (today the Gulf of Paria). He proceeded to explore the south coast of Trinidad where he named *Punta de la Playa* (presently Erin Point), *Punta del Arenal*, and *Isla Sancta* (the latter was not actually an island but part of the continent and is known today as Punta Bombeador in Venezuela). In Golfo de la Ballena, he also named two visually impressive points: a rock standing in mid-*boca*, *El Gallo* (not mentioned in the *Diario*), and a hill he believed to be part of another island, *Isla de Gracia*, which, in fact, was part of the Venezuelan promontory.[65] Desiring to explore the latter, he went back across Boca de la Sierpe, crossed and explored Golfo de la Ballena (where he named *Punta del Aguja* and *Isla Sabeta* [also spelled as *Ysabeta*]), and then returned to Boca del Drago.

Place names he assigned during the third and fourth voyages, which appear in the additional pages Las Casas copied, include those inspired by religious thoughts (*Isla de la Asumpción*, *Isla Santa Cruz*, *Isla Santa Chaterina*, *Tierra de Gracia*, *Isla El Romero*); the natural world, namely, that of birds (*Isla Martinet*) and shapes of the landscape (*Cabo Luengo*, *Punta Llana*, *Isla Alto Velo*); life among the local inhabitants (*Puerto de las Cabañas*); and sensory experiences such as taste, very possibly related to encounters with the local inhabitants (*Cabo de Sabor*, *Cabo Rico*). *Islas Abre-el-ojo* reminds navigators to keep an open eye for the dangers of the natural environment or, perhaps, for those flesh-eating Caribs. (For a complete list of toponyms, see the appendix.) Despite the meaningful naming of *Isla de la Trinidad* and *Tierra de Gracia*, not a great number of place names Columbus assigned during the last two voyages evoke the ideas of spiritual salvation. Besides the aforementioned two toponyms, only one other, *Jardines*, is perhaps related to the idea of the Garden of Eden. The additional summary Las Casas made of the ship log of the third voyage includes a handful of place names inspired by the sacred realm and the names of saints, something that is no different from the toponymic discourse of the first and second voyages. The toponymic discourse of the fourth voyage, however, marks quite a sharp turning point, as it contains almost no such toponyms. *Relación del cuarto viaje* contains only two toponyms that clearly express a positive religious meaning (*Cabo de Gracias a Dios* and *Puerto Belén*) and another one that potentially refers to the Virgin (*Puerto Gordo*). Even the section of Las Casas's *Historia de las Indias* that focuses on the fourth voyage offers just two more such toponyms (*Puerto Santa Gloria* and *Puerto Santo Domingo*). The motifs of fear, danger, and physical as well as moral suffering fragment the discourses of the proximity of the Earthly Paradise and of spiritual salvation. They permeate the narratives of the two *relaciones*, thus producing the "breaking" of the subject, "quiebra del sujeto [del paraíso terrenal]," to use the words of Mignolo.[66] Both the *Relación del tercer viaje* and the *Relación del cuarto viaje* insist repeatedly on the extreme heat, noise, and the sensation of being pulled inwards that Columbus and his crew experienced, which bring to the reader's mind familiar infernal imagery.

Perhaps sensing that the entitlement which he believed had been granted to him by God himself to create a new order in the New World no longer belonged to him, Columbus was languid about inventing place names during the final voyage. The list of toponyms he assigned during the fourth voyage is short and thematically scattered, and its imaginative quality is limited. The *Relación del cuarto viaje* introduces just eight new Castilian toponyms, and in his *Historia de las Indias*, Las Casas mentions fourteen more, bringing the total to twenty-two (the authorship of the toponyms in the latter group is not always explicitly stated). Because of the scarcity of place names invented during this last voyage, the lack of toponymic context further diminishes the expressive quality of the existing toponyms and the overall cohesiveness of the fabric of the toponymic discourse. The sombre quality of the toponyms Columbus invented during the fourth voyage (as of *Puerto del Retrete*) as well as their practical intention (*Puerto de Bastimentos* and *Puerto Gordo*)[67] attest to the tired mind of the explorer whose imagination and energy were both running dry, while his physical and emotional health was reaching precarious limits. Some of the toponyms that could be interpreted in various ways gain a more negative meaning based on the narrative context in which they appear. *Puerto del Retrete*, which could be thought of as a peaceful name referring to a sheltered place (from the verb *retirarse*, to move back or away), in the narrative context of the *Relación del cuarto viaje* is clearly a glum name pronounced during circumstances that were far from comforting:

"fallé en el camino al Retrete, adonde me (retruse con harto perigro y enojo) y bien fatigado yo, los navíos y la gente."[68] Columbus also named the greedy-sounding *Río de la Posesión*, the bizarre *Costa de la Oreja* (based on the observation of the pierced ears of the natives), and the anxious *Río Desastre* (all three are included in Las Casas's description of the fourth voyage in his *Historia* but they are absent from the *Relación del cuarto viaje*). The two positive-sounding toponyms *Puerto Belén* and *Belporto* (*Puerto Bello*, *Bel Puerto*) mark but brief interludes of temporary relief in a stream of troubling events described in anxious paragraphs and summed up in gloomy toponyms. Even some of the positive-sounding toponyms were actually introduced under distressed circumstances, which taints their meaning to a more negative light. For example, Columbus's crew suffered great danger on the way to Puerto Santa Gloria and inside it they also found the navigation to Puerto Santo Domingo very dangerous: "Pasar desta isleta [Beata], para venir a este puerto de Sancto Domingo es muy difícil."[69] As a whole, the toponymy and the narrative of the fourth voyage continue with the motif of suffering and desperation articulated in the *Relación del tercer viaje*.

Overall, most of the toponyms Columbus invented in Castilian during the third and fourth voyages fall into three categories. Toponyms in the first category refer to neutral subjects that are unrelated to spiritual or ideological realms: these include practical necessities (*Puerto de Bastimentos*) as well as natural and landscape features (*Puerto de Gatos* and *Punta Llana*). Toponyms in the second category document feelings of anxiety and desperation either directly or indirectly (*Río Desastre*, *Boca del Drago*, *Puerto del Retrete*, *Puerto Santa Gloria*, and *Puerto Santo Domingo*).[70] And toponyms in the third category are based on Taino and other indigenous toponymy, chieftains' names, words, and word fragments. The toponymic discourse of the third and fourth voyages can be distinguished clearly from that of the first two voyages based on these last two categories. Feelings of anxiety and desperation were almost entirely absent from the place names Columbus assigned during the first two voyages, whereas they occupy a prominent place in the last two voyages. Furthermore, the place names based on Taino and other indigenous toponymy, words, and chieftains' names are notably more numerous than the place names invented in Castilian.

Regardless of the gloomy nature of many of the toponyms invented during the third and fourth voyages, *Boca del Drago* and *Boca de la Sierpe* could still be thought of either as passing points in the journey towards the Earthly Paradise or as the feared final destination. Passage through the belly of the beast – that is, being swallowed by the beast and then either released into salvation or fighting one's way into freedom – is a motif in several legends that speak about spiritual and physical renewal. Jonah, according to the Bible, was swallowed by a whale and spent three days and three nights in its belly repenting his sins, after which he emerged spiritually reborn. St Margaret of Antioch was swallowed by a dragon and then released (the toponym *Isla Margarita*, which Columbus also invented during the third voyage, may be a reference to this saint, though it may also be a reference to pearls). St Brendan, the legendary Irish monk who searched for the Earthly Paradise, encountered a whale and celebrated Easter Mass on its back (as portrayed in an image from *Nova typis transacta navigation*, printed in 1621; figure 6.7). In Columbian toponymy, the theme of Christian pilgrimage is suggested by the toponym *Golfo de la Ballena*, and it is also present in toponyms from the third voyage: *Isla El Romero* ("The Pilgrim Island"), *Isla Caracol*, and *Cabo de Conchas* (the meaning of the final toponym is related to the tradition that, upon their return from the Holy Land, crusaders wore a shell, usually a scallop shell, as a symbol of their pilgrimage).[71] Columbus himself carried out a pilgrimage after the first voyage. When they feared that the *Niña* would sink, crew members drew beans from a hat. Columbus drew one marked with a cross and thus he was chosen to make a pilgrimage to the Church of Saint Mary of Guadaloupe should they return safely to Spain. The stormy sea, which was used profusely in literature as an allegory of Christian pilgrimage and, more generally, of the trials of human life, is another textual element that supports the presence of the theme of Christian pilgrimage.[72] Similarly, the serpent (in the toponyms *Cabo de Sierpe* and *Boca de la Sierpe*) is a symbol of a sinner who renews himself both physically and spiritually.[73]

Given the discursive context in which it was named, the toponym *Isla de la Trinidad* directly expresses the idea of salvation while other toponyms inspired by the sacred realm and names of saints do so in a more marginal way: *Puerto de la Navidad*, *Puerto de Sancto Domingo*, *Isla de la Asumpción*, *Isla Concepción*, and others (these are mentioned in the summary Las Casas made of the ship log of the third voyage but they are not included in the transcription known as the *Relación del tercer viaje*). Naming the three peaks *Isla de la Trinidad* immediately *after* describing sailing through and naming the two *bocas* suggests that Columbus felt as though he had escaped into salvation from a grave danger. In the *Relación del tercer viaje*, the section that follows directly after the descriptions of sailing through the two *bocas* deals with the location of the Earthly Paradise and the pear-like shape of the earth. Oliva states that the vision of

6.7. St Brendan and the whale island. *Nova typis transacta navigatio* (Linz, 1621). Courtesy of the John Carter Brown Library, Providence, RI.

the high hills of Trinidad liberated Columbus from the fears he was experiencing, referring to the tremendous waves that threatened to bury the caravels: "Así fatigados, al fin alcanzaron aire suave y templado y vieron de las gavias unas sierras altas, *cuya vista los libró de tan gran temor* en que estaban de no poder haber reparo de agua."[74] Based on Peter Martyr's description, it appears that the true reason for joy was the belief that the Earthly Paradise was located at the top of the three peaks of Trinidad: "Y así afirma y sostiene que *en la cima de aquellos tres montes*, que hemos dicho vio desde lejos el marino vigía desde la atalaya, *está el paraíso terrenal.*"[75] The celebratory nature of *Isla de la Trinidad* suggests a victory against the imaginary beast and its naming marks a point of joyful culmination in the narrative of the *Relación del tercer viaje*. The tone of the narrative shifts notably as the dangers of the *bocas* are replaced by relief at the sight of the hills of Trinidad. *Isla de la Trinidad*, *Tierra de Graçia*, *Jardines*, and *Isla de Gracia* – all named in the vicinity of the *bocas* – echo the juxtaposition of the gates to Earthly Paradise and the two dragons in the Hereford Cathedral map (see figure 6.4). These toponyms suggest that

Columbus emerged from the dangerous *bocas* unscathed and renewed, both literally and metaphorically. Contrary to the names of the *bocas*, these toponyms speak about the holiness of the place and, thus, the proximity of the Earthly Paradise. Their tone is joyous and uplifting in celebration of an escape from great dangers. After being plagued by the most challenging natural conditions in the *bocas*, the navigators enjoyed the pleasant, temperate climate near *Isla de la Trinidad* and *Tierra de Graçia*. After entrapment by the geographic space and their view being impaired by great waves near the *bocas*, free vision and beautiful sights characterize their arrival at Isla de la Trinidad, Tierra de Graçia, and Isla Sancta.

Incongruous in the *Relación del tercer viaje*, however, is the sequence in which places were named. The tone of the narrative shifts from one expressing anxiety associated with sailing through the *bocas* to one expressing the joy and relief they felt as they sighted the three peaks of the Isla de la Trinidad in the east and the peak of Tierra de Graçia in the west. So much emphasis is placed on the quasi-miraculous apparition of the three high peaks that it seems logical that Columbus named them to celebrate his successful escape. The narrative of the *Relación del tercer viaje* states that Columbus named Trinidad *after* escaping from the *bocas*: "subió un marinero a la gavia y vido al Poniente tres montañas juntas. Diximos la *Salve Regina* y otras muchas prosas, y dimos todos muchas graçias a Nuestro Señor. Y después … bolví fazia la tierra … después de aver nombrado a la isla de la Trinidad."[76] However, a statement is made earlier in the *Relación del tercer viaje* that Columbus had already named *Isla de la Trinidad* before he approached either of the *bocas*. Las Casas informs us, in fact, that *Isla de la Trinidad* was the first place name Columbus pronounced during the third voyage.[77] Likewise, he had also already named *Tierra de Graçia* and *Isla Sancta* before entering the *bocas*.

The toponyms, therefore, and the order in which they were pronounced tell us something that the *diarios* do not: the trajectory of the events that Columbus experienced did not bring relief but did the contrary. Columbus first believed he had arrived at a beautiful, tranquil, and safe landscape, the high hills of which signalled the vicinity of the Earthly Paradise, but then he experienced all the signs, such as heat, noise, and a swallowing force, of having arrived near the gates to Hell. Columbus knew that this was not a message he could articulate to the Spanish Crown in his ship log, especially if he was to present the case for yet another voyage of exploration and conquest or at least to prove that his voyages had not been fruitless. After the dramatic description of his navigation through the *bocas*, he wisely emphasized the beauty of the high hills and the safety of the bay.

The toponymy, however, reveals his true sense about the precarious spiritual and ideological destination which he was afraid he had reached.

Discourse of Chaos

The final characteristic of the two *bocas* that must be addressed is chaos and the notable absence of a force to control it. The *Relación del tercer viaje* describes the overwhelming sense of disorder that the navigators experienced as soon as they left the Cape Verde islands: "todo de un golpe vino, atán *desordenado*, que no avía persona que osase desçender debajo de cubierta a remediar la basija y mantenimientos."[78] Elements in the narrative of the *Relación del tercer viaje*, such as salty and fresh water mixing, waves rising above the caravels, currents simultaneously pulling and pushing, are all indications that the natural order of things had been disturbed. In the Western literary tradition, two foundational narratives involve the concept of chaos. The first is the biblical narrative of the creation of the world from primordial chaos at the beginning of time; the second is that of destruction as the world, overwhelmed by increasing chaos, perished in an apocalyptic battle.[79] In the paradigm of the narrative of creation, according to various Western ancient myths and literary traditions, the hero battles the forces of primordial chaos, typically represented by a dragon or a sea beast. The scholar of world myths Mircea Eliade has insightfully described this as "the ancient scenario of the combat and the victory of the divinity over the marine monster, incarnation of chaos."[80] Saints' or heroes' battles with dragons also represented the struggle between the sacred and the diabolic, between good and evil. It is both surprising and telling that although Columbus included in his toponymy symbols of chaos, he excluded names of any of those heroes or saints who were celebrated for having vanquished a serpent or a dragon.

In medieval and Renaissance art, Archangel Michael and St George are both often shown battling a dragon. Christ and the Virgin Mary are also sometimes shown trampling a serpent or a dragon, which symbolizes their victory over death, sin, and evil. Other male and female saints believed to have defeated a dragon are the apostle Philip, St Sylvester, St Martha of Bethany, St Catherine, and St Margaret. Columbus does not include references to these saints in his toponymy nor does he point out a relationship between the dragon or the serpent and the saints who were believed to have vanquished them. The names of Catalina and Margarita in the toponyms are two exceptions, but their connection to the saints St Catherine and St Margaret is unclear.[81] The same is true for Christ or the Virgin Mary;

references to the Marian events in the toponyms *Isla de la Asumpción* and *Isla Concepción* and to Christ in *Puerto de la Navidad* bear no relationship to the serpent or the dragon. The absences are particularly notable in the case of the two celebrated male saints Archangel Michael and St George who were most commonly shown battling a dragon in medieval and Renaissance art, both of which had inspired the Portuguese in the naming of two islands in the Atlantic: *Sam Miguel* and *Sam Jorge* in the Azores.[82]

Also notably absent is a celebrated demigod who fought and vanquished several different monsters. He was particularly venerated in Spain, and Columbus was often compared to him. Hercules, immortalized by Hesiod in his *Theogony* and Dante in his *Divine Comedy*, fought the invulnerable lion which had been terrorizing the inhabitants of the hills around Nemea, strangling the beast with his bare arms (the First Labour). Hercules also defeated the nine-headed Lernean hydra, which enabled him to expand the frontier of the known world (the Second Labour) and he overcame the three-headed dog Cerberus, which had a snake or a dragon for its tail and snakes for its hair and which was guarding the entrance to the underworld of Hades (the Twelfth Labour). Spain had a particular attachment to Hercules and some claimed him to be the founder of the Spanish empire. Legend tells us that, as part of his Tenth Labour ordered by Euristeo, Hercules separated the continents of Europe and Africa and placed columns on two mountains, thus marking the Strait of Gibraltar. The pillars, as well as the phrase "plus ultra," both symbolizing the extension of existing limits of knowledge, were frequently featured on coins and coats of arms. Carlos I (V) (1500–58) adopted the Herculean pillars for Spain's coat of arms as a symbol of its worldwide power and had the words "plus ultra" written underneath, referring to the extension of the Spanish empire from the peninsula all the way to the recently annexed America. The pillars were even marked on maps.[83] Spanish historians writing about Columbus's voyages frequently alluded to Hercules and likened Columbus's voyages of discovery to the way a Hellenic demigod had once expanded the limits of the known world. Oliva, in an attempt to reconcile history and myth, states that both Columbus's courage and his achievements were greater than those of Hercules: "Partieron éstos ... con mayor confianza que tuvo Hércules y, dejando atrás los fines que él puso, navegaron treinta días al occidente."[84] The Spanish Crown in the Americas also adopted the Herculean pillars and the words "plus ultra," or sometimes simply "plus," and had them inscribed on coins.[85] As in the case of religious figures known to have battled a dragon, any references to Hercules are decidedly absent in the Columbian toponymy.

These significant absences likely attest to Columbus's desire to plant himself on the landscape of the unfamiliar lands and dangerous waters that extended far beyond the Pillars of Hercules. At the same time, they point to another absence that turns out to be even more significant: that of Columbus's own name. Columbus did not name any places after himself, nor after his sons Diego and Ferdinand or his brothers Bartholomew, Giovanni, and Giacomo. Nor did he name places after the women he loved, his first wife Felipa Moniz Perestrello or his mistress Beatrice. He did not name places after his native village near Genoa (if that is where he was actually born). Even the name of his flagship, to which he only refers as *la nao* and never by name, is entirely absent from the narrative of discovery and conquest and, by consequence, from the toponymic discourse. While many conquistadors later inserted their own names as they named places in the Americas, Columbus did this very little, if at all. For example, the captain of *Pinta*, Martín Alonso Pinzón, during the course of the first voyage disobediently sailed in search for Baveque on his own and named a river after himself, *Río Martín Alonso*. Seeking to erase the record of such rash behaviour, Columbus promptly changed this name to *Río de Gracia*. Rivalry aside, already in the first voyage Columbus instituted a principle to not attribute places in the lands he was claiming for the Crown after specific individuals, including himself or anyone else in the crew. He stayed true to this principle through to the end of the final voyage. Some exceptions can be found. These include the names of islands Columbus pronounced after monasteries that had provided support to him, *Isla Santa María de Guadalupe* and *Isla Santa María de Monsarrate*. Another exception is the Holy Trinity, to which he was passionately devoted, and the name of his name saint, St Christopher, spiritual entities to which Columbus was most devoted. *El Romero* may allude to Columbus's own pilgrimages in addition to the general idea of pilgrimage. Other toponyms that may have had some personal significance for Columbus include those that explore various human relationships such as brotherhood (*Los Dos Hermanos*, first mentioned on 19 December 1492), fatherhood (*Cabo de Padre y Hijo*, 12 January 1493), and romantic love (*Cabo del Enamorado*, 12 January 1493). However, all of these place names express broad human relationships and general feelings of spiritual devotion. The *diarios* contain no commentary as to whether or not Columbus's personal relationships inspired the naming of these places. None of them are direct testaments to Columbus's persona in the way that toponyms such as *Río Martín Alonso* or *America*, the toponym that was bestowed on the entire land mass in honour of Amerigo Vespucci, are. Columbus's presence on the Caribbean landscape is at best implicit. Therefore, ultimately the toponymic discourse of the third and fourth voyages reveals the absent figure of Columbus or of any other "creator" or "hero" who could institute order in the chaotic landscape. At best, this discourse reveals the figure of a pilgrim and a sinner, overwhelmed by fear caused by the surrounding dangers and suffering physically and morally.

Broken Naming Patterns and the Proliferation of Indigenous Toponymy as Symptoms of Chaos

The third and fourth voyages document a significant increase in the absorption of indigenous toponyms into the Columbian toponymic discourse, and a declining cohesiveness and expressive quality of the place names invented in Castilian. The number of Taino and other indigenous toponyms incorporated during the third voyage is still modest: five toponyms of indigenous origin are introduced in Las Casas's *Historia de las Indias*, in contrast to the eight and thirty-four Castilian toponyms that are introduced in the *Relación del tercer viaje* and the additional pages by Las Casas not included in the transcription, respectively. However, the situation changes dramatically during the fourth voyage. In contrast to the twenty-four Castilian toponyms introduced in the *Relación del cuarto viaje*, Las Casas's *Historia de las Indias*, and Ferdinand Columbus's *Historia* (eight, fifteen, and one, respectively), an impressive thirty-six toponyms of indigenous origins are introduced in the same sources (nine, twenty, and seven, respectively). For purposes of comparison, the *Diario del primer viaje* registers seventy Castilian toponyms and twenty-six toponyms of Taino origin, in addition to two more toponyms of Taino origin registered in letters. The portion of Las Casas's *Historia de las Indias* dealing with the first voyage introduces four Castilian toponyms and four of Taino origin. The *Relación del segundo viaje* introduces ten new Castilian toponyms and no new toponyms of indigenous origins. The section in Las Casas's *Historia de las Indias* dedicated to the second voyage introduces fifteen Castilian toponyms and five of Taino origin, while the relevant section in Ferdinand Columbus's *Historia* introduces seven and two, respectively. To sum up, the various sources that document Columbus's naming consistently show that his naming in Castilian was prolific during the first, second, and third voyages and that proportionally the numbers of Taino toponyms that he acquired were significantly less than those he introduced in Castilian. However, during the fourth voyage the situation changed dramatically and Columbus incorporated into his toponymic discourse almost twice as many toponyms of Taino and other indigenous origins as he invented in Castilian. Though the numbers are not exact because we do not know how many of the indigenous toponyms found in Las Casas's *Historia de las Indias* were also toponyms that Columbus knew and that had affected his understanding of the landscape, the trend is nevertheless hard to ignore.

At the same time, the toponymic discourse of the last voyage manifests broken thematic patterns, unfinished sequences, and an overall impoverishment in the creativity of the place names. The eight place names introduced in the *Relación del cuarto viaje* do not exhibit hierarchical sequences, patterns of symmetry, or the principle of centre the way the toponyms of the first, second, and the third voyages did. Even the thematic cohesiveness is difficult to establish: *Puerto de Bastimentos* and *Puerto Gordo* speak to the practical concerns of the voyage; *Cabo de Gracias a Dios* and *Puerto Belén* are two spiritual names; *Puerto del Retrete* is a pessimistic name initially inspired by the narrowness of the channel; *Belporto* is a safe and insipid name that speaks to the aesthetics of the place; and *Isla de las Bocas* (or *Isla de las Pozas*) may allude once again to the fear that the landscape was capable of swallowing ships, lands, and people. The existing patterns of symmetry and hierarchies in the Columbian toponymic discourse of the first, second, and, to some extent, the third voyage are expressions of the acts of ordering and of trying to make sense of the disorderly and unknown. Symbolically, they repeat the act of Creation during which chaos was transformed into order, an act that ancient societies also performed by inhabiting or using territories.[86] The dramatic breaking of the process of Creation is reflected in the toponymy of the third and fourth voyages during the pronouncement of the toponyms *Boca del Drago* and *Boca de la Sierpe*. In addition to being expressions of Columbus's eschatological mindset and of his fear of the proximity of Hell, these toponyms also articulate the overwhelming sense of the return of chaos.

Finally, the narratives documenting the last two voyages exhibit a tendency towards the demonization of the local peoples and the infernalization of the Caribbean landscape. The natural signs that can be interpreted as indicating the proximity of the gates to Hell were explored in detail in the earlier pages of this chapter. In addition, descriptions of the local peoples focus on their ugliness, blackness, and monstrous features. For example, the toponyms *Costa de la Oreja* was provoked by the sight of natives who had pierced their ears. Ferdinand Columbus describes their blackness, nakedness, savageness, and cannibalism:

> los habitantes ... son casi negros, de mal aspecto, van completamente desnudos y se muestran en todo muy salvajes; según decía el indio que capturamos, comen carne humana y el pescado crudo, tal como lo pescan; y se perforan las orejas haciendo unos agujeros tan grandes, que cómodamente cabría por ellos un huevo de gallina. Por este motivo, el Almirante bautizó a aquella costa con el nombre de Costa de la Oreja.[87]

Furthermore, according to Ferdinand Columbus's description of an encounter with a local tribe during the fourth voyage, Columbus also began associating some of the indigenous peoples with the devil:

> Llevan los brazos y el cuerpo adornados con arabescos trazados con fuego, lo que les da una extraña apariencia ... Cuando se preparan para sus fiestas, se pintan la cara de negro o de rojo, se trazan en el rostro líneas de distintos colores, se dibujan un pico de avestruz o se pintan de negro los ojos. Son las maneras que ellos tienen de embellecerse, cuando en realidad *asemejan a diablos*.[88]

Together, the infernalization of the natural landscape and the increasing influence of indigenous onomastics (which may be Taino or other) in the Columbian toponymic discourse reveal Columbus's disillusion caused by his inability to subdue the landscape physically or metaphorically through acts of verbal mapping.

Conclusion

The naming of *Boca del Drago* and *Boca de la Sierpe* during the third voyage express a breaking point in the Columbian toponymic discourse. As they bring together an entire range of symbols and metaphors with which dragons and serpents have been associated in the Christian, classical, and cosmographic traditions, as well as in Asian and American contexts, they create a transoceanic space that escapes cultural definition. However, rather than being in control of this space, Columbus is overwhelmed by it. The naming of the two *bocas* expresses his deepest anxieties and the unsettling sense of physical and spiritual danger. While significant portions of the narratives of the third and fourth voyages are dedicated to the location of the Earthly Paradise, many of the natural signs of its proximity can also be interpreted as indicating that the gates to Hell could also be nearby.

Columbus's inability to establish clear patterns indicative of a strong rhetoric and his failure to insert himself, through references to his own name or places directly associated with himself, his family, or the place where he was born, carves out vacuums that are filled with anxiety and fear. These vacuums are further reinforced by the broken patterns and lack of control due to an increasing proportion of indigenous place names. The meanings of many of the indigenous place names are unknown to Columbus and hence they are incorporated into his own naming fabric in a disconnected, haphazard fashion that contrasts sharply with the discursive manifestations in the toponymic discourse of the earlier voyages based on thematic groupings, hierarchical sequences, and symmetrical arrangements. The occasional demonization of the native inhabitants and the repeated and insistent infernalization of the landscape create a vision of a world that was hostile and overwhelming. They also indicate his greatest fear that, instead of the Earthly Paradise, the gates to Hell could be nearby. At the dusk of his exploration efforts, the fact that his scattered toponymic discourse in Castilian was completely overwhelmed by indigenous onomastics suggests that Columbus felt that that he was being devoured by the very landscape he had been attempting to subdue.

Conclusion

The extensive list of place names Columbus invented in Castilian, which can be pieced together from several historical accounts, reveals a series of verbal mapping acts through which Columbus built a fictional landscape. The letter to Santángel, which announced the official version of the "discovery" of a world previously unknown to Europeans, presented to readers only a small group of toponyms. Carefully chosen from the much longer list, they effectively communicated the idea that, through his acts of naming, Columbus generated in this region yet unexplored by Europeans patterns of hierarchy, progression, and centre, and that these patterns faithfully represented the European ideals of order in society, nature, and aesthetics. They also projected the idea that the toponymic discourse as a whole was clear, uncluttered, easily understandable, and thus that this structure, and the place names that had created it, would endure. Some elements of this structure and clarity can be found in the longer list of toponyms known to us today, and among its patterns and progressions is the creation of thematic groups and toponymic clusters as well as the establishment of principles of symmetry, hierarchy, and chronology. And yet, despite repeated attempts, an overall order was not achieved, and the patterns became increasingly fragmented as the voyages continued. The haphazard emergence of themes as well as unfinished and broken patterns suggest that the process of naming was far from systematic and controlled. Many of the thematic groups are left wanting completion, which cannot be found in the pages of the *diarios* or contemporary histories; hierarchies appear imperfect as some of the entries seem to be misplaced.

The linguistic unity and the narrative flow that were created through the invention of place names in Castilian were furthermore repeatedly interrupted and broken by Taino place names, which, for Castilian readers, were difficult to pronounce and whose meanings were entirely obscure. Not only did Taino place names warp the layout of the Castilian toponymic discourse but they also substantially impacted Columbus's verbal mapping of the American landscape. This was due to the remarkable influence that the Taino people had on his search for desired treasures, his conceptualization of his location in relation to the mainland of Asia, and his overall efforts in mapping. As illustrated by examples such as Columbus's focus on the name of *Baveque* while trying to find the hidden source of gold, dismissing the presence of Taino toponymy and language in the Columbian toponymic discourse as a whole would result in a rather impoverished understanding of the processes that shaped it. The definition of their corpus as one consisting of *both* the place names that Columbus invented in Castilian *and* the fragments of the Taino language and toponymy that he appropriated, translated, or even mechanically repeated allows us to study the process of naming in greater depth.

A study of the list of Columbian place names as a whole reveals that Columbus's language of naming was not a rigid instrument with which a one-directional flow of power and single-handed appropriation of spaces was achieved, as the letter to Santángel led his readers to believe; instead it was a verbal testament of the multidirectional linguistic, epistemological, and material exchanges that both enabled and complicated progress in Columbus's voyages and that subsequently shaped what soon became know as European visions of America. It also reveals that Columbian names were not only projections of a theoretical certainty or mirages of desire, but were also products of negotiation, translation, manipulation, and subversion. Ultimately, Columbus did not achieve either of the two distinct goals stated in the prologue to the *Diario del primer viaje*. The first, the practical goal of drawing a navigational chart with new Castilian names of places, which, by making it easy for Europeans to pronounce and to remember those names, would tame and render readable the otherwise opaque landscape, was achieved only in part. A rather significant portion of the place names were not easy either to transcribe or to pronounce, and the names meant nothing to European eyes and ears. The second – the more abstract, political, but ultimately philosophical – goal of making sense of the world of the Other through a verbal mapping of it and by imposing on it a familiar order was undermined from its very beginning. The system of onomastics that had existed long before continued to exist and threatened the newly invented names by infiltrating and subverting the theoretically orderly toponymic discourse in Castilian.

Ironically, perhaps, the influence that the Taino inhabitants exerted on Columbus's decisions for naming, exploring, and mapping stems from the clashing objectives contained in his own promise. Before making the lands and their people subjects of the Spanish Crown and imposing a new ideological, political, and spiritual order onto their lives, a deeper understanding of them had to be achieved first and the exotic lands had to be made familiar to those who were claiming ownership. Columbian toponymy reflects these dual and conflicting processes of imposing and inquiring, erasing and translating, taking possession and submitting himself to the mercy of the Taino people who were willing to help as often as they intentionally manipulated and derided Columbus.

The lack of order and control in the Columbian toponymic discourse is also visible in the failures that spanned beyond the toponymic discourse itself. Columbus's failures to institute order include his unsuccessful tenure as a governor and his quickly deteriorating relationships with the authorities of the New World, including the king and queen themselves. His failure to establish an effective administrative order is mirrored in his failure to institute a linguistic and cartographic order, something to which he had dedicated an enormous amount of energy throughout his voyages. One of the more direct expressions of Columbus's failure to institute order through his toponymy is the fact that, despite his initial promise, none of the maps we know he drew, as there are several references to them in the *diarios*, have survived.[1] Some of the maps were probably lost at sea, as were some original letters and documents, including the letter of 14 February. Some did make their way across the ocean, but since they were regarded as highly secret official documents, their use was limited to a very select circle of individuals. None of Columbus's maps ever became public nor did they become institutionalized or become the accepted and commonly known versions of how Europe mapped America. The only exception is the sketch of the coast of Hispaniola attributed to Columbus that has reached posterity. However, this sketch includes only six toponyms and thus it fails to render a complete picture of the scope of the Columbian naming, just like the letter to Santángel. Columbus fell short of bridging the distance between the list of toponyms to be inscribed on a new map and making them part of one. Hence, according to Ptolemy's instructions, he failed to complete the fundamental step in making a map of the known part of the world. The absence of any surviving maps leaves Columbian place names in a particularly precarious position: rather than serving their intended practical function of marking places on a map or navigational chart, they survived instead only as a list. In its unfinished and unfulfilled state, this list further underlines their enduring rhetorical and discursive, rather than the intended scientific and pragmatic, functions.

Columbus's inability to inscribe himself on the landscape he had spent more than a decade mapping and appropriating is only one item on his list of missed opportunities. That list also included making a clear statement of a geographic accomplishment and asserting an allegorical victory of virtue against sin and of Good against Evil through his toponymic discourse. While the narrative of the *Relación del tercer viaje* vehemently affirms the proximity of the Earthly Paradise, the toponyms invented during this voyage, especially the place names *Boca de la Sierpe* and *Boca del Drago*, speak to the fear that was starting to overpower Columbus; instead of the gates of the Earthly Paradise, he felt he could be coming closer to the gates to Hell.

Due to the fact that they never became established on maps, only a handful of the place names Columbus invented are still known today. The great majority of them were quickly replaced by place names invented by others or even by the original Taino names. Some places were renamed so quickly that the apparent inconsistency in naming frustrated Las Casas, who remarked in the margins of the *Diario*: "no entiendo cómo a este puerto puso arriba Puerto María y ahora de San Nicolás" (6 December 1492).[2] Some places were renamed by explorers and conquerors of other nationalities: for example, the noble-sounding *Isabela* is known today by the more prosaic name, *Crooked Island*; and not a trace of the spirituality of *Santa Maria de la Concepción* is left in the current name of the place, *Rum Cay*. As some of these place names were removed from European maps of the New World very soon after Columbus had imposed them, Las Casas nostalgically wrote about them: "Andando por la costa delante halló [Colón] muchos cabos; a uno llamó del Angel, a otro llamó la Punta del Hierro, a otro el Redondo y a otro el Francés, a otro el Cabo del Buen Tiempo, a otro Tajado. De todos estos nombres de cabos no queda hoy alguno."[3] This, no doubt, caused significant frustration for Columbus as he saw his already disorderly discourse being disassembled, which would cause confusion and danger for navigators. Hence, rather than producing an enduring list of place names, Columbus's efforts to name places resulted in deleted and changed toponyms and Castilian toponyms used in conjunction with Taino ones; as a result, there was significant confusion both in theoretical terms for contemporary historians and in practical terms for sailors. Finally, as a result of his neglect to assign a common name to the whole territory, Columbus was unable to claim the territory;

instead, it is known by the name of another explorer, as Amerigo Vespucci's America. In the end, this cost Columbus not only the toponymic discourse he had created for the foreign landscape over the course of many years, but also the most important name of all; not inscribing his own name onto the landscape he otherwise so eagerly named is perhaps a testament to his most significant failure. This notable absence is an open admission of a battle lost against the local landscape and languages which had, in the end, appropriated the space and devoured him as well.

In some cases future conquistadors maintained the names that Columbus had originally assigned: thus after claiming the island that Columbus had named *Marigalante* and the group of islands he named *Todos los Santos*, the French maintained their names, and the islands are still known today as *Mariegalante* and *Les Saintes*. Of a few others that are still used, *Cabo de Gracias a Dios* (Cape God be Thanked), named on 14 September 1502 during the fourth voyage, designates the most prominent point on the cape on the east coast of Central America, on the border between Honduras and Nicaragua. Other names that are still in use include that of the island Tortuga which, according to Morison, "is the first place name given by Columbus that has never been changed"; *Monte Christi* in the Dominican Republic; *Puerto Bello* in Panama; and *Golfo de las Flechas* (Gulf of the Arrows, part of Samaná Bay in the Dominican Republic).[4] Most of the place names Columbus invented, however, have slipped into oblivion. No one even knows for certain where Columbus's first landfall on the island he named *San Salvador* was, as several different islands are trying to claim this dubious honour.

Another factor that contributes to the increasing sense of disorder and control slipping from Columbus's hands as the inventor of the names is that of their authorship. Columbus frequently affirmed his authorship of place names: "puse nombre." We also know from the *diarios* that when the captain of *Pinta*, Martín Alonso Pinzón, named a river after himself, Columbus right away renamed it *Río de Gracia*. This incident demonstrates two things. On the one hand, this act of renaming demonstrates Columbus's unwillingness to give up the exclusive right of assigning names. Martín Alonso had sailed in search of the island of Baveque on his own, disobeying the orders of his admiral in hopes of finding gold. Independent exploration and naming were privileges available only to the captain general of the fleet, and Martín Alonso had usurped them. The record of such brass disobedience needed to be erased, and Columbus quickly changed the name of the place. At the same time, Columbus refused to assign places names after individuals. Aside from the names of members of the royal family and one name possibly dedicated to a royal functionary, the landscape he was naming was not to become a map of tributes or a list of acknowledgments. It is doubtful that Columbus chose the name of the island *Saona* to honour the crew member Michel de Cuneo, though the latter claims so in his infamous letter in which he also describes, in detail, his raping of an indigenous woman.[5] The only references to Colombus himself, if there are any, are faint and unspecific. One such example is the place name *El Romero*, pronounced during the third voyage, which may refer to the pilgrimages Columbus made in Spain and perhaps reflect the idea of his voyages in the Indies as metaphoric pilgrimages. The name of Martín Alonso inscribed on the new map would have been not only an insult to Columbus as a captain, but also inconsistent with Columbus's overall naming strategies. His names instead evoked concepts and visions using the reality in front of him in a symbolic way. Columbus also assigned place names after names of saints and after abstract human relationships (*Cabo de Padre y Hijo*, *Cabo del Enamorado*, *Peña de los Enamorados*); but never, at least not in the first voyage, did he choose his own name or names of any of his family members, friends, or lovers. Today, various places in Latin America bear the name of the captain, the country of Colombia being a prominent example. However, all these names were established later and by individuals other than Columbus.

The authorship of some names pronounced during the third and fourth voyages mentioned in contemporary chronicles is less certain than that of the first two. Two circumstances explain the increasing uncertainty about Columbus's authorship of names in the later voyages. First of all, Columbus's descriptions of the earlier voyages are more detailed than those of the later voyages. The *Relación del cuarto viaje* in particular is written in an apocalyptic, tragic, and nearly delirious tone that leaves little space for facts and names. It contains only eight new place names that Columbus invented during this voyage, and Las Casas frequently expresses his uncertainty about the authorship of the additional names given during the last voyage. The second circumstance is the explosion of exploratory voyages to the New World by others. By his third voyage, the king and queen's trust in Columbus was deteriorating, while many other voyages of exploration and conquest were being authorized.[6] As other Europeans began embarking on such voyages of exploration, they joined the frenzy of inventing whatever new names pleased their fancy. In the first half of 1499, Hojeda discovered the Gulf of Maracaibo and named it *Venezuela*, Little Venice.[7] The Florentine explorer Amerigo Vespucci, who explored Paria with Alonso de Hojeda, Bartolomé Roldán (a pilot of Columbus's first voyage), and Juan de la Cosa (the map maker from Columbus's second voyage who sent the account of his voyage to the leading European map maker Waldsemüller), claimed the name of the entire continent, America. Las Casas made comments in his *Historia de las Indias* about the uncertainty of the authorship of some of the place names he was copying, as in the case of Puerto de Cartagena: "De lo cual parece que no puso el Almirante nombre al puerto que hoy llamamos de Cartagena, según algunos han dicho … Yo creo que aquel nombre debió poner Rodrigo de Bastidas y Juan de la Cosa o quizá Cristóbal Guerra, que fueron los que aquella tierra primero que otros descubrieron y cognoscieron y también la escandalizaron."[8] As the voyages advanced, Las Casas speculated more often about the authorship of some of the names: "muy nombrado Marañón; no sé por quién ni por qué causa se le puso aquel nombre."[9] The proliferation of name-givers, names of uncertain authorship, and lack of conclusive evidence about the nature of place names were frustrating to Las Casas. The most exasperating aspect had to do with the frequent changes of already existing Castilian names and the resulting confusion on maps. Las Casas observes: "Todas estas islas y muchos puertos y partes de la tierra firme están ya descognoscidas, por mudalles los nombres los que hacen las cartas de marear, en que no poca confusión engendran, y aun son causa de hartos yerros y perdición de navíos."[10] Therefore, the proliferation of name-givers and the resulting uncertainty of authorship of place names, repeated renaming of places, and confusion on the maps must be taken into consideration when addressing the lists of Columbian place names, especially those invented during the last two voyages.

Columbus's admission of his failure to institute order is expressed in the *relaciones* of the third and fourth voyages. The toponymy of the final two voyages reveals that which Columbus knew though he did not spell it out in his narrative: that this attempt to institute a new order had failed and that he was facing linguistic, administrative, and spiritual chaos. This chaos, emblems of which are *Boca de la Sierpe*, *Boca del Drago*, and *Isla de las Bocas*, named during the third and fourth voyages, is overarching: as in a literary text, the disturbed order in nature is a metaphor for a tormented human mind; as in a spiritual tale, the unruly sea is an allegory of a restless soul.

The toponymy of the last two voyages, when compared to that of the first two, is characterized by a notable shift in tone and perspective. As discussed earlier in this book, the toponymy of the first voyage encompasses a wide range of themes, motifs, and metaphors, ranging from aesthetics to human emotions to weather conditions, and its dominating tone is hopeful, as demonstrated by such examples as *Cabo Hermoso*, *Cabo Lindo*, *Cabo Belprado*, *Cabo del Enamorado*, and *Cabo del Buen Tiempo*. Despite the devastating news Columbus faced when he returned to the Caribbean on his second voyage and found that all of the colonizers who had stayed on the island (and many of the native inhabitants as well) had been killed as a result of a violent conflict with the local inhabitants, the tone of the toponymic discourse of the second voyage remains neutral, inexpressive of the dismay he must have felt. The prevalent theme in the toponymy of the second voyage is religious (seven of the eleven Columbian place names were inspired by Christian motifs, and five of those honour Christian saints).

In contrast, the place names of the third and the fourth voyages present a decided shift in both the subjects they reference and their overall tone and character. The toponyms of the fourth voyage are not thematically uniform, and they reveal a more haphazard way of naming. Strong emotions – fear for life, desperation, exasperation, elation, and gratefulness – emerge during this final voyage. The names given during the fourth voyage are disconnected from one another in their meanings, as Columbus appears to be torn between the practical (*Puerto de Bastimentos*) and the spiritual (*Puerto Belén*). Some of the place names invented during this final voyage appear to be reflections of the fear and desperation that Columbus must have felt (*Puerto del Retrete* and *Isla de las Bocas* or *Isla de las Pozas*). Others express feelings of joyful relief (*Cabo de Gracias a Dios*).[11] Two names – *Costa de los Contrastes* (The Coast of Contrarieties) and *Alpha et Omega* – document especially well the state of a mind torn by extremes, caught between the gentle breezes of the Earthly Paradise and the scorching tempests from Hell.

Boca de la Sierpe and *Boca del Drago* reflect the culmination of the fear and distress that permeates the narrative of the *Relación del tercer viaje* to which the relief and the celebratory tenor of *Isla de la Trinidad*, *Tierra de Graçia*, and *Isla Sancta* provide a stark contrast. Even the religious toponyms invented during the third voyage become testimonies of Columbus's exasperated attitude rather than being statements of peace and joy. Together with the toponyms *Boca de la Sierpe* and *Boca del Drago*, they document the continuous shifts of his focus from salvation to perdition and from hope to despair. The order in naming *Isla de la Trinidad* first and then *Boca del Drago* and *Boca de la Sierpe* implies that salvation was a theoretical projection that was replaced by overwhelming experiences of danger. The continuous juxtaposition of deliberations about the Earthly Paradise and observations of landscape qualities associated with Hell, such as the scorching heat and the overwhelming sensation of being pulled inwards, suggest that Columbus felt torn between these two ideas and uncertain about where he had arrived. The names *Boca del Drago* and *Boca de la Sierpe* express Columbus's distressed attitude at the end of his journeys of exploration and conquest that had lasted twelve years, at the conclusion of which his health was quickly declining, his imagination soaring, and his life approaching its end. However, beyond communicating Columbus's desperation due to his deteriorated physical and mental state as well as the conflictive relationships with the native inhabitants and Old World administrative structures, the toponymy of the third and fourth voyages records Columbus's realization that his attempt to establish a symbolic order of places through language had failed.

The increasing fragmentation of naming patterns during the final two voyages and the proliferation of Taino and hybrid toponyms in proportion to the Castilian ones attest to Columbus's inability to assert a new toponymy and the resulting linguistic and epistemological chaos. The unsuccessful attempt to produce a clear chart and an orderly list of new place names reflects the breaking down of the way in which language was used to describe the world in Europe prior to its acquaintance with the Americas and the rising awareness of a need for a different way of articulating knowledge. The broken order in the list of place names represents not only Columbus's own failure to establish a larger epistemological system and administrative command but also a much deeper crisis affecting the newly born conceptual and physical relationship between several worlds – the Americas, Europe, Asia, and Africa – during the earliest stage of encounter. Columbian toponymy narrates the story of disillusion, as previous knowledge was discovered to be inadequate; frustration, as the search for the riches of the Asian lands and for the peace of the Earthly Paradise turned out to be fruitless; and growing anxiety, as physical danger was accompanied by an awareness of an increasingly difficult-to-control linguistic, epistemological, administrative, and natural chaos.

One other tendency that can be observed in the toponymic discourse as a whole has to do with Columbus's engagement with the Caribbean landscape. The toponyms representative of Columbus's outlook during the first and the second voyages are exemplary of his removed, abstract relationship with it. The toponyms invented early during the first voyage reflect a glance that reaches as far as celestial bodies and traces their supposedly real but intangible connection to the metals he imagined developing in the womb of the earth. The toponyms *Cabo de Sierpe* and *Monte Cristo* invented later during the first voyage demonstrate that

Columbus's glance had commenced to draw closer to the visible and the physical surface of the landscape, rather than looking for imagined, theoretical links between the skies and the depths of the earth. This glance was still very broad and surveyed large areas from a position of a distant, unaffected observer; however, Columbus began to see the outlines of the actual lands before him rather than theorizing about vast spaces and prime elements such as air and earth. Furthermore, through the names of metals and planets in the *Diario del primer viaje*, Columbus approached the territories beyond the limits of the known world as a mouldable mass and a chaotic space wanting order. His goal was to place or situate all seas and lands in their proper places ("toda la mar e tierras del mar Occéano en sus proprios lugares, debaxo su viento"). This promise marked the beginning of universal time and started the creation of the cosmos, as Columbus repeated the scheme set up before him endless times in the medieval genre of a universal history. The naming of *Cabo de Sierpe*, analysed in chapter 3, marks a different beginning in time: the start of the Christian era, marked with the birth of the Christ Child and with Christ's physical death on the cross and spiritual rebirth. Therefore, already in the first voyage, two visions of the world were presented simultaneously, distinguishing the creation of the pre-Christian world and the birth of the Christian era.

The toponymy of the third and the fourth voyages demonstrates a much more engaged and immediate relationship between the observer and the landscape and, as a result of this, the change in Columbus's role as an imposer, which he assumed during the first two voyages, to one of receiver, as he moved closer to the lands and began to sense them with all of his five senses. During the final two voyages, his gaze drew ever nearer to the concrete objects, animals, shapes, and features of the landscape he was exploring. His ear became more open to the sounds of the foreign Taino language; by the final voyage indigenous toponymy even began to overpower the one he was attempting to create. In this context, *Boca de la Sierpe* and *Boca del Drago* express Columbus's angst as he was losing all the battles: the physical fights with the surrounding natural environment, the administrative challenges, the physical and cultural conflicts with local indigenous groups, and even the toponymic battle symbolic of his desire to establish a metaphoric order. His proximity to Hell had to be underplayed because of the message that needed to be articulated for the king and queen. However, the demonization of the indigenous people, the infernalization of nature, and the inclusion of infernal imagery in the toponymic discourse reveal one of Columbus's greatest fears.

The examination of the entire known corpus of Columbian place names reveals that Columbus did not so much *invent* America, as Edmundo O'Gorman has brilliantly proposed, for he could not have envisioned the places he was naming as existing in a perfectly sterile space void of previous names and meanings. Instead, he constructed, through the repeated acts of negotiating between the American, Asian, and European worlds (landscapes, visions, and nomenclatures) a fictional world that was hybrid and transoceanic. Rather than being an expression of a single mind's flight of imagination, Columbus's act of mapping America was a product of complex and multidirectional relationships between peoples, languages, and landscapes, compound interactions which resulted in many alterations and in the construction of a new, staged reality. The corpus of Columbian place names is a unique expression of these earliest exchanges, no matter how asymmetrical, among various geographic and cultural entities, the result of which was the production of a new world.

Appendix A Comprehensive List of Columbian Place Names

Below is a comprehensive list of what I consider to be Columbian place names; it includes toponyms of Taino and other indigenous origins as well as some that refer to Asia. I have extracted these toponyms from the following primary sources: Consuelo Varela and Juan Gil, editors, *Cristóbal Colón: Textos y documentos completos*, both 2003 and 1982 editions; Ferdinand Columbus (Hernando Colón), *Historia del Almirante*, edited by Manuel Carrera Díaz; Bartolomé de Las Casas, *Historia de las Indias*, edited by Agustín Millares Carlo; Bartolomé de Las Casas, *Las Casas on Columbus: The Third Voyage*, edited by Geoffrey Symcox; and Peter Martyr d'Anghiera (Pedro Mártir de Anglería), *The Discovery of the New World in the Writings of Peter Martyr of Anghiera*, edited by Ernesto Lunardi et al., translated into English by Felix Azzola.

The place names are listed in the order in which they are introduced in the *diarios*. Toponyms from other primary sources are listed next, also arranged in the order in which they appear in those sources. Those place names already included in the list compiled from the *diarios* are omitted to avoid repetition. Likewise, if a toponym appears in the *Diario del primer viaje* and then again in the *relaciones* of the second, third, or fourth voyages, it is listed in this appendix only in the list from the first voyage or in whichever voyage it is mentioned for the first time. Toponyms of indigenous origin, which include Taino toponyms as well as hybrid place names consisting of Castilian and Taino components, are listed in separate sections with the headings "toponyms of indigenous origin," and they are also organized according to when they were first mentioned in the *diarios* and the other sources. Any alternative spellings used in the sources and the date on which the place name appears in the *Diario del primer viaje* for the first time are provided in parentheses. If the toponym is first mentioned in the margin, I make a note "margin," and provide the date on which the toponym is mentioned in the body of the *diarios* for the first time. Any notable comments about these place names in the sources are given next, and the English translations are provided in the endnotes. Whenever a reputable English translation was available, I used it; when no translation was available or when my interpretation of the name or the phrase was different, I provided my own translations.

Except for the first voyage, sources do not include consistent references to dates, thus there is no data about when a particular name appeared in Columbus's original ship log for the first time or when Columbus assigned it. In the rest of this appendix, place names are listed in the order in which they appear in the sources used here; however, dates are not provided. When a contemporary historian, such as Las Casas, provides a date or another circumstance related to the naming of the place, this information is included in an endnote.

First voyage

Diario del primer viaje: Toponyms in Castilian. Source: Varela and Gil

1. **San Salvador, isla de** (Sant Salvador) (14 Oct 1492). The Taino name of this island was *Guanahaní.*
2. **Santa María de la Concepción, isla de** (Conçepçión) (15 Oct). Its modern name is Rum Cay.[1]
3. **Fernandina, isla** (Ferrandina) (15 Oct). Originally called *Yuma* in Taino.[2] See *Yuma, río* on page 177.
4. **Isabela, isla** (Yslabela; Ysabela; Ysavela) (19 Oct). The Taino name of this island was *Samoet.*
5. **Hermoso, cabo** (Fermoso) (19 Oct). During Columbus's time, it was also known as Puerto Escondido.[3]
6. **Laguna, cabo de la** (20 Oct)
7. **Isleo, cabo del** (21 Oct)
8. **Arena, islas de** (27 Oct)
9. **San Salvador, río** (28 Oct). The mountains facing Río San Salvador reminded Columbus of "the Peña de los Enamorados in the kingdom of Granada, the Lover's Leap whence Christian Manuel and Moorish Laila leapt to their death when pursued by angry father."[4] Las Casas comments on this association in the *Diario del primer viaje*: "Señala la disposiçión del río y del puerto que arriba dixo y nombró San Salvador, que tiene sus montañas hermosas y altas como la Peña de

los Enamorados, y una d'ellas tiene ençima otro montezillo a manera de una hermosa mezquita."[5]

10. **San Salvador, puerto** (28 Oct)
11. **Luna, río de la** (29 Oct)
12. **Mares, río de** (29 Oct)
13. **Palmas, cabo de** (30 Oct). This toponym appears to be inspired by the physical properties of the place: "y vido cabo lleno de palmas y púsole Cabo de palmas."[6]
14. **Mares, puerto de** (5 Nov). *Río de Mares*, introduced on 29 October, and *Puerto de Mares* may refer to the same body of water. Columbus commonly assigned the same name to the river and its mouth calling them *río* and *puerto*.
15. **Sol, río del** (12 Nov)
16. **Poniente, río del** (12 Nov)
17. **Nuestra Señora, la mar de** (14 Nov). This toponym also refers to a group of islands in the bay. It documents Columbus's religious devotion to the Virgin Mary and his promise to do a pilgrimage in her honour: "Después d'esto el Almirante y toda la gente hizieron voto de, en llegando a la primera tierra, ir todos en camissa en proçessión a hazer oraçión en una iglesia que fuese de la invocación de Nuestra Señora."[7] The high mountains on the islands also inspired this religious name: "Púsoles nombre la mar de Nuestra Señora. Dize tantas y tales cosas de la fertilidad y hermosura y altura d'estas islas que halló en este puerto, que dize a los Reyes que no se maravillen de encareçellas tanto, porque les çertifica que cree que no dize la çentessima parte: algunas d'ellas que pareçía que llegan al çielo y hechas como puntas de diamantes; otras que sobre su gran altura tienen ençima como una mesa, y al pie d'ellas fondo grandíssimo, que podrá llegar a elas una grandíssima carraca, todas llenas de arboledas y sin peñas."[8]
18. **Príncipe, puerto del** (Prínçipe) (18 Nov)
19. **Santa Catalina, puerto de** (Sancta Cathalina) (24 Nov). This toponym may refer to Saint Catherine and also to a real-life woman named Catalina. The latter was an indigenous woman the Spaniards had captured who escaped from their caravel and swam over three miles to recover her freedom. See also *Santa Chaterina, isla* on page 187.
20. **Llana, isla** (24 Nov)
21. **Pico, cabo del** (26 Nov). There was also the island of Pico in the Azores.[9]
22. **Campana, cabo de** (27 Nov). Las Casas implies that the cape reminded Columbus of Campana in Andalusia: "Y porque los aguajes y

corrientes lo avian echado aquella noche más de çinco o seis leguas al Sueste adelante de donde avía anocheçido, y le avía pareçido la tierra de Campana."[10]

23. **Santo, puerto** (Sacro) (1 Dec)
24. **Lindo, cabo** (4 Dec)
25. **Monte, cabo del** (4 Dec)
26. **Juana, isla** (5 Dec). This is the Castilian name that Columbus gave to the island of Cuba: "A la siguiente que encontró, es decir, Cuba, la llamó Juana, en honor del príncipe don Juan, heredero de Castilla, teniendo cuidado, con estos nombres, de rendir honor tanto a lo spiritual como a lo temporal."[11] *Historia del Almirante*, in the same chapter, also establishes a bizarre connection between the name *Juana* and the Taino name of an iguana: "Había en aquella tierra [La Fernandina] muchas aguas y lagos, junto a uno de los cuales vieron una serpiente de siete pies de longitud, con un vientre de más de un pie de ancho ... Los indios le llaman *juana*."[12] The spelling of the word could be due to a copyist or translator's mistake.
27. **María, puerto** (6 Dec)
28. **Estrella, cabo del** (cabo de la) (6 Dec)
29. **Tortuga, isla de la** (6 Dec)
30. **Elefante, cabo del** (Elifante) (6 Dec). In *Tesoro de la lengua castellana o española*, the first monolingual dictionary of the Spanish language, Sebastián de Covarrubias, who began editing the dictionary in 1605, cites several classical authors such as Pliny, Cicero, Aristotle, and Seneca who all discuss the superior qualities of the elephant. For example, Pliny begins Book Eight of *Natural History* with a description of an elephant since it is the largest of all animals and closest to man in its abilities ("en los sentidos parece ir a los alcances al hombre"). Covarrubias says that the elephant fights the serpent and wins, thus symbolizing the emperor or the king.[13]
31. **Cinquin, cabo de** (6 Dec)
32. **San Nicolao, puerto de** (Sant Nicolás) (6 Dec). According to Las Casas, Columbus assigned this name based on the liturgical calendar: "A oras de bísperas, entró en el puerto dicho, y púsole nombre Puerto de San Nicolao, porque era día de Sant Nicolás, por honra suya, y a la entrada d'él se maravilló de su hermosura y bondad."[14]
33. **Concepción, puerto de la** (Conçepción) (7 Dec). The Spaniards renamed it *Bahía de los Mosquitos*; it is known today as Moustique Bay.[15]
34. **Española, isla** (Hispaniola) (9 Dec). Columbus identified *Española* with the biblical Ophir of King Solomon.

35. **Pierna, punta** (14 Dec)
36. **Lançada, punta** (14 Dec)
37. **Aguda, punta** (14 Dec)
38. **Valle del Paraíso** (15 Dec)
39. **Guadalquivir, río** (15 Dec)
40. **Los Dos Hermanos** (19 Dec)
41. **Torres, cabo de** (19 Dec)
42. **Sancto Thomás, isla de** (19 Dec)
43. **Alto y Baxo, cabo** (19 Dec)
44. **Sancto Thomás, puerto de la mar de** (Sancto [Santo] Thomé) (21 Dec). The liturgical calendar and the vast waters inspired this religious toponym, *Puerto de la mar de Sancto Thomás*, as the comment of Las Casas in the text of the *Diario del primer viaje* suggests: "Púsole nombre el Puerto de la mar de Sancto Thomás, porque era oy su día; díxole mar por su grandeza."[16]
45. **Amiga, isla** (24 Dec)
46. **Sancta, punta** (25 Dec)
47. **Navidad, villa de la** (4 Jan 1493)
48. **Sancto, cabo** (4 Jan)
49. **Sierpe, cabo de** (4 Jan). Covarrubias comments that, among its many other meanings, the serpent also symbolizes "la redondez de la tierra y sus provincias, que para conquistarlas son necesarias muchas fuerzas, excesivo ánimo y suma prudencia."[17]
50. **Cristo, monte** (el Monte Cristi; Montechristo) (4 Jan). Known today as Isla de Cabra.[18]
51. **Bezerro, cabo del** (5 Jan). Sources do not give any information about the naming of this cape. Covarrubias provides several definitions of the word *becerro* or *bezerro*: in addition to "calf," it also means "becerro marino, es una bestia anfibia, que vive en la mar y en la tierra" (*becerro marino* is an amphibian animal that lives in the sea and on land) referring perhaps to a sea cow or a manatee. *Becerro* is also the name for the book of communities, town, and city councils ("El libro de las comunidades, cabildos y ayuntamientos, suelen llamar becerro"). The term is borrowed from the Jewish community in which the Torah of Moses and any book of laws or acts of the community was called *becerro* because it was bound in calf skin for better protection ("por ventura se tomó de los judíos, que llaman al libro de la ley de Moisén Tora … *Tora, lex*, que comúnmente dicen la Tora, y por alusión debieron llamar becerro el libro en que consiste todo el gobierno y actos de la comunidad; o porque está encuadernado y guarnecido con piel de becerro, para mayor custodia y

entereza"). Furthermore, the children of Israel idolized the golden calf, *el becerro de oro*, in the desert. And finally, *Becerril* is also "the name of two places [in Castile], one of which is called Becerril de Campos so as to distinguish it from the other one, and that is where they raise very good mules" (Becerril, nombre propio de dos lugares, que a diferencia llaman al uno Becerril de Campos, donde se crían muy buenas mulas).[19]

52. **Ioana, isla** (6 Jan)
53. **Oro, río del** (8 Jan). According to Las Casas, Columbus himself later renamed it as *Río de las Cañas* (see *Cañas, río de las* on page 180).
54. **Roxa, punta** (9 Jan)
55. **Gracia, río de** (10 Jan)
56. **Belprado, cabo** (11 Jan)
57. **Plata, monte de** (11 Jan)
58. **Angel, cabo del** (11 Jan). The local name for this island was *Samaná*.[20]
59. **Hierro, punta del** (11 Jan)
60. **Seca, punta** (11 Jan)
61. **Redondo, cabo** (11 Jan)
62. **Françés, cabo** (11 Jan)
63. **Buen Tiempo, cabo del** (11 Jan)
64. **Tajado, cabo** (11 Jan)
65. **Padre y Hijo, cabo de** (12 Jan)
66. **Enamorado, cabo del** (12 Jan). Known today as Cabo Cabrón.
67. **Plata, puerto de** (13 Jan)
68. **Flechas, golfo de las** (16 Jan)
79. **Flechas, puerto de las** (16 Jan). "bahía de las Flechas, ahora llamada de Samaná."[21]
70. **Sant Theramo, cabo** (16 Jan). Name of a cape on Hispaniola: "Este cabo es Sant Theramo creo cierto que es el que llaman agora el Cabo del Engaño."[22]

Diario del primer viaje: Toponyms of indigenous origin.
Source: Varela and Gil

1. **Guanahaní** (Guanafaní) (11 Oct 1492). Cambiaso notes that another documented spelling of this place name is *Iguanani*. The critic hypothesizes that the name refers to the serpent-like or iguana-like shapes of the island or of its parts.[23]
2. **Samoet, isla** (17 Oct). Columbus named it *Isla Isabela*.

3. **Cuba, isla** (Colba) (21 Oct). According to Coll y Toste, the word *cuba* is formed from two Taino roots – *coa*, place, and *bana*, large or great – and it means "a great place."[24]
4. **Bohío** (Bofío, tierra de Bohío) (21 Oct). The word *bohío* means a native-style hut. Columbus incorporated this place name into his toponymic discourse mistakenly assuming it was a Taino toponym; it refers to the northern part of Hispaniola.[25]
5. **Cibao** (Çibao) (23 Oct [margin]; 23 Dec). An extensive region in the north of Hispaniola, under the rule of the cacique Maguana. The name, *sibao*, means "mountain of stones"; according to Cambiaso, *cibe-ao* means "many stones."[26]
6. **Faba** (30 Oct). Neither Coll y Toste nor Cambiaso provide any explanations about this toponym. It could be a corrupted version of a Taino word or toponym or it could be a toponym referring to a place in Asia, perhaps an alternative spelling of *Bafan*, the name of a province ruled by the Great Khan mentiond by Marco Polo.
7. **Haiti** (4 Nov [margin]). Taino name for Hispaniola meaning "high lands."[27]
8. **Cuba, cabo de** (12 Nov)
9. **Baveque, isla de** (isla [islas] del Baneque, Babeque) (12 Nov). The Spaniards associated it with large quantities of gold: "afirmando que había mucho oro (y creo, cierto, que es la que llamaban el viaje primero Baneque, que tantas veces la nombraban, pues que no veo que aquí el Almirante haga mención de Baneque)."[28] Some critics believe that *Baveque* refers to the island of Santo Domingo, others that it refers to *tierra firme* or other islands, and yet others do not believe that it refers to any place in particular. According to Coll y Toste, prefixes applied to the beginnings of words were used as pronouns. The word *aneque* meant *why* and thus *b-aneque* meant *why you?* Therefore, proceeds the scholar, when Columbus inquired the natives about places where gold could be found, they pointed to the horizon and exclaimed "baneque, baneque," that is, "and you, who are you? Who are you?" The word *baneque* was taken for a name of an island when in reality it was an expression of surprise.[29]
10. **Jamaica, la isla de** (17 Dec [margin]; Janahica; Yamaye [6 Jan 1943]; Yamaya). *Jamaica* means "a great place with water."[30]
11. **Caribata, provinçia** (19 Dec)
12. **Caribata, monte** (Caritaba, Caribana) (19 Dec). Refers to the region under the rule of the cacique Marien in Haiti.
13. **Caribata, cabo de** (20 Dec)

14. **Guarionex** (29 Dec). The main cacique of Magua in Hispaniola.[31]
15. **Macorix** (29 Dec). A port, a river, and a region in Hispaniola.[32]
16. **Mayonic** (29 Dec). Neither Coll y Toste nor Cambiaso provide any explanations for *Mayonic*. This could be a corrupted version of the Taino name of the river in Cuba, *Mayabón*.
17. **Fuma** (29 Dec). Fuma was the name of an elderly woman from Cibao. It is also a woman's name in general.[33]
18. **Coroay** (29 Dec). The location of the chiefdom of Maguana on Hispaniola.[34]
19. **Yaqui, río** (8 Jan 1493 [margin]). Name of two important rivers that flow through the Jaragua and Managua regions of Hispaniola. One crosses most of *Cibao* and is the "true Yaki"; the other flows south and is also known by the name of *Neyba*. The tallest mountains where both rivers start are also known with this name.[35]
20. **Matininó, isla de** (Mateninó) (13 Jan). Columbus believed this island was inhabited by Amazon-like women.
21. **Goanin, isla de** (Guanín) (13 Jan). According to different interpretations, *guanín* refers to gold of low quality, gold, copper, an alloy of gold and copper, or an alloy of gold, silver, and copper. It also refers to plates made of one of those metals or alloys that the chieftains wore around their necks.[36] According to Las Casas, *goanin* was made up of thirty-two parts, of which eighteen were gold, six were silver, and eight were copper ("halló que de treinta y dos partes las diez y ocho eran de oro y las seys de plata y las ocho de cobre").[37]
22. **Carib, isla de** (Caniba) (13 Jan). The word *caribe* or *karibo* is still used in Haiti and it means "bad, bitter, fierce, and spicy."[38] Coll y Toste points out Navarrete's mistake in applying this term to Puerto Rico, instead of *Boriquén*. The name is derived from *caribo*, meaning "courageous man." In various dialects, the people are referred to as *caribná*, *carifná*, *calina* and *calinago*.[39]
23. **Higuay** (13 Jan). Name of the central village in the chiefdom Yguayagua in the extreme East of Hispaniola.[40] It was subdivided into regions of Asua, Maniex, Bonao, Cayemú, Cacao, Hicayagua, and Boyá. The following rivers flowed through it: Ozama, Yamasá, Guabanimo (today Isabela), Quabón, Yuma, Yabacoa, Anamuya, Jaina, and Sabita (Jiguero).[41]
24. **Samana, golfo de** (Xamaná, Samaná, Zamaná; in Peter Martyr, Sant Telmo de Xamaná) (16 Jan [margin]). Refers to the peninsula and the bay to the east of Hispaniola.[42] According to Cambiaso, it is the peninsula to the north of the island inhabited by the Ciguayo people.[43]

Samaníes was a group of these Ciguayo people who were great warriors and who gave their name to the island. They protected the island from the attacks of the Caribes. It was a matriarchal society who associated themselves with the water element.[44] Xamaná was the Taino name of the place; Columbus renamed the place both by using the original Taino toponym and by adding to it the name of a Spanish saint. Later, it was renamed to the more Spanish-sounding *Cabo del Angel.*

25. **Yuma, río** (16 Jan [margin]). An important river in the east of Hispaniola, in La Altagracia province. *Yuma* was also the original name of the island inhabited by the Lucayo Tainos which Columbus called *Fernandina* (today called Long Island).[45]
26. **Tamo, río** (16 Jan [margin]). Neither Coll y Toste nor Cambiaso provide any comments about river Tamo.

Carta a Luis de Santángel (15 February 1493): Toponym of uncertain origin, possibly Taino. Source: Varela and Gil

1. **Auan.** Neither Coll de Toste nor Cambiaso provide any comments about Auan.

Carta a los Reyes anunciando el Descubrimiento (4 March 1493): Toponym of Taino origin. Source: Varela and Gil

1. **Boriquén** (Borinquén). Taino name of the island of Puerto Rico. It is denoted thus in Juan de la Cosa's 1500 map and Martin Waldsemüller's *Tabula Terrae Novae* (1508). One of the interpretations of its meaning is "lands of a courageous landlord."[46]

Las Casas, Historia de las Indias: Toponyms in Castilian. Source: Millares Carlo

1. **Alpha et Omega, cabo**. Not mentioned in the *diarios*. According to Las Casas, the cape was named on 5 December. Its Taino name was *Bayatiquiri*: "que él llamó el primer viaje, cuando la descubrió, Alpha et Omega, y agora se llama la Punta de Bayatiquiri, en lengua de los indios."[47]
2. **Vega Real**
3. **El Nombre de Dios a Panamá, río**
4. **San Rafael, cabo de**. The tip of the Hispaniola island which the Spanish promptly renamed *Cabo del Engaño*: "que agora se llama

el Cabo del Engaño, y el Almirante en su primer viaje le puso nombre el Cabo de San Rafael."[48]

Las Casas, Historia de las Indias: Toponyms of indigenous origin. Source: Millares Carlo

1. **Cubanacán**. The central region of Cuba.[49]
2. **Maicí, punta de**. Neither Coll y Toste nor Cambiaso comment about this toponym. Coll y Toste indicates that *maisí* means "corn."[50]
3. **Baracoa**. A port in Cuba.[51]
4. **Mayonix**. Neither Coll y Toste nor Cambiaso comment about this toponym.

Second voyage

Relación del segundo viaje: Toponyms in Castilian. Source: Varela and Gil

1. **La Dominica, isla** (Domenica). According to Columbus, he named the island because he arrived there on Sunday: "Llegué domingo … a una isla de altísima montaña, a la cual llamé la Dominica a conmemoración del mismo día."[52] Both Peter Martyr and Ferdinand Columbus concur: "Hanc, quoniam die dominico sors obtulerat, *Dominicam* placuit vocari" and "por haberla descubierto un domingo por la mañana."[53] It could also have been one of the islands inhabited by the fierce Caribs: "o alguna de los caníbales que oy llaman los caribes."[54]
2. **La Galana, isla** (Marigalante). Both Las Casas in his *Historia de las Indias* and Ferdinand Columbus use the version of the name *Marigalante*, and the latter claims that the naming of the island was inspired by the name of the flagship: "por llamarse así la nao capitana."[55]
3. **Santa María de Guadalupe, isla** (isla Guadalupe). According to Peter Martyr, the name of this island was inspired by its resemblance to the Guadalupa mountain in the Old World where the Virgin was venerated. According to Peter Martyr, the island was inhabited by Island Caribs and its native name was *Caracueria*: "Hanc vocant *Guadalupeam* insulam, a montis Guadalupi similitudine ubi Intemeratae Virginis mirabile colitur simulacrum. *Carucueriam* incolae appellant, est Caribium primaria habitation."[56]

4. **Santa María de Monsarrate, isla.** According to Peter Martyr, the height of the mountains inspired this religious name: "quoniam altis montibus instructa esset, *Montem Serratum* illam vocant."[57]
5. **Todos los Santos, isla**
6. **De Santa Húrsula, isla**
7. **Las honze mill vírgenes**
8. **Sant Juan Baptista, isla de.** This island, which we know today as Puerto Rico, was also known with its Taino name *Boriquen*, as Peter Martyr tells us: "Ab hoc tractu procedentes itinere in medio iacet insula, dicta ab indigenis *Burichena*: hanc *Sancti Ioannis* insulam appellavit."[58]
9. **Fin D'España, cabo**
10. **Ysabela, villa**

No new toponyms of Taino or of other indigenous origin are listed in the *Relación del segundo viaje*.

Las Casas, Historia de las Indias: Toponyms in Castilian.
Source: Millares Carlo

1. **Santa María la Redonda, isla.** According to Peter Martyr, the round shape of the island inspired this religious name: "Altero die quandam aliam vident cui, quod sphaerica esset, *Sanctae Mariae Rotundae* nomen indidit Praefectus."[59]
2. **Santa María la Antigua, isla** (in Peter Martyr, *Isla Bienaventurada Virgen Antigua*). It was common to name ships after the Virgin. *La Gorda* and *El Antigua* were names of Bobadilla's ships. The master of the former obtained his appellation due to the name of the caravel and was named Andrea Martín de la Gorda.[60]
3. **Sant Martín, isla**
4. **Santa Cruz, isla de.** Its Taino name was *Ayay* and the other of its recorded two names of apparent Taino origin was *Cibuqueira*.[61] According to Peter Martyr, Columbus's authorship of this place name is uncertain: "ocurrit quam currit quam Ay Ay ab indigenis vocitatam, *Sanctae Crucis*, nomine appellari voluerunt."[62] Today it is known as St Croix.
5. **Los Hidalgos, puerto de.** The place was named in honour of the noblemen who accompanied the workers up the nearby mountain

range: "mandó el Almirante ir a ciertos hidalgos con gente de trabajo delante, la sierra arriba … y por esta causa puso nombre a aquel puerto el Puerto de los Hidalgos."[63]

6. **Las Cañas, río de.** This is another name for *Río del Oro*: "al cual llamó el Almirante el río de las Cañas, no se acordando que en el primer viaje lo nombró Río del Oro, cuando estuvo a su boca, que sale a Monte-Christi."[64]
7. **Cruz, cabo de**
8. **Evangelista, isla del.** Its Taino name was *Guanaja* and it is known today as *Isla de Pinos*, as it was renamed promptly by the Spaniards: "creo que es la isla que después llamamos y hoy se llama la isla de Pinos."[65] Columbus also named *Isla de Pinos* (see *Pinos, isla de* on page 191).
9. **Fin de Oriente, cabo.** Columbus seems to have assigned three different names to this cape: *Cabo Fin de Oriente*, *Cabo de Cuba*, and *Alpha et Omega*: "el cabo de Cuba … que llamó Fin de Oriente, y por otro nombre Alpha et Omega."[66]
10. **Farol, cabo del**
11. **San Miguel, isla.** Later known as *Isla del Tiburón*: "al cual puso nombre Cabo de Sant Miguel, que agora se llama el Cabo o Punta del Tiburón."[67]
12. **Madame Beata, isla.** Las Casas comments: "Y esta tierra era una isleta chequita que llamó Madama Beata, y oy comúnmente nombran La Beata … Creyó que La Beata era … una isleta que se llama Sancta Caterina, quando vino por esta costa del sur del descubrimiento de la isla de Cuba."[68]
13. **Alto Velo, isla.** According to Las Casas, the island received its name due to its resemblance to the sails of a ship: "Está junto a ella [La Beata] otra más chequita que tiene una serrezuela altilla que desde lejos parece vela, y púsole nombre Alto Velo."[69] According to Las Casas, a similar name, *Cabo de la Vela*, was not assigned by Columbus but rather by Juan de la Cosa and Alonso de Hojeda during Columbus's fourth voyage. They also probably invented the name *Isla de los Gigantes*.[70]
14. **Cathalina, tierra de.** Named after a native cacique woman known to the Spaniards as Cathalina: "y esta tierra debía ser la que agora llaman de Cathalina, por una cacica o señora, que después cognoscieron los cristianos, señora de aquella tierra."[71]
15. **Magdalena, fortaleza**

Las Casas, Historia de las Indias: Toponyms of indigenous origin. Source: Millares Carlo

1. **Buenicún, río**. The Spaniards renamed it *Río Seco*: "que los cristianos, el tiempo andando, llamaron Río Seco."[72]
2. **Coatenicuz, río**. *Coa* means "place" in Taino.[73]
3. **Cibú, río**. *Ciba* means "stone" in Taino. Neither Coll y Toste nor Cambiaso mention river Cibú.
4. **Saona, isla.** The island was also known with the Taino or Carib name *Adamaney*: "una isleta que los indios llamaban Adamaney, que agora llamamos la Saona, el cual nombre creo que le puso el mismo Almirante o su hermano el Adelantado."[74] Oliva begins his narration suggesting that the name was inspired by Columbus's birth place, which according to him was *Saona*: "Cristóual Colón, genoués, natural de Saona."[75] However, Cambiaso argues that the name of the island was derived from the name of its cacique: "Este nombre no es una corrupción del nombre Savona (ciudad de la Liguria, y que clamó un tiempo de haber sido cuna del inmortal genovés) como se ha pretendido, impuéstole por Colón en memoria de la tierra de sus antepasados. *Adamanaí* debe nombre de un cacique que vivió en esa isla."[76] Saona is located near the southeastern coast of Hispaniola and it faces Cape Palmillas in Hispaniola. At the time of conquest, it was occupied by the Caribs.[77]
5. **Mona, isla** (in Ferdinand Columbus's *Historia*, Amona). A small islet between Puerto Rico and Hispaniola.[78] The editor of *Historia de las Indias*, Millares Carlo, comments that Columbus's decision to name the island *Mona* may have been influenced by the island bearing the same name in England, which is mentioned by Pliny, Julius Cesar, and Cornelius Tacitus.

Ferdinand Columbus: Toponyms in Castilian. Source: Díaz

1. **Ángel, cabo del**
2. **Verde, río**
3. **Fuerte, cabo**. Known today as Punta Negro.
4. **Grande, puerto**. Known today as Guantánamo.
5. **Bueno, puerto**. Las Casas criticizes the choice for this name: "La víspera de Sant Juan llegaron a un puerto de Jamaica, llamado Puerto Bueno, y aunque bueno para contra la tormenta de la mar, pero malo

para se mamparar de la sed y de el hambre, porque ni agua ni población de indios alguna tenía."[79]

6. **Santa Marta, isla**
7. **Las Vacas, bahía de**. Ferdinand Columbus implies an unclear connection between the name and the fact that there were nine small islands near the coast: "una bahía que llamó de las Vacas, por haber allí nueve isletas próximas a la costa."[80] Díaz, the editor of Ferdinand Columbus's *Historia*, notes that this was the Bay of Portland (Bahía de Portland) and that the meaning of the name is uncertain: "Estas islas no parecen razón suficiente para justificar tal nombre. Este se debe, probablemente, a que los expedicionarios pudieron ver allí numerosos manatees, que los europeos comparaban a una especie de vacas marinas."[81]

Ferdinand Columbus: Toponyms of indigenous origin. Source: Díaz

1. **Cibao, puerto.** There also was a province called *Provincia de Cibao*,[82] an extensive region in the northern part of Hispaniola that was under the rulership of the cacique Maguana. The name is derived from *siba*, "stone," and *o*, "mountain," meaning "rocky mountain."[83]
2. **Guacanagarí, puerto de**. Guacanagarí was a Haitian cacique with whom Columbus developed close diplomatic ties. Neither Coll y Toste nor Cambiaso mention the port named in his honour.

Peter Martyr: Toponyms in Castilian. Source: Décadas

1. **San Martín, isla**
2. **Real, puerto**. It seems that Columbus himself did not assign this name. According to Peter Martyr, it was named thus because it was an excellent and secure port: "Fluvii alicuius grande ostium arbitrates, portum ibi valde commodum ac tutum adinvenit, *Portum Regalem* propterea nominandum consuerunt."[84]

Peter Martyr: Toponyms of indigenous origin. Source: Décadas

1. **Caracueria.** This is the native name of Isla Guadalupe. Neither Coll y Toste nor Cambiaso explain this toponym. It might be related to the Taino word *caracurí*, meaning a jewel for the nose.[85]

Relación del viaje a Cuba y Jamaica (26 February 1495): Toponyms of indigenous origin. Source: Varela and Gil

1. **Macaca, provincia**. Neither Coll y Toste nor Cambiaso explain this toponym. Taino words that may be related to it include *macagua* (a type of tree) and *macana* (a thick wooden weapon used by the Taino warriors). *Maguaca* is a tributary river of the Yaque in the north of Hispaniola. *Maguana* is one of the five chiefdoms of Haiti, governed by the cacique Caonabo.[86] *Machaca*, which is likely not of Taino origin, is the name of mountains in Cuba.[87] Accordingly, *Macaya* was the Taino name of mountains on one of the islands (Haiti, Boriquen, and eastern Cuba).[88] See also *Macaca, pueblo* on page 194.
2. **Hornofay, provincia**. Neither Coll y Toste nor Cambiaso explain this toponym.

Third voyage

Relación del tercer viaje: Toponyms in Castilian. Source: Varela and Gil

1. **Galea, cabo de la**. This is a mistake for *Cabo de la Galera*. According to the *Relación del tercer viaje*, Columbus named the cape after naming Trinidad: "yo llegué … a un cavo a que dixe de la Galea, después de aver anombrado a la isla de la Trinidad."[89] Cabo de la Galera (Galley Cape) is now called Galeota Point. According to Morison, who sailed those waters, "the resemblance of it to a many-masted galley under sail was striking. In addition to the bright-peaked cliffs which resemble lateen sails, there are diagonal marks on the rocks that look like a bank of oars."[90] Centuries earlier, Las Casas made a similar observation: "un cabo que parecía estar al poniente al qual llamó cabo de la Galera por una peña grande que tenía que desde lexos parecía galera que yva a la vela."[91]
2. **Trinidad, isla de la**. According to Las Casas, this was the first name that Columbus assigned during the third voyage: "Puso nombre a esta tierra la isla de La Trinidad porque así lo llevava determinado [que] la primera tierra que descubriese así se nombrase. 'Y plugo' – dize él – 'Nuestro Señor por su alta magestad que la vista primera fueron todos juntos tres mogotes. Digo tres montañas todas a un tiempo y en una vista. Su alta potencia por su piedad me guie'–

dize él – 'en tal manera que aya el muncho servicio y Vuestras Altezas muncho placer, que es cierto que la fallada desta tierra en esta parte fue gran milagro a tanto como la fallada del primer viaje.' Estas son sus palabras."[92]

3. **Arenal, punta** (del). Named because of the animal footprints they saw in the sand: "se halló toda la tierra hollada de una [sic] alimañas que tenían la pata como de cabra."[93]
4. **Graçia, tierra de**
5. **Jardines**. The place reminded Columbus of gardens: "Llamé allí a este lugar Jardines, porque ansí conforma con el nombre."[94]
6. **Perlas, golfo de las**. Columbus invented this name: "el golfo que yo dixe, al cual llamé de las Perlas."[95] Las Casas added a comment in the margin of his *Historia*: "A este golpho puso nombre Golpho de las Perlas, aunque no ay creo yo ninguna."[96] Interestingly, Las Casas also dedicated his entire, rather extraordinary chapter 135 to pearls.[97] See also *Margarita, isla* on page 187.
7. **Sierpe, boca de la**. Columbus claims authorship of the name but he does not make comments about its meaning: "En esta boca del austro, a que yo llamé de la Sierpe." Las Casas attributes it to the greater danger Columbus and his crew experienced near the *boca*: "Porque este gran peligro puso a esta boca nombre la Boca de la Sierpe."[98]
8. **Drago, boca del**. As in the case of *Boca de la Sierpe*, Columbus does not make comments about the meaning of this name, while Las Casas once again attributes it to the great danger experienced there: "en aquella otra el setentrión, a que yo llamé del Drago"; "Dizen que dixo aquí el Almirante, aunque no lo hallé escripto de su mano como hallé lo susodicho, que si de allí se escapaban podía hazer cuenta que se escapaban de la boca del drago."[99]

Additional pages by Las Casas not included in the transcription: Toponyms in Castilian. Source: Varela and Gil

1. **Ysabella Nueva**. It was promptly renamed *Santo Domingo*.
2. **Sant Raphael, isla de**
3. **Galera, cabo de la**. See *Galea, cabo de la* on page 183.
4. **Sancta, isla**. *Isla Sancta* was part of the continent, but Columbus mistook it for an island: "ésta es la tierra firme de la qual, como vido un pedazo, parecióle que sería isla. A esta puso nombre la isla Sancta. Dize aquí que no quiso tomar algunos indios por no escandalizar la tierra." Later, Columbus renamed *Isla Sancta* as *Isla de Gracia*:

"entre dos islas (La Trinidad y la que llamó Sancta, y después adelante llamó isla de Gracia." Neither of the two names survived for very long, as Las Casas observes: "[Finalmente], de todos los nombres que puso a islas y cabos e la tierra firme, que tenía por isla de Gracia, no han quedado [y] no se platican oy sino la isla de La Trinidad y la Boca de Drago, y los Testigos y la Margarita."[100]

5. **Playa, punta de la**
6. **Vallena, golpho de la** (Ballena). Now known as the Gulf of Paria. There, Columbus suffered the danger of losing all his ships.
7. **Gracia, isla de**. This is the Paria Peninsula, on the mainland, which Columbus believed was an island. *Tierra de Gracia*, listed in the summary, refers to the same landmark.
8. **Lapa, cabo de**. This cape was on the tip of the Paria Peninsula.[101]
9. **Boto, cabo**. According to Morison, it is known today as Cape Blunt.[102] Columbus named it because of its shape: "vido en aquel cabo dos isletas en medio de esta boca [Boca de la Sierpe] que hacen aquel cabo de la tierra firme, el qual llamó Cabo Boto, por ser gruesso y romo, y otro cabo de La Trinidad que nombró de Lapa." Las Casas also describes fish that are called *botos*: "Y parecieron unos pesces que se llaman botos, que son poco menos que grandes terneras que tienen la cabeza muy roma (o bota)."[103]
10. **Caracol, isla**. Now called Chacachacare, "probably because of its intricate outline."[104] Cambiaso believes that *caracol* is a Haitian word meaning "coarse," "rough," and says that it is found in several compound words. The word in Castilian means "sea shell" as well as "land in the form of a spiral," and the Italian *caracolare* refers to the turns and jumps of a horse.[105]
11. **Delfín, isla**. Now named Huevos. It is located in the vicinity of the island Columbus had named *Isla Caracol*: "La una isleta nombró el Caracol y la otra del Delfín."[106] According to Morison, "when seen from the westward it is very like a dolphin fish or dorado, with a large head looking down the Gulf."[107]
12. **Belaforma, isla**. This island was probably Tobago. According to Las Casas, Columbus named it because of its beauty: "Púsole nombre Belaforma, porque devía tener de lexo buen parescer."[108]
13. **Aguja, punta del** (Punta de L'Aguja). According to Morison, the Island of the Needle "was the modern Punta Alcatraz or Guaraguara."[109] Las Casas writes that the date when Columbus named it is unknown.[110] *Aguja* was also the name of one "of the least seaworthy" ships in Bobadilla's fleet that brought 4,000 *pesos* in gold back to Castile.[111]

14. **Sabeta, isla**. Las Casas's transcription says nothing about the meaning of this name: "Llegando a la Punta del Aguja dize que vido otra isla al sur 15 leguas que yva al sureste-norueste muy grande y tierra muy alta, y llamola Sabeta."[112] Morison could not identify the island: "I cannot imagine what Sabeta was."[113]
15. **Ysabeta, isla**. Likely, *Isla Ysabeta* and *Isla Sabeta* are variants of the same name.
16. **Tramontana, isla**
17. **Llana, punta**. No commentaries about this place name are available. A similar toponym, *Isla Llana*, was introduced on 24 November in the *Diario del primer viaje*.
18. **Sara, punta**. Las Casas observes that Columbus introduces these names as if they were already familiar to the reader despite the fact that no comments about them have been made: "Haze mención aquí de la Punta Seca, de la isla Isabeta [de la isla Tramontana], de la Punta Llana, de la Punta Sara, suponiéndolas. Empero, ninguna cosa a dicho dellas o de algunas dellas."[114]
19. **Gatos, puerto de**. According to Morison, "'Monkey Harbor,' in the outer part of which he anchored, was undoubtedly Chacachacare Bay on the island of that name, which Columbus called *El Caracol*."[115]
20. **Cabañas, puerto de las**
21. **Conchas, cabo de**. Las Casas includes this name along with the next three, but he provides no commentary about them: "Por aquella costa abaxo vido munchas islas hazia el norte y munchos cabos [en la tierra firme], a los quales todos puso nombres, y a uno Cabo de Conchas, a otro Cabo Luengo, [a otro Cabo de Sabor, a otro Cabo Rico], tierra alta y muy hermosa."[116]
22. **Luengo, cabo**
23. **Sabor, cabo de**
24. **Rico, cabo**
25. **Asumpción, isla de la**. Named the day before the vigil of the Assumption of the Virgin.[117]
26. **Concepción, isla**. Not to be confused with *Santa María de la Concepción* (today Rum Cay, Bahamas), which was one of the first names given during the first voyage and first mentioned in the *Diario del primer viaje*, on 15 October 1492. Morison does not believe *Isla Concepción* existed: "La Concepción, I imagine, was only a cloud."[118]
27. **Los Testigos, islas**. Three islets comprising *Los Testigos* are known today in English as The Witnesses. This is one of the few names from

the third voyage that survived until the time when Las Casas was writing.[119]

28. **El Romero, isla**. The Pilgrim "was probably the solitary islet now called *La Sola*."[120]
29. **Las Guardias, islas**. The Sentinels or Watches "are obviously the group of islets now called *Los Frailes* near Margarita."[121]
30. **Margarita, isla**. The meaning of this place name is ambiguous. According to Covarrubias, *margarita* is a precious stone, *latine margarita et unio*, described by Pliny the Elder. St Margaret was a virgin and a martyr. The name of the island could also refer to Margaret of Austria (1480–1530), daughter of Maximilian I and wife of the prince of Asturias, Juan.
31. **Martinet, isla**. The Martlet "is identified by Las Casas as the island now called *Blanca* or *Blanquilla*, northwest of Margarita."[122] According to *Real Academia*, "Martinete" in modern Spanish means "martlet," that is, a bird from the swallow family, short-tailed or resembling a swallow, which lives near rivers and lakes, and comes to Spain in the spring and emigrates towards San Martín. According to the *Oxford Dictionary*, however, a martlet also refers to a mythical bird "with tufts or feathers for legs and no feet, borne as a charge."
32. **La Navidad, puerto de**
33. **Santa Chaterina, isla** (Catalina). It is possible that *Isla Chaterina* was *Isla Madama Beata* or *La Beata*. During the second voyage, Columbus or perhaps one of his men baptized an indigenous woman whom they had captured with the name Catalina; she soon after escaped from their caravel and swam more than three miles to recover her freedom.[123] The port bearing the name of the same saint, *Puerto de Santa Catalina*, is mentioned on 24 November in the *Diario del primer viaje*. See also *Madame Beata, isla* on page 180.
34. **Sancto Domingo, puerto de**. Columbus's son suggests Columbus named this port for his father: "puso inmediatamente rumbo a oriente en demanda de Santo Domingo, en cuyo puerto o río entró el 30 de agosto, puesto que el Adelantado había decidido establecer el emplazamiento de la ciudad en la parte oriental del río, donde hoy se encuentra, llamándola Santo Domingo en memoria de su padre, que se llamaba Domingo."[124] See also *Ysabella Nueva* on page 184.

Las Casas, Historia de las Indias: Toponyms in Castilian. Source: Symcox

1. **Puerto Rico, isla**
2. **Abre-el-ojo.** It seems that these were not islands but rather underwater cliffs that threatened ships because they could not be seen easily: "Destas perlas que dize aquí el Almirante que se hallaron en las islas de Babueca, nunca supe destas perlas que se hallasen en las islas de Babueca, que son cerca del Puerto de Plata en esta isla Española, y éstas más son baxos debaxo del agua que no islas que hacen harto daño a los navíos que por allí pasan, si no están sobre aviso y así tienen título Abre el ojo."[125]
3. **Asunción, isla de la**
4. **Coche, isleta.** "la una se llama Coche, que quiere decir venado."[126]
5. **Blanca, isla.** The island was promptly renamed *Isla Margarita*: "Y ésta es la isleta de la parte del norte cercana a la Margarita, que agora se llama isla Blanca, y dista las ocho o nueve leguas de la Margarita, [como dixe]."[127] See also *Margarita, isla* on page 187 and *Cubagua, isla* on page 189.
6. **La Vega Grande**
7. **Concepción, fortaleza.** The fortress is located in La Vega Grande: "Esta provincia [de Bonao] dista de Sancto Domingo veynte leguas y de La Vega grande, digo de la fortaleza de Concepción, que están en La Vega, diez."[128]

Las Casas, Historia de las Indias: Toponyms of indigenous origin. Source: Symcox

1. **Paria.** The coastal region of South America, today in Venezuela.[129] Las Casas makes the following observations: "Estando en esta Punto del Arenal que es el fin de la isla de La Trinidad, vido hazia el norte, quarta del nordeste, a distancia de quinze leguas, un cabo o punta de la misma tierra firme, y esta fue la que se llama Paria. El Almirante, creyendo que era otra isla distinta, púsole nombre la isla de Gracia"[130]; "De aver llegado a Paria el Américo en este su primer viaje, él mismo lo confiesa en su primera navegación diciendo: '*Et provincia ipsa parias ab ipsis nuncupata est, hec ille*'"[131]; "Mas pensava hazer en este año de quinientos enviar a edificar una fortaleza en la tierra de Paria por la pesquería de las perlas, de donde pudiese a Sus Altezas enviar cada un año una gran cantidad dellas. Porque no se podía decir el número y peso y valor

que tenían. Y que quando las descubrió, si no fuera por los bastimentos que se le dañaban, tenía cierto que enbiara una pipa dellas llena."[132] Neither Coll y Toste nor Cambiaso comment on the toponym Paria.

2. **Yuyaparí, río**. Now the Orinoco river.
3. **Cubagua, isla**. It is first mentioned as a place where pearls can be found: "Y dezían verdad, que veynte y cinco leguas o treynta … de allí hasta el poniente está la isla de Cubagua de que luego se dirá, donde las [perlas] cogían." According to Las Casas, Columbus renamed this island as *Isla Margarita*: "la una se llama Coche, que quiere decir venado, y la otra Cubagua, que es la que arriba en el cap 137 dixe donde se an cogido infinitas perlas. De manera que el Almirante, aunque no sabía que en aqueste golphete se criaban las perlas, parece que adevinó en llamar esta isleta la Margarita y [estuvo muy cerca] della puesto que no lo expressa."[133] Neither Coll y Toste nor Cambiaso include this toponym in their dictionaries.
4. **Ayremarí, río**. Las Casas mentions the toponym in passing: "los ríos Yuyaparí y el otro que sale cerca dél que llamamos Ayremarí."[134] Neither Coll y Toste nor Cambiaso provide any comments about this toponym.
5. **Bonao, pueblo and provincia**. A region in Hispaniola.[135] The name of a minor cacique; the name means "great river."[136] Francisco Roldán established this village: "[Francisco Roldán] acordóse acercar con buena parte de su gente a esta villa y así se vino hazia la provincia de Bonao, donde ay una muy fértil y granosa vega muy llena y poblada de gente de indios, abundantíssima de comida y pan cazabi, donde ya estaban algunos christianos poblados y [después se pobló] la villa de Bonao."[137]

Fourth voyage

Relación del cuarto viaje: Toponyms in Castilian.
Source: Varela and Gil

1. **Las Figueras**
2. **Gracias a Dios, cabo de**
3. **Puerto de Bastimentos**. Though Columbus assigned this name, it was quickly renamed as *El Nombre de Dios*: "el puerto que llamamos el Nombre de Dios, al cual llamó el Almirante puerto de Bastimentos, porque todas aquellas comarcas y tres isletas que estavan por allí eran llenas de labranzas y maizales."[138]
4. **Retrete, puerto del**. Columbus probably named this small port due to its small size and distant location: "un portezuelo, al cual puso

el Almirante nombre Retrete, por su estrechura, porque no cabían en él arriba de cinco o seis navíos juntos." According to Ferdinand Columbus, "un pequeño puerto al que se dio el nombre de Retrete."[139]

5. **Gordo, puerto**
6. **Belén, puerto**. Based on the liturgical calendar, Columbus named the river Belén; its native name was *Yebra*.[140]
7. **Belporto** (Puerto Bello; Bel Puerto; Portobelo)
8. **Bocas, isla de las** (according to another interpretation of the manuscript, *Isla de las Pozas*. *Pozas* in Varela, *Textos y documentos completos* [1982], 300; *Pozzas* in Ferdinand Colombus; *Bocas* in Varela and Gil [2003], 494). *Poza* in Spanish means "pool of water, puddle," a word that may refer to the waters surrounding the island; *boca* is the geographic term meaning "mouth"; the two names are, thus, somewhat synonymous in their literal meaning, though they have distinct metaphoric implications.

Relación del cuarto viaje: Toponyms of indigenous and Asian origin. Source: Varela and Gil

1. **Cariay**. Perhaps related to the Taino word *carey*, which refers to a type of turtle (*Chelonia imbricata*).[141]
2. **Çiamba**. Neither Coll y Toste nor Cambiaso provide an explanation.
3. **Çarabarú**. Neither Coll y Toste nor Cambiaso provide an explanation.
4. **Yebra, río.** Columbus named it *Puerto Belén*. Neither Coll y Toste nor Cambiaso provide an explanation for this name.
5. **Çiguare, provincia** (Cyguare, ciudad or provincia). *Sigua* refers to a small seashell.[142] *Ri* means "place" or "village," but it can also mean "value" or "fortress."[143] Therefore, *siguare* probably means "a place of seashells." Las Casas believes that Ciguare refers to a city or a province under the rulership of the Great Khan: "[Cyguare] debía ser alguna ciudad o provincia de los reinos del Gran Khan, y que de allí a diez jornadas estaba el río de Ganges."[144]
6. **Quivián, pueblo del** (Quibián). Quivián was the name of the indigenous ruler of the territory.
7. **Magón, tierra de**. Neither Coll y Toste nor Cambiaso comment about Tierra de Magón. *Provincia Mango* is an Asian toponym and *Tierra de Magón* may refer to the same place.
8. **Braxil, puerto del** (Brasil). According to Las Casas, this is *Puerto de Yaquimo*, which Columbus named *Puerto del Brasil*.[145]

9. **Pego, reino de**. Neither Coll y Toste nor Cambiaso comment about *Reino de Pego*. It is probably not a Lucayo Taino toponym, but more likely refers to the Asian province rich in rubies, according to the description by Marco Polo.

Las Casas, Historia de las Indias: Toponyms in Castilian. Source: Millares Carlo

1. **El Jardín de la Reina, isla**. A name that Columbus pronounced.[146]
2. **Pinos, isla de**. A name inspired by nature: "porque había en ellas muchos pinos, púsole el Almirante por nombre la Isla de Pinos."[147]
3. **Honduras, cabo**. The word *honduras* in Spanish means "depth." According to Morison, Columbus gave the name *Cabo Honduras* to *Punta de Caxinas*, which he derived from the Taino name of a tree that they found there, probably *Chrysobalanus Icaco*.[148] A few years later, the Spaniards founded the city of Trujillo there: "el cabo que agora llaman de Honduras, donde está o estuvo la ciudad de españoles que llamaron Trujillo."[149] The place name Honduras never makes an appearance in the *diarios*, and Columbus may not have actually invented this name nor did he name the city of Trujillo. See also *Caxinas, punta de* on page 193.
4. **Trujillo, ciudad**. Columbus did not assign this name.
5. **La Nueva España**
6. **Oreja, costa de la**. The name was inspired by the sight of natives who had pierced their ears: "había otras gentes por aquella costa que tenían las orejas horadadas y tan grandes agujeros que cupiera un huevo de gallina bien por ellos, puso nombre a aquella ribera la costa de la Oreja"; and, in Ferdinand Columbus's words, "los habitantes … son casi negros, de mal aspecto, van completamente desnudos y se muestran en todo muy salvajes; según decía el indio que capturamos, comen carne humana y el pescado crudo, tal como lo pescan; y se perforan las orejas haciendo unos agujeros tan grandes, que cómodamente cabría por ellos un huevo de gallina. Por este motivo, el Almirante bautizó a aquella costa con el nombre de Costa de la Oreja."[150]
7. **Desastre, río**. Columbus assigned this name.[151]
8. **La Huerta, isla**. Columbus assigned this name.[152] According to Las Casas's description of the island, it looked like a garden and thus deserved such name.
9. **Contrastes, costa de los**. This name expresses the adverse weather conditions that the navigators experienced: "Por todos estos temporales tan adversos y diversos, que parece que nunca hombres

navegantes padecieron en tan poco camino, como desde Bel Puerto hasta Veragua, otros tales, puso por nombre a aquella costa la costa de los Contrastes."[153]

10. **San Cristóbal, montañas**. This religious name was inspired by the height of the mountain peak, which looked like a hermit's chapel: "las montañas muy altas que están sobre Veragua, que llamó el Almirante de Sant Cristóbal, porque el pico de la más alta parece exceder a la región del aire, porque nunca se ve sobre aquél nube alguna, sino todas quedan muy más bajas y a quien lo mira parece que es una ermita."[154]
11. **Las Barbas, isletas**. Columbus assigned this name, which Las Casas comments on as he expresses his dismay about how quickly names get changed on maps: "De allí pasaron arriba del puerto del Retrete, a una tierra que tenía junto muchas isletas, que el Almirante llamó las Barbas, y creo que hoy es el que pintan en las cartas el Golfo de San Blas; y cuando no nos catáremos, éstos que hacen cartas les pornán de Sant Nicolás, según cada día se escriben novedades."[155]
12. **Cartagena, puerto**. Most likely, Columbus did not assign this name, but since Las Casas discusses its authorship in the context of Columbian naming, I include it in this list. Las Casas writes that Columbus's authorship is unlikely since Ferdinand Columbus omits this name from his account and that normally he records all the names that his father had assigned, including much more minor ones. According to Las Casas, the name was probably assigned by Rodrigo de Bastidas and Juan de la Cosa or perhaps by Cristóbal Guerra, who went to that area first.[156]
13. **Las Tortugas, dos isletas**. Las Casas tells us these islands were named for the many turtles near them. He also informs us that the islands were soon renamed as *Los Caimanes* when marked on navigational charts.[157]
14. **Santa Gloria, puerto**. According to Las Casas, Columbus's crew suffered great danger on the way to this port and inside it.[158]
15. **Santo Domingo, puerto**. Navigating to this port was also very dangerous: "Pasar desta isleta [Beata], para venir a este puerto de Sancto Domingo es muy difícil."[159]

Las Casas, Historia de las Indias: Toponyms of indigenous origin. Source: Millares Carlo

1. **Guanaja, isla** and **Las Guanajas, islas**. According to Las Casas, this was a native name that the Spaniards adopted: "Al cabo, con grandes

dificultades, peligros y trabajos inefables, llegó y descubrió una isla pequeña, que los indios llamaban Guanaja, y tiene por vecinas otras tres o cuatro islas menores que aquélla, que los españoles llamaron después las Guanajas."[160] It is Isla de Pinos in the southwest of Cuba. *Guanajo* is the Taino word for "turkey."[161]

2. **Yucatán, tierra de**. This name's origins are in the Nahuatl language.
3. **Veragua, provincia**
4. **Caxinas, punta de** (Caxina, punta). Columbus adopted this name from the name of a certain fruit from a tree, which the natives called *caxinas*, as Ferdinand Columbus comments: "una punta que llamó de Cajinas por haber en ella muchos árboles que dan unos frutos algo arrugados y con el hueso esponjoso, sabrosos sobre todo si se toman cocidos, y a los que los indios llaman *cajinas*."[162] Now called Cape Honduras.
5. **Quiribri, isla**. Neither Coll y Toste nor Cambiaso provide any comments about this name or the following six.
6. **Cariarí, pueblo.**
7. **Aburená, provincia.**
8. **Catiba, provincia.**
9. **Hurira, puerto.**
10. **Cubiga o Cubija, pueblo.**
11. **Guija o Guiga, provincia.**
12. **Veragua, río**. According to Las Casas, this is a native name: "Adelante deste río está otro, una legua o dos, que los indios decían Veragua."[163]
13. **Urirá, pueblo**. This was the village of chieftain Quibián's enemies.[164]
14. **Urirá, río**. *Río Urirá* and *Puerto Hurira* above may be the same name.
15. **Dururi**. This was the name of the chieftain of a village. Neither Coll y Toste nor Cambiaso provide any comments.
16. **Cobrava, pueblo** (Cobraba). Neither Coll y Toste nor Cambiaso provide any comments. See also *Cateba, pueblo* below.
17. **Cateba, pueblo**. Las Casa says this was a village where Columbus's brother received hospitable treatment. The natives gave him food and the Spaniards exchanged items for gold mirrors.[165]
18. **Macaca, pueblo**. This was another village where the natives received the Spanish hospitably, Las Casas says. The natives gave the Spaniards cassava bread and other things.[166]
19. **Navasa, isleta**. Neither Coll y Toste nor Cambiaso provide any comments.

20. **Mayma, pueblo** (Maima in Ferdinand Columbus). This was likely not a Taino name since neither Coll y Toste nor Cambiaso provide any comments. Later, the Spanish built a town in its place and named it Sevilla.[167]

Ferdinand Columbus: Toponyms in Castilian. Source: Díaz

1. **Desgracia, río de la**. In chapter 41 of his *Historia*, Ferdinand Columbus relates the many difficulties his father encountered when navigating along the Costa de la Oreja towards the Cabo de Gracias a Dios. In this chapter, he also describes the unfortunate incident during which Columbus sent ashore a smaller boat to get water and wood and the boat sank and all the men that were in it drowned: "y al chocar contra la corriente de la desembocadura golpeó con tanta furia a las lanchas que una de ellas se hundió, muriendo todos los que la ocupaban."[168] The place was named to commemorate this event.

Ferdinand Columbus: Toponyms of indigenous origin. Source: Díaz

1. **Cerobaró, canal de**. Neither Coll y Toste nor Cambiaso provide any comments.
2. **Aburemá, canal**. Neither Coll y Toste nor Cambiaso provide any comments.
3. **Guaiga, río**. Another conflict with an indigenous tribe occurred by the river: "Al llegar a Guaiga, que es un río a doce leguas de Aburema, el Almirante ordenó que las lanchas fuesen a tierra; mientras lo hacían, vieron a más de cien indios en la playa, quienes las atacaron furiosamente, metiéndose en el agua hasta la cintura, arrojándoles sus azagayas, haciendo sonar unos cuernos y un tambor en son de guerra para defender su territorio, lanzando agua salada hacia los cristianos y masticando hierbas y escupiéndolas hacia ellos."[169]
4. **Cobraba, pueblo**. Neither Coll y Toste nor Cambiaso provide any comments.
5. **Guigua, región**. According to Ferdinand Columbus, there were two regions known with this name: "del mismo nombre que otra que se encuentra entre Veragua y Ciguaré."[170]
6. **Huiva, peñón**. Neither Coll y Toste nor Cambiaso provide any comments.

7. **Aomaquique, provincia**. Neither Coll y Toste nor Cambiaso provide any comments.

Seventeen Spanish settlements ("villas") named by the Spanish. Source: Millares Carlo

1. **Santo Domingo**
2. **Buenaventura**
3. **El Bonao**
4. **La Concepción**
5. **Santiago**
6. **Puerto de la Plata**
7. **Puerto Real**
8. **Lares de Guahaba**. Guajaba was the region in the chiefdom of the cacique Marien where the Spanish founded a village, which they named *Lares de Guahaba.*[171]
9. **El Árbol Gordo**
10. **El Cotuy**
11. **De Açua**
12. **Sant Juan de la Maguana**
13. **Xaraguá**. A lake and a region in Haiti.[172]
14. **De Yaquimo**. A place and a port in the chiefdom Jaragua.
15. **De Salvatierra**
16. **De Salvaleón**
17. **Santa Cruz de Aycayagua**

Notes

Introduction

1 "*whatever* things and merchandise of *whatever* kind, *name*, or manner that *they might be.*" Djelal Kadir sees "Columbus's vacillation in grammar" as "symptomatic of a larger shift of the ground on which his tenacious vision had previously discerned and legitimated a world-altering endeavor, the enterprise he launched across the Ocean Sea" (*Columbus and the Ends of the Earth*, 197).
2 "*that* which has been discovered." This vaguely phrased objective has supported the thesis of the unknown pilot, as Juan Manzano Manzano, among others, has argued in *Colón y su secreto*.
3 Todorov, *Conquest of America*, 27.
4 "Instrucción dada por el Rey à Pedrarias Dávila," quoted in Stewart, *Names on the Land*, 12.
5 A number of scholars have referred extensively to Columbian toponymy, not so much as an object of study in its own right, but as a useful tool for reconstructing the geographic and historic realities of the Columbian enterprise. Notable among them are Thacher, *The Continent of America*; Morison, *Admiral of the Ocean Sea*; and Levillier, *América, la bien llamada*.
6 Subirats, *El continente vacío*, 52.
7 Todorov, *Conquest of America*, 26–7.
8 The paradisiacal metaphor for describing the world Columbus found has found popular appeal among scholars as well as popular writers. The use of this metaphor is frequent in analyses and titles of works: Paiewonsky's *Conquest of Eden, 1493–1515* and Sale's *The Conquest of Paradise* are some examples.
9 Varela and Gil, 96–7. "And for this I thought to write down upon this voyage in great detail from day to day all that I should do and see, and encounter, as hereinafter shall be seen" (Morison, *Journals and Other Documents*, 49).

10 Varela and Gil, 97. "In addition, Lord Princes, to noting down each night what that day had brought forth, and each day what was sailed by night, I intend to make a new chart of navigation, upon which I shall place the whole sea and lands of the Ocean Sea in their proper positions under their bearings, and, further, to compose a book, and set down everything as in a real picture, by latitude north of the equator and longitude west" (Morison, *Journals and Other Documents*, 49).

11 Varela and Gil, 97. "and above all it is very important that I forget sleep and labor much at navigation" (Morison, *Journals and Other Documents*, 49).

12 Recent works dealing with mapping in Columbus include Alison Sandman, "Mirroring the World: Sea Charts, Navigation, and Territorial Claims in Sixteenth-century Spain," in *Merchants and Marvels*, ed. Smith and Findlen, 83–108; Padrón, *Spacious Word*; Darcy, "Visualizing Discovery."

13 Adorno, *Polemics of Possession*, viii.

14 There has been a significant production of criticism and theory related to maps as rhetorical instruments and of the ideological, rather than representational, intents in maps, and my book is inspired by these studies as well. Some of the notable works that offer valuable ways of thinking about territoriality, appropriation, representation, and translation include the following: Kagan, *Urban Images of the Hispanic World, 1493–1793*; Katchor, "Literary Legends: The Realm of the Literary Map"; Arias and Meléndez, *Mapping Colonial Spanish America*; Padrón, *The Spacious Word*; Casey, *Earth-Mapping*; Cosgrove, "Maps, Mapping, Modernity"; Jacob, *The Sovereign Map*; Abrams and Abrams, *Else/where*; Akerman, *The Imperial Map*. The work of unsurpassed importance that has defined the field of cartography is, of course, *The History of Cartography* by Harley and Woodward. Select studies on cartography and mapping in literature include Edson, *Mapping Time and Space*, and Scafi, *Mapping Paradise*.

15 Harley, "Silences and Secrecy," in Harley and Woodward, *History of Cartography*, 1:57.

16 For studies on Spanish naming in the Americas, see two articles by Val Julián: "Albores de la toponimia indiana," and "La toponomía conquistadora." Nito Verdera has also published a study of Columbian toponymy, *De Ibiza y Formentera al Caribe*. In a geographically different colonial context, notable is Carter's *The Road to Botany Bay*, which studies James Cook's naming of places in Australia.

17 Zamora, *Reading Columbus*, 11.

18 For the discussion of Rumeu de Armas's and Ramos's hypotheses, see Zamora, *Reading Columbus*, 11–12.

19 Varela and Gil, 220. "To the first island which I found I gave the name *Sant Salvador*, in recognition of His Heavenly Majesty, who marvelously hath given all this; the Indians call it *Guanahani*. To the second I gave the name

Isla de Santa Maria de Concepcion: to the third, *Ferrandina*; to the fourth, *La Isla Bella*; to the fifth, *La Isla Juana*; and so to each one I gave a new name" (Morison, *Journals and Other Documents*, 182).

20 In reality, this was a group of cays (keys) – Seal, Sister, North, South, and Nurse – that form the eastern edge of the Great Bahama Bank, which Columbus believed to be a group of islands. Morison, *Admiral of the Ocean Sea*, 252.

21 Varela and Gil, 152. "Here it seems that he assigned to Cuba the name Juana" (my translation).

22 Varela and Gil, 122. "which I believe must be Japan, according to the description of these Indians whom I carry, and which they call *Colba*" (Morison, *Journals and Other Documents*, 78).

23 "A la siguiente que encontró, es decir, Cuba, la llamó Juana, en honor del príncipe don Juan, heredero de Castilla, teniendo cuidado, con estos nombres, de render honor tanto a lo spiritual como a lo temporal" (Díaz, 117) ("and the island that he next found, Cuba, he named Juana in memory of Prince Juan, heir apparent to the throne of Castile. Thus he aimed to honour both the spiritual and temporal powers"; Keen, *Life of the Admiral*, 67). And in the next paragraph: "Había en aquella tierra [La Fernandina] muchas aguas y lagos, junto a uno de los cuales vieron una serpiente de siete pies de longitud, con un vientre de más de un pie de ancho ... Los indios le llaman *juana*" (Díaz, 118) ("That country has many streams and lakes and near one of these they saw a serpent seven feet long and a foot wide in the middle ... The Indians call it iguana"; Keen, *Life of the Admiral*, 67).

24 Ferdinand Columbus wrote his father's biography in Spanish; however, the original was lost and only the translation into Italian published in Venice in 1571 has survived. The Spanish editions published subsequently are translations from Italian back into Castilian.

25 Varela and Gil, 109–10. "daylight [on] Friday, when they arrived at the island of the Bahamas that was called in the Indians' tongue Guanahani" (Morison, *Journals and Other Documents*, 64).

26 Zamora, *Reading Columbus*, 74.

27 Varela and Gil, 113 (emphasis mine). "and those men whom I had captured made signs to me that they were so many that they could not be counted, and called by their names more than a hundred" (Morison, *Journals and Other Documents*, 68).

28 Díaz, 37. "In reality it was Guanahaní, which the admiral named San Salvador" (Keen, *Life of the Admiral*, 7).

29 Wilson, *The Indigenous People of the Caribbean*, 2.

30 Ibid., 7.

31 Highfield, "Some Observations on the Taino Language," 161.

32 More recently, scholars have become increasingly interested in the contribution by the indigenous peoples as active agents during the encounter and early colonial

history. Select studies include Vizenor, "Manifest Manners"; Mignolo, *The Darker Side of the Renaissance*; Mundy, *The Mapping of New Spain*; Mazzotti, *Coros mestizos del Inca Garcilaso*, and his edited volume, *Agencias criollas*; Brokaw, "Indigenous and European Discursive Modes," and "Ambivalence, Mimicry, and Stereotype"; Deagan and Cruxent, *Columbus's Outpost among the Taínos*; Stone, *In Place of Gods and Kings*; and Keegan and Carlson, *Talking Taíno*.

33 Highfield, "Some Observations on the Taino Language," 161.
34 Among others, see "The Garifuna of Central America" by Nancie L. Gonzalez (197–205); "The Legacy of the Indigenous People of the Caribbean" by Samuel M. Wilson (206–13); and "Five Hundred Years of Indigenous Resistance" (214–22) by Garnette Joseph in Wilson, *Hispaniola*.
35 Arrom, "The Creation Myths of the Taino," 79.
36 Tucker, "Place-Names, Conquest, and Empire," 25.
37 Todorov, *Conquest of America*, 27.
38 Varela and Gil, 113. "and [they] called by their names more than a hundred" (Morison, *Journals and Other Documents*, 68).
39 Foucault, *Archaeology of Knowledge*, 107.
40 Zelinsky, "Slouching toward a Theory of Names," 248.
41 Zelinsky, "By Their Names You Shall Know Them," 87.
42 Berg and Vuolteenaho, "Towards Critical Toponymies," in *Critical Toponymies*, ed. Berg and Vuolteenaho, 7.
43 Kearns and Berg, "Proclaiming Place: Towards a Geography of Place Name Pronunciation," in *Critical Toponymies*, ed. Berg and Vuolteenaho, 156.
44 Highfield, "Some Observations on the Taino Language," 161.
45 Rouse, *Tainos*, 5.
46 Highfield, "Some Observations on the Taino Language," 155–7.
47 Wilson, *Indigenous People of the Caribbean*, 7.
48 Gen. 32:28–9, 35:10.
49 Zamora, *Reading Columbus*, 139.
50 Greenblatt, *Marvelous Possessions*, 82.
51 Genette, *Mimologics*, 5.
52 "Later on, having more or less used up the religious and royal hierarchies, he resorts to a more traditional motivation – by direct resemblance – for which he immediately gives us a justification" (Todorov, *Conquest of America*, 27).
53 Carter, *The Road to Botany Bay*, 7.
54 Though writing about a different geographic and cultural context in which the science and the scientific methodology had evolved to a state quite different from that in which Columbus was undertaking his transatlantic voyages, Carter similarly rejects the idea of the supremacy of imperial naming: "The idea of Cook spontaneously generating an imperial mythology is a biographical myth. It ignores the fact that exploration, no less than, say, botany was an

intellectual discipline with its own distinctive scientific method, its own rules of description and classification" (*The Road to Botany Bay*, 8).

55 Two distinct positions have dominated the centuries-long intellectual debate about the origin of language: the relationship between names and things is either inherently correct, one that perhaps has gone awry over time as language gradually lost its divinely inspired form, but one that can still be traced back to the origins; or this relationship is an arbitrary one, based on convention and its acceptance within a community. In Plato's philosophical dialogue *Cratylus*, the first work dedicated to this question, Cratylus defends the thesis of a natural relationship between names and things, while Hermogenes defends the nominalist or the conventionalist thesis, according to which names are accepted by an agreement within a certain community or group of people. The third interlocutor, Socrates, probes into the weaknesses of both stands and, in the process, crystallizes two ways through which the relationship between words and things can be evaluated: through an examination of the way words are derived (an approximation to an etymological analysis) and through sound symbolism. While the reliance on etymologies proves to be a circular and ultimately self-defeating method since sooner or later it leads us to the root of the original word from which the others were derived and for which this method no longer works, the attempt to understand the logic behind the choice of sounds turns out to be equally untrustworthy; because of the corruption that languages have undergone over time, fully understanding this logic is difficult or perhaps impossible.

56 Genette, *Mimologics*, 252. The context of the phrase used here is in connection with Proust's *Remembrance of Things Past*. Genette's final chapters peruse the persistence of mimeticism in literary works by Marcel Proust, Stéphane Mallarmé, Paul Valéry, and Gaston Bachelard, among others.

57 "Navigat igitur eius semper littora abradens ad occidentem duas lequas et viginti supra bis centum, ut ipse ait, hoc est millia passuum circiter tercentum et mille septingentisque insulis nomen imposuit, in laevam plusquam tribus millibus passim, ut ipse dicere audit, relictis" (Peter Martyr, 260) ("So he sailed West always bordering its coasts, for 222 leagues, that is 1,300 miles, as he gives to understand, and named 700 islands, leaving behind to the left more than 3,000 here and there, as he himself dared to say"; ibid., 261).

1. "Named Incorrectly": The Geographic and Symbolic Functions of Columbian Place Names

1 Varela and Gil, 97. "In addition, Lord Princes, to noting down each night what that day had brought forth, and each day what was sailed by night, I intend to make a new chart of navigation, upon which I shall place the

whole sea and lands of the Ocean Sea in their proper positions under their bearings" (Morison, *Journals and Other Documents*, 49). According to Virgil Milani, the word "situar" is an Italianism meaning "to describe" as in the following sentence: "fue necesario traer á esto el decir é opinion de aquellos que escribieron é situaron el mundo" ("it was necessary to bring to this the words and the opinion of those who wrote about the world and described it"; Navarrete, 1:367, quoted in Milani, *The Written Language*, 107); it has been used this way in Italian texts, such as in *Volgarizzamento di Palladio* (c. 1340) and by Pier Francesco Giambullari (1495–1555).

2 Wey Gomez's recent translation of this quotation in his *Tropics of Empire* elucidates this part of its meaning: "in their proper places under their compass bearings [*debaxo su viento*], and moreover, [I will] compose a book and place all of the same in a map [*por pintura*], by latitude from the equinoctial line and by longitude from the west" (391).

3 Zamora convincingly argues that "the so-called prologue to the *Diario* [should be read], not as the preface Las Casas claimed it was, but rather as an autonomous textual entity, the Letter of 1492, that Las Casas chose to append to his edition of Columbus's journal" (*Reading Columbus*, 57).

4 Campbell, "Portolan Charts," in Harley and Woodward, *History of Cartography*, 1:372.

5 Zamora, *Reading Columbus*, 108.

6 Campbell, "Portolan Charts," in Harley and Woodward, *History of Cartography*, 1:415.

7 Ibid., 415–28.

8 Woodward, "Reality, Symbolism, Time, and Space in Medieval World Maps," 510–21.

9 Campbell, "Portolan Charts," in Harley and Woodward, *History of Cartography*, 1:415–28.

10 Woodward, "Medieval *Mappaemundi*," in Harley and Woodward, *History of Cartography*, 1:286–370. With these words Woodward sums up the argument laid out in Anna-Dorothee von den Brincken's work available in German. Her most relevant article by is "Mappa mundi und Chronographia." For a more extensive bibliography of Brincken's work and for Woodward's discussion of the way medieval *mappa mundi* fulfilled "a secular as well as a spiritual need," see Harley and Woodward, *History of Cartography*, 1:288–92.

11 My definition of "map" is based on that by Harley and Woodward, *History of Cartography*, vol. 1. Furthermore, my definition of "mapping" is that which Denis Cosgrove provides in his "Introduction: Mapping Meaning" in the volume he edited titled *Mappings*: "The measure of mapping is not restricted to the mathematical; it may equally be spiritual, political or moral.

By the same token, the mapping's record is not confined to the archival; it includes the remembered, the imagined, the contemplated ... Acts of mapping are creative, sometimes anxious, moments in coming to knowledge of the world, and the map is both the spatial embodiment of knowledge and a stimulus to further cognitive engagements" (2).

12 See Varela and Gil, 444–8.

13 Genette draws our attention to the way in which Augustine points out the pitfall in the analysis of etymological origins of words in that the process may become infinite: "Because it would be easy to refute them by saying that this would be an infinite process, for by whichever words you interpret the origin of any one word, the origin of these words would in turn have to be sought, they [the Stoics] assert that you must search until you arrive at some similarity of the sound of the word to the thing" ("*De origine verbi*" [*On the Origin of Words*], ch. 6 of *De dialectica* [*On Dialectic*], attributed to Augustine, quoted by Genette, *Mimologics*, 31).

14 Quoted in Zamora, *Reading Columbus*, 103.

15 Berggren and Jones, *Ptolemy's* Geography, 81.

16 Ibid., 4. For a useful explanation of the three parts of the work, its reliance on and response to an earlier cartographer, Marinos of Tyre, and of its original contributions, see Berggren and Jones, introduction to *Ptolemy's* Geography (3–54), as well as their translations of selected parts of *Ptolemy's* Geography.

17 Berggren and Jones, *Ptolemy's* Geography, 57.

18 Ibid., 59.

19 According to D.A. Brading, in his "The Two Cities," Augustine's views on politics, war, and empire "influenced the manner in which the discovery and conquest of the new World was interpreted and justified in Spain" (99).

20 Augustine, *Expositions*, 411.

21 Varela and Gil, 269. "And as we arrived at the islands of Cape Verde, which is a false name because they are so dry that there is nothing green on them and all their people are sick, I decided not to linger on" (my translation).

22 Díaz, 256. "Proceeded to another island called Boa Vista – a name that certainly does not correspond to the truth, for it is a miserable and melancholy place" (Keen, *Life of the Admiral*, 176).

23 This deliberation appears amid the description of the Portuguese explorations along the western coast of Africa: "Dicen algunos que se le había dado este nombre, sustituyendo al suyo original de Agesingua, por ser el cabo y el fin de la buena esperanza de su conquista y descubrimiento, aunque otros sostienen que se llamó así por tratarse deun cabo que le daba esperanzas de mejor tierra y navegación" (Díaz, 73). ("Which name [the Cape of Good Hope] according to some was given that cape in place of its proper one, Agesingua,

because it marked the end of those fine hopes of conquest and discovery; others claim it got that name because it gave promise of the discovery of richer lands and of more prosperous voyages"; Keen, *Life of the Admiral*, 35).

24 West and Kling, *The* Libro de las Profecías *of Christopher Columbus*, 101.

25 See Milhou, *Colón y su mentalidad mesiánica*, 80–90. The quote is as follows: "la Trinidad completada con la Virgen, esposa del Padre, fecundada por el Espíritu Santo y madre del hijo" (ibid., 56).

26 "Suele la divinal Providencia ordenar que se pongan nombres y sobrenombres a las personas que señala para se servir conformes a los oficios que les determina cometer, según asaz parece por muchas partes de la Sagrada Escriptura, y el Filósofo, en el 4.° de la *Metafísica*, dice que los nombres deben convenir con las propiedades y oficios de las cosas" (Millares Carlo, 1:28) (Divine Providence commonly orders things so that the names and surnames that are given to people indicate the deeds they will commit, as it seems according to many places of the Scripture, and the Philosopher [Aristotle] in his fourth chapter of *Metaphysics* says that the names must conform to the properties and functions of things; my translation).

27 Millares Carlo, 1:51. "So that now we find that some of the lands or islands in these Indies have sunk, which are some of the first ones that we find when going that way, and they are called the *Sunker Isles*" (my translation). "Because of which one cannot navigate by the compass, and it has happened that ships got lost there" (my translation).

28 Millares Carlo, 1:52.

29 Ferdinand Colón gives three instances that elucidate the meanings of the Hesperides Islands: Hercules fighting the dragon that guarded the Hesperides; Euristeus sending Hercules to get the golden apples from the Hesperides; and finally, in the chapter about the planets, Hyginus's explanation that the planet Venus was often named Hesperus because it sets just after the sunset (Díaz, 65–71). The Venetian edition of *De poetica astronomia* to which Ferdinand Columbus refers is *Poeticon astronomicon* (Venice: Erhardus Ratdolt, 1485).

30 Varela and Gil, 366. "in order to spread his sacred name and faith to so many peoples" (my translation).

31 Las Casas, *Obras Completas*, vol. 6, *Apologética Historia*, ch. 1 and 2.

32 Ferdinand Columbus writes about the metaphor of the dove contained in his father's first name in Italian: "puesto que llevó la gracia del Espíritu Santo al Nuevo Mundo que descubrió, mostrando, como en el bautismo de san Juan Bautista el Espíritu Santo bajo figura de paloma mostró, al hijo amado de Dios a quien allí no conocían; y porque, como la paloma de Noé, llevó también sobre las aguas del Océano el olivo y el óleo del bautismo para que

pacíficamente se integraran en la Iglesia aquellas gentes que hasta entonces estaban encerradas en el arca de las tinieblas y la confusión" (Díaz, 32) ("because he carried the grace of the Holy Ghost to that New World which he discovered, showing those people who knew Him not Who was God's beloved son, as the Holy Ghost did in the figure of a dove when St. John baptized Christ; and because over the waters of the ocean, like the dove of Noah's ark, he bore the olive branch and oil of baptism, to signify that those people who had been shut up in the ark of darkness and confusion were to enjoy peace and union with the Church"; Keen, *Life of the Admiral*, 4).

33 Ferdinand Columbus mentions no less than five distinct individuals known by the last name Colón: the one described by Cornelius Tacitus, two "ilustres Colones," "illustrious Coloni" described by the Venetian Sabellicus, as well as Colón el Mozo and Colón el Viejo (Keen, *Life of the Admiral*, 4). The interpretation of *Colón* as meaning "member" is as follows: "Porque en griego significa 'miembro,' y así, teniendo como nombre de pila Cristóbal, se sabía de quién era miembro, es decir, de Cristo, por quien iba a ser mandado entre aquellas gentes para la salvación de las mismas" (Díaz, 32) ("Because in Greek it means "member," and by his proper name Christopher, men might know that he was a member of Christ, by Whom he was sent for the salvation of those people"; Keen, *Life of the Admiral*, 4). The full argument is as follows: "si queremos reducir su nombre a la pronunciación latina, que es Christophorus Colonus, diremos que así como se dice que San Cristóbal tuvo aquel nombre porque pasaba a Cristo por la profundidad de las aguas con tanto peligro, por lo cual fue llamado Cristóbal, y así como llevaba y traía a las gentes, las cuales otra persona no fuera bastante para pasarlos así el Almirante, que fue Cristóbal Colón, pidiendo a Cristo su ayuda y que le favoreciese en aquel peligro de su pasaje, pasó él y sus ministros, para que fueran aquellas gentes *indianas* colonos y moradores de la Iglesia triunfante de los cielos; pues es bien de creer que muchas almas, las cuales Satanás esperaba haber de gozar, no habiendo quien las pasase por aquella agua del Bautismo, hayan sido hechas por él colonos o ciudadanos y moradores de la eterna Gloria del Paraíso" (Díaz, 32) ("And if we give his name its Latin form, which is Christophorus Colonus, we may say that just as St. Christopher is reported to have gotten that name because he carried Christ over deep waters with great danger to himself, and just as he conveyed over people whom no other could have carried, so the Admiral Christopher Colonus, asking Christ's aid and protection in that perilous pass, crossed over with his company that the Indian nations might become dwellers in the triumphant Church of Heaven. There is reason to believe that many souls that Satan expected to catch because they had not passed through the waters of baptism were by the

Admiral made dwellers in the eternal glory of Paradise"; Keen, *Life of the Admiral*, 4).

34 "Considerando esto, me convencí de que, de la misma manera que la mayor parte de sus actos fueron realizados por algún misterioso designio, tampoco lo que se refiere a tal nombre y apellido se produjo al azar. Podríamos aducir al ejemplo de muchos nombres que, no sin oculta causa, fueron puestos como indicio del efecto que iba a derivarse, como si se tratara de pronosticar las maravillas y novedades de lo que llevaron a cabo" (Díaz, 32) ("Reflecting on this, I was moved to believe that just as most of his affairs were directed by a secret Providence, so the variety of his name and surname was not without its mystery. We could cite as examples many names which a hidden cause assigned as symbols of the parts which their bearers were to play. Just so, the Admiral's name foretold the novel and wonderful deed he was to perform"; Keen, *Life of the Admiral*, 4).

35 "Instrucción a Mosen Pedro Margarite" (9 April 1494), in Varela and Gil, 272. "With the help of Our Lord you should travel through much land, and that will be good and always, wherever you go, along all the roads and pathways put some tall crosses and *mojones* and also put crosses on the trees and crosses in any place that you deem to be convenient and where they will not be able to fall ... because, may the Lord be venerated, the land belongs to the Christians, and you will have great profits from the eternal memory that will be made of them; and another thing that you should do is carve onto some tall and large trees the names of their Highnesses" (my translation).

2. Words and the World: The Known Corpus of Columbian Place Names

1 "Navigat igitur eius semper littora abradens ad occidentem duas lequas et viginti supra bis centum, ut ipse ait, hoc est millia passuum circiter tercentum et mille septingentisque insulis nomen imposuit, in laevam plusquam tribus millibus passim, ut ipse dicere audit, relictis" (Peter Martyr, 260) ("So he sailed West always bordering its coasts, for 222 leagues, that is 1,300 miles, as he gives to understand, and named 700 islands, leaving behind to the left more than 3,000 here and there, as he himself dared to say"; ibid., 261).

2 This excludes any place name recorded in historical sources other than the ones listed in the appendix; however, this is a reasonable count of Columbian place names available to us. A preliminary count was done in my doctoral dissertation, though these numbers are slightly different: Evelina Gužauskytė, "The Places of Places: Naming and Ordering the World in Christopher Columbus's 'Diario de a bordo' (1492–1504)," PhD dissertation at Columbia University, 2005.

3 The additional thirty-four toponyms Las Casas lists in the summary are listed in the appendix. The paragraphs comprising the summary are included in Varela and Gil's 2003 edition of *Textos y documentos completos* immediately after the text of the *Relación* (Varela and Gil, 384–406).

4 Varela and Gil, 140, 132.

5 The toponyms are listed in the appendix in the order in which they are introduced in the *diarios*.

6 Arguably, the unknown pilot who shared with Columbus news about formerly unknown lands may have shown him a sketch of them, according to the theory of pre-discovery argued by Juan Manzano Manzano and several other scholars.

7 *Cabo Redondo* may also have been inspired by the Virgin Santa María la Redonda.

8 One of the meanings of *becerro* is a sea cow or a manatee, according to the first monolingual dictionary of the Spanish language titled *Tesoro de la lengua castellana o española* by Sebastián de Covarrubias (see the appendix for further commentary).

9 See Levillier, *América, la bien llamada*, 1:87–93, for a discussion of the naming of *Isabela* and the confusion about its true location, including Humboldt's theory that Columbus gave the name of the queen to two different places.

10 Varela and Gil, 401. "They found some fisherman huts … He named the place Port of Huts" (my translation).

11 Varela and Gil, 238–9. "They fought ferociously, and three of our men were wounded with arrows" (my translation).

12 Varela and Gil, 162 and 145. "He called … the river Guadalquivir, because it is said that it flows as large as the Guadalquivir at Cordova" (Morison, *Journals and Other Documents*, 121); "and it reminded him of the land of Campana" (my translation). Flowing into the Ocean Sea, the river Guadalquivir served as the point of embarkation for Columbus's ships taking off to and coming back from the transatlantic voyages. Columbus recalls it frequently in his *Diario*, usually when comparing the idyllic landscape and the Paradise-like climate of the New World to the sights and the feeling of mid-April Andalusia. Manuel Álvar speaks of "the gentle memory of Andalusia" (el recuerdo encariñado de Andalucía), and the desire to compare the New World to Andalusia as well as to the familiar Old World, including Portugal, Castille, Valencia, and Sicily, although often purposely avoiding references to Portugal and Italy, covering these memories with "a heavy slab of silences" (una pesada losa de silencios) (Manuel Álvar, *Diario del descubrimiento*, 22).

13 Varela and Gil, 125. "which he called *las islas de Arena*, owing to the slight depth which they had in the southerly direction, for a distance of six leagues" (Morison, *Journals and Other Documents*, 81).

14 For more on the influences of Italian, Portuguese, and other languages on Columbus's discourse, see two classical works: Milani, *Written Language*, and Menéndez Pidal, *La lengua de Cristóbal Colón*.

15 A few examples include these commentaries: about *Puerto de San Nicolao*: "entró en el puerto dicho, y púsole nombre Puerto de San Nicolao, porque era día de Sant Nicolás, por honra suya" (Varela and Gil, 154) ("he entered the said harbor, and gave it the name *Puerto de San Nicolao*, because it was the feast of St Nicholas, for his honor"; Morison, *Journals and Other Documents*, 112); *Puerto de la Mar de Sancto Thomás*: "Púsole nombre el Puerto de la mar de Sancto Thomás, porque era oy su día" (Varela and Gil, 172) ("he gave it the name *Puerto de la Mar de Sancto Thomas*, for today was his feast"; Morison, *Journals and Other Documents*, 130); and *Villa de la Navidad*, according to Las Casas's note in the margin of the transcription: "porque llegó allí día de la Navidad, como parece por lo de arriba" (Varela and Gil, 186) (because he arrived there on Christmas Day, as it can be deduced from the above; my translation).

16 Varela and Gil, 126 and 176. "Saw another river much greater than the others, so the Indians told him by signs … Called de river *Rio de Mares*" (Morison, *Journals and Other Documents*, 83); and "a small flat island which lies near the middle and which he named La Amiga" (ibid., 134).

17 According to Coll y Toste, *Cuba* means "a great place" formed from two Indo-Antillian roots: *coa*, place, and *bana*, large or great. *Caribata* refers to the region under the rule of the cacique Marien in Haiti. *Xamaná* (spelled in sources also as *Samaná* and *Zamaná*) refers to the peninsula and the bay to the east of Hispaniola (Coll y Toste, *Prehistoria*, 205, 252). According to Cambiaso, it is the peninsula to the north of the island inhabited by the Ciguayos (*Pequeño diccionario*, 126).

18 18 December 1492, Varela and Gil, 166. "I sent for more beads, among which for a symbol I had a gold *excelente* on which was portrayed Your Highnesses, and showed it to him, and told him again, as yesterday, that Your Highnesses ruled and were lords over the better part of the world, and that there were none such great princes; and showed him the other banners and the others with the cross. With this he was much impressed and said before his counselors, 'what great lords Your Highnesses must be!'" (Morison, *Journals and Other Documents*, 125).

19 I would like to thank the American Numismatic Society and its staff for their generous help in providing access to their collections and for their guidance in finding materials regarding the study of the Spanish coin *cinquin*.

20 Milhou, *Colón y su mentalidad mesiánica*, 56.
21 Milhou analyses Columbus's siglum in *Colón y su mentalidad mesiánica*, 90.
22 See Juan Gil's detailed discussion of this place name in "El enigma de una denominación: el cabo de Alfa et O," in *Mitos y utopías del descubrimiento*, 89–96.
23 Mâle, *Religious Art*, 5.
24 Kolve, *Chaucer and the Imagery of Narrative*, 316.
25 Eliade, *Myth of the Eternal Return*, 12.
26 Various civilizations used celestial archetypes in their interpretation of terrestrial geography. Creations of such archetypes are a way of assimilating chaos and of appropriating the landscape, as Mircea Eliade eloquently argues: "This is why, when possession is taken of a territory – that is, when its exploitation begins – rites are performed that symbolically repeat the act of Creation: the uncultivated zone is first 'cosmicized,' then inhabited" (*Myth of the Eternal Return*, 9–10).
27 Eliade, *Myth of the Eternal Return*, 11.
28 For interpretations of the Columbian siglum or cryptogram, see Pistarino, *Cristoforo Colombo*, and related bibliography. In addition, *Puerto Santo* may have a more personal meaning for Columbus. The mountainous landscape of the *Puerto Santo* island may have also reminded him of the Portuguese island Porto Santo near Madera where he spent his honeymoon with Felipa Moniz Perestrello.
29 Mignolo, "Cartas, crónicas y relaciones del descubrimiento y la conquista," 71.
30 Ibid.
31 Ibid., 72.

3. "Y saber dellos los secretos de la tierra": Taino Toponymy and Columbian Naming

1 Nader and Formisano, *The Book of Privileges Issued to Christopher Columbus*, 99.
2 Zamora, *Reading Columbus*, 11–12.
3 Ibid.
4 Varela and Gil, 220. "To the first island which I found I gave the name *Sant Salvador*, in recognition of His Heavenly Majesty, who marvelously hath given all this; the Indians call it *Guanahani*. To the second I gave the name *Isla de Santa María de Concepción*; to the third, *Ferrandina*; to the fourth, *La Isla Bella*; to the fifth, *La Isla Juana*: and so to each one I gave a new name" (Morison, *Journals and Other Documents*, 182).
5 Díaz, 37. "In reality it was Guanahaní, which the Admiral named San Salvador" (Keen, *Life of the Admiral*, 7).

6 It seems that *Guanahaní* was likely first included in Columbus's ship log of the first voyage, since it appears in the *Diario del primer viaje* significantly before the mention of the Castilian *San Salvador*. It was then deleted from the letter of 4 March to underline the strategy of naming places in Castilian and the ideology articulated in it, and it was included again in the letter to Santángel. The letter of 4 March stresses the Castilian linguistic dominion through naming even more by omitting the Taino *Guanahaní* altogether: "A la primera puse nombre la isla [de] Sant Salvador a memoria de su Alta Magestad; a la segunda, de Santa María de Conçibiçión; a la tercera, Fernandina; a la cuarta, la Ysavela; a la quinta, la Juana" (Varela and Gil, 228) (To the first [island] I gave the name island of *Sant Salvador*, in recognition of His Heavenly Majesty; to the second, of *Santa María de Conçibiçión*; to the third, *Fernandina*; to the fourth, la *Ysavela*; to the fifth, *la Juana*; my translation). This is consistent with Zamora's observation that the letter to Santángel contains comments and structure both of which aim to underscore Columbus's noble Christian behaviour towards the native inhabitants, an important part of the image to be projected to the European audience. Both of these messages are absent from the letter of 4 March, which instead focuses on the "messianic" goals by explicitly articulating the reconquest of Jerusalem as the purpose of the transoceanic voyages (Zamora, *Reading Columbus*, 20, 14–17).

7 "El día viernes que llegaron a una isleta de los lucayos, que se llamava en lengua de indios Guanahaní" (Varela and Gil, 109–10) ("And lay-to waiting for daylight Friday, when they arrived at an island of the Bahamas that was called in the Indian's tongue Guanahaní"; Morison, *Journals and Other Documents*, 64). Ferdinand Columbus maintains the structure of the *diario* and introduces the Taino toponym before the Castilian one; he does so as he writes to correct the twelve misconceptions, "falsedades," about his father, one of which was that the first island his father had discovered was Hispaniola: "Se trató, por el contrario, de Guanahaní, a la que el Almirante llamó San Salvador" (Díaz, 37) ("In reality it was Guanahaní, which the Admiral named San Salvador"; Keen, *Life of the Admiral*, 7).

8 Morison, *Admiral of the Ocean Sea*, 254.

9 In addition, in his *Relación acerca de las antigüedades de los indios*, Pané lists Taino toponyms referring to smaller geographic bodies, such as mountains (*Cauta*), caves (*Cacibajagua* and *Amayaúna*), and provinces (*Caonao*), among many others, as well as mythical names of places and gods. Pané's account of the toponymy is also limited, and its accuracy was further complicated during the processes of transcribing, editing, and translating the original text.

10 Varela and Gil, 113. "And saw so many islands that I could not decide where to go first; and those men whom I had captured made signs to me that they were so many that they could not be counted, and called by their names more than a hundred" (Morison, *Journals and Other Documents*, 68).

11 Varela and Gil, 128. "And the captain of *Pinta* said he understood that this Cuba was a city, and that that land was a very great continent that trended far to the N, and that the King of that land made war with the Grand Khan, whom they called *Camí*, and his land or city, *Faba*, and many other names" (Morison, *Journals and Other Documents*, 84–5).

12 The island, which both he and Columbus referred to as "La Española," is today shared by Haiti and the Dominican Republic.

13 Wilson, *Indigenous People of the Caribbean*, 5.

14 Irving Rouse classified the islands into three major cultural zones based on the archaeological record: Classic Taino (Haiti and Boriquen, including the nearby Ayay [St Croix], before the Carib intrusion); Western Taino (Cuba, Jamaica, and Lucayos); and Eastern Taino (the islands of the northern Lesser Antilles, to the east of Boriquen and the Virgin Islands).

15 Stevens-Arroyo, *Cave of the Jagua*, xliii.

16 Highfield, "Some Observations on the Taino Language," 164. In addition, recorded Taino names of male caciques include *Amanex*, *Behechio*, *Cotubanamá*, and *Guacanagarí*; and those of female caciques include *Anacoana*, *Higuanamá*, and *Cabomba*. *Ganauvariu* was one of the first persons encountered by Pané and *Guaticavá*, the first Indian who died baptized (ibid.).

17 Coll y Toste, *Prehistoria*, 138.

18 Saviñón in Cambiaso, *Pequeño diccionario*, 10. Among the latter are Pedro Henríquez Ureña and the scholar from the Dominican Republic José Gabriel García.

19 Highfield, "Some Observations on the Taino Language," 155. This thesis is also supported by Douglas Taylor, José Juan Arrom, and Antonio M. Stevens-Arroyo.

20 Highfield, "Some Observations on the Taino Language," 157.

21 Stevens-Arroyo, *Cave of the Jagua*, xlii.

22 Arrom prefers the term "Arahuacan," which has not been anglicized.

23 Taylor, *Languages of the West Indies*, 13–14. According to Taylor, these languages were spoken in the following regions: Arawak or Lokono was spoken in Trinidad and the Guianese coastal region from the Orinoco as far east as the Oyapock; Igneri or Island-Carib was spoken in the Lesser Antilles except Trinidad and Tobago, and from Stann Creek in British Honduras, south and east around the Gulf of Honduras to the Black River; and Karina or Carib

was spoken in Tobago, Grenada, and probably other parts of the Lesser Antilles, the Guianas from north of the Orinoco eastward to the Amazon (the modern Galibi peoples of the Guianas are part of this linguistic family).

24 Stevens-Arroyo, *Cave of the Jagua*, 32–3.

25 Ibid., 33.

26 Wilson, *The Indigenous People of the Caribbean*, 7.

27 Taylor, *Languages of the West Indies*, 14–16.

28 Stevens-Arroyo, *Cave of the Jagua*, xliv.

29 For more on Island Caribs and their language, see Vincent O. Cooper, "Language and Gender among the Kalinago of Fifteenth-century St. Croix" (186–96), and Louis Allaire, "The Caribs of the Lesser Antilles" (177–185) in Wilson, *Hispaniola*.

30 Quoted in Highfield, "Some Observations on the Taino Language," 156, citing Marshall Durbin, "A Survey of the Carib Language Family," in *South American Indian Languages: Retrospect and Prospect*, ed. Harriet E. Manelis Klein and Louisa R. Stark (Austin: University of Texas Press, 1986), 325–70; Philip P. Boucher, *Cannibal Encounters: Europeans and Island Caribs, 1492–1763* (Baltimore: Johns Hopkins University Press, 1992); and Peter Hulme and Neil L. Whitehead, *Wild Majesty: Encounters with Caribs from Columbus to the Present Day: An Anthology* (Oxford; Clarendon Press, 1992).

31 Highfield, "Some Observations on the Taino Language," 156.

32 Wilson, *Indigenous People of the Caribbean*, 7.

33 Highfield, "Some Observations on the Taino Language," 155 and 157.

34 Ibid., 155.

35 One of the two words preserved from the language of the Ciguayo is *tuob*, or gold (R. Fuson, ed., *The Log of Christopher Columbus* [Camden, ME: International Marine, 1992], 172, quoted in Highfield, "Some Observations on the Taino Language," 155).

36 Varela and Gil, 147. "And also I do not know the language, and the people of these lands do not understand me" (Morison, *Journals and Other Documents*, 105).

37 Varela and Gil, 277 (emphasis mine). "Thus I say this again and once again, that I lack nothing else but to be able to speak and preach in their language before they all become Christian" (my translation).

38 Varela and Gil, 279 (emphasis mine). "Thus, in addition that these people are not all Christians, which is *because I do not know the language*, I also cannot reach the great quantities of gold and other riches that are hidden in this island of spices, which they would extract for us, but *I do not know the language in which I could speak to them*" (translation and emphasis mine).

39 Varela and Gil, 171. "The only thing missing is to know their language and to command them, because they do everything they are told without any contradiction" (my translation).

40 For a discussion of language in Columbus, see Zamora, "'If Cahonaboa Learns to Speak.'"

41 Highfield, "Some Observations on the Taino Language," 158. According to Highfield, the Spanish chroniclers recorded primarily words for things that were unfamiliar for them, thus, names for root crops such as *yucca* and *age*, animals such as *hutía* and *manatí*, and cultural artefacts such as *canoa* and *zemi*. Incidentally, Arrom points out that the word *manatí* was one that the Tainos borrowed from the Island Carib language (Arrom, "La lengua de los taínos," 62). The majority of the known Taino lexicon comes from the following categories: toponymy, names of prominent people, such as caciques, terms related to agriculture and mining, terms for plants and animals, and the lexicon of religion and mythology. Some of the categories that the Spaniards did *not* record include plants and animals that had apparent counterparts in the Old World, avifauna, and parts of the human face and body (Highfield, "Some Observations on the Taino Language," 158). For a more extensive survey of the Taino lexicon, see Highfield, 160–8, and Coll y Toste, *Prehistoria*, 146–54.

42 Coll y Toste, *Prehistoria*, 142.

43 Highfield, "Some Observations on the Taino Language," 161.

44 Ibid.

45 Ibid., 161–2.

46 Ibid., 161.

47 Arrom, "La lengua de los taínos," 56.

48 Ibid., 56–8.

49 Ibid., 53.

50 Ibid., 54.

51 Ibid., 55.

52 The following authors have discussed the justification of possession based on the then-current European law: Marrero-Fente, *La poética de la ley*; Greenblatt, *Marvelous Possessions*; Rabasa, *Inventing A-M-E-R-I-C-A*; and Subirats, *El continente vacío*.

53 *Guanahaní* means "iguana" (Morison, *Admiral of the Ocean Sea*, 233).

54 According to Marco Polo, Quinsay was the greatest city in the world. Like Venice, it was situated on a lagoon and had mansions, towers, bridges, and sanctuaries. It boasted the poetic name meaning "city of heavens." This Chinese city is now called Hangchow.

55 Varela and Gil, 128. "And the captain of *Pinta* said he understood that … the King of that land made war with the Grand Khan, whom they called *Camí*" (Morison, *Journals and Other Documents*, 84–5).
56 Varela and Gil, 122. "And afterwards to depart for another much larger island which I believe must be Japan, according to the description of these Indians whom I carry, and which they call Colba" (Morison, *Journals and Other Documents*, 78).
57 Cibao was a region of Haiti where gold was indeed mined.
58 Some of the other early Spanish cosmographers also realized that the natives possessed highly valuable information. Alonso de Santa Cruz, the unofficial cosmographical advisor to the Council of Indies, whose cosmographical works were denied publication, in his *Islario general* urged discoverers to gather information from native informants whose knowledge he valued over that of Spanish explorers (Portuondo, *Secret Science*, 113–14).
59 Millares Carlo, 2:279.
60 Ibid. "The admiral commanded that some of those Indians be captured by force, so that they would bring them along and *learn from them the secrets of the lands*. They captured seven, not without great protest by the others, and of those seven he chose two who appeared the most honest and respected. The others they let go with a few gifts from Castille, and they let them understand by signs that they were taking the other two as guides and that later they would send them back" (my translation).
61 Millares Carlo, 2:280. "They took from them [the ten canoes that they encountered] two men who seemed most respected by others, so that they could learn from them as well as from the other two from Cariarí, *the secrets of the lands*" (my translation).
62 Coll y Toste, *Prehistoria*, 146.
63 Millares Carlo, 2:277. "There were other people living along that coast who had their ears pierced and the holes were so large that a hen's egg would have fit through, and he named that coast *Coasta de la Oreja*" (my translation).
64 Morison suggests Columbus called it *El Caracol* "probably because of its intricate outline" (*Admiral of the Ocean Sea*, 538).
65 Coll y Toste, *Prehistoria*, 143–4.
66 Robin Kearns and Lawrence Berg, "Proclaiming Place: Towards a Geography of Place Name Pronunciation," in *Critical Toponymies*, ed. Berg and Vuolteenaho, 156.
67 Varela and Gil, 145, 179, 153.
68 Ibid., 158, 176, 179.
69 Ibid., 128, 180, 129.

70 We also find similar parallel structures in the works by Las Casas and Pané. Las Casas's attitude towards and treatment of indigenous toponymy also changed over time, but it followed the opposite trajectory from that of Columbus. In the early pages of the *Historia de las Indias* dedicated to Columbus's first voyage, the Dominican friar used the Castilian toponyms he invented to argue in favour of the Spanish ownership of the Indies. At this stage, he did not yet question the legitimacy of the Castilian toponymy or its relationship to the Taino toponymy. Occasionally, Las Casas recorded both the Taino and the Castilian place names using the same parallel structure Columbus did. However, more frequently he included only the Castilian name. Another instance in which he emphasized the supremacy of the Castilian language was when he defined the native language spoken in the island of Hispaniola, in Castilian, as "lengua desta isla Española," without even mentioning its Taino name.

71 Highfield, "Some Observations on the Taino Language," 167.

72 Millares Carlo, 2:276 (emphasis mine). "Of which, since it was all told in signs, *either the Indians ridiculed him on purpose*, or he did not understand anything except what he wanted to understand" (translation and emphasis mine).

73 Symcox, 221 (emphasis mine). "As Francisco Roldán knew that the admiral now would not be long in coming – or perhaps he had heard of the admiral's arrival from friends in this village that informed him about anything new that happened or because he had spies among the Indians or Christians, and the Indians fly with the news wherever they are – he decided to approach this village with many of his people. And so he came toward the province of Bonao" (Symcox, 80–1, emphasis mine).

74 Varela and Gil, 119. "And then all these Indians began to say that this island was smaller than the island *Samoet*, and that it would be well to turn back, to be there sooner … and so I came about and sailed all this night to the ESE, sometimes to due E and sometimes to the SE; and this to keep clear of the land, for there were very heavy clouds and the weather very oppressive. There was little [wind], and it didn't permit me to reach the land to anchor … And we find ourselves at the SE cape of the island where I expect to anchor until it clears off, to see the other islands where I have to go" (Morison, *Journals and Other Documents*, 74).

4. Heavenly Bodies and Metallurgy in Columbian Toponymy

1 *Puerto de Plata* does not appear in the body of the *Diario* but rather in its margins, in Las Casas's note about the river Martín Alonso: "Este es el río que

dicen de Martín Alonso, qu'está cinco leguas de Puerto de Plata" (Varela and Gil, 192) (This is the river they call Martín Alonso, which is five leagues from Puerto de Plata; my translation). *Cabo de Luna* and *Río de la Fuente* do not appear in the *Diario* but have been mentioned by critics. According to Gil, during his fourth voyage Columbus discovered coasts from Cabo de Luna all the way to Puerto del Retrete (Gil, *Mitos y utopias del descubrimiento,* 184). The dates for when Columbus assigned these place names are unknown.

2 Anna Friedman Herlihy, "Renaissance Star Charts," in Woodward, *History of Cartography*, 3:99.

3 Manzano Manzano, *Colón y su secreto*, 423.

4 Coll y Toste, *Prehistoria*, 209.

5 Ibid., 423–4.

6 Ibid., 425.

7 Varela and Gil, 47. "Ultimately, clearly African names are projected onto the toponymy of the Indies: Cabo do Monte, Cabo Verde, Cabo Roxo, Cabo das Palmas, Río do Ouro, Porto Santo, etc., among others that are evidently Portuguese, such as Valle del Paraíso" (my translation).

8 Seed suggests that a similar Portuguese toponym, *Gold Coast*, relates to the mercantilist discourse: "When the Portuguese writers renamed, they did not pick Portuguese places, but rather the principal economic trade good of an area: Gold Coast, Ivory Coast, Malagueta Coast (after a West African spice)" (*Ceremonies of Possession*, 176). The place name "Malagueta coast" is an interesting example of how a plant (the spice) found in one continent (Africa) resulted in a place name that was later applied to a different plant in a different continent (South America). *Malagueta* (*capsicum frutescens*) is a hot chilli used in Brazil, especially Bahia, as well as in Portugal and Mozambique; *Melegueta* (*aframomum melegueta*), also known as "grains of paradise," is the spice native to the West African coast, namely the countries Ghana, Liberia, Ivory Coast, Togo, and Nigeria. The Portuguese named the coast in West Africa after the spice and later applied the name *melegueta* to the local wild type of chilli in Brazil, which became known as *malagueta*. The coast extending from Cape Mesurado to Cape Palmas along present-day coastal Liberia is called the Grain Coast or Malagueta Coast.

9 In medieval art, golden rays of the sun represent the revelation of sacred truth and gold itself symbolizes Christ, while in Christian churches, gold decorations on the ceilings, walls, and the altar represent rays of divine light. For a discussion of gold as a religious symbol for Columbus, see Milhou, *Colón y su mentalidad mesiánica*, 125–32.

10 Several Columbian place names echo place names from the Old World, including names given by Spanish and Portuguese colonists in Africa and

the Canary Islands. Columbian texts also make reference to European place names inspired by celestial bodies and metals, such as the "ruta de la Plata" in Spain, mentioned in Columbus's letter to his son dated 28 November 1504, as "the easiest route to arrive there [to Valladolid where the court was then stationed] from Seville" (el camino más fácil para llegar allí desde Sevilla) in Spain (Varela and Gil, 511). Columbus's *Punta del Hierro* reflects the name of the most western of the Canary Islands, *Isla de Hierro*, which Columbus used as a point of reference at various times during his voyages. Columbian toponym *Punta de Plata* is an echo of the Castilian *Punta de Plata* (today, the name of a long beach in Malaga), a toponym that is not mentioned in the *Diario*.

11 Morison, *Admiral of the Ocean Sea*, 337.

12 Varela and Gil, 25.

13 Ibid., 126. "Proceeded another league, saw a river not so wide at the entrance, which he named *Rio de la Luna*. Continued until the hour of vespers; saw another river much greater than the others, so the Indians told him by signs, near it he saw good villages of houses. Called the river *Rio de Mares*" (Morison, *Journals and Documents*, 83).

14 The narrative also reflects the relative scarcity of silver: the inhabitants of the islands that Columbus visited during his first voyage possessed only small quantities. Spaniards did not discover significant deposits of silver until 1531 when they found silver mines west of Tenochtitlán (Bedini, *Christopher Columbus and the Age of Exploration*, 466).

15 Varela and Gil, 111. "They bear no arms, nor know thereof; for I showed them swords and they grabbed them by the blade and cut themselves through ignorance" (Morison, *Journals and Other Documents*, 65). Ferdinand Columbus affirms similarly: "Tampoco conocían el uso del hierro, porque hacen sus azagayas, a las que antes nos referimos, de varillas con la punta afilada y endurecida al fuego, armándola con un diente de pez en lugar de con hierro" (Díaz, 111) ("Nor have they anything of iron, for their darts are sticks with sharpened points that they harden in the fire, arming the end with a fish's tooth instead of an iron point"; Keen, *Life of the Admiral*, 61).

16 Varela and Gil, 129. "The Admiral saw no gold on any one of them. But the Admiral says that he saw on one of them a piece of worked silver hanging to his nose, which he considered a sign that there was silver in the land" (Morison, *Journals and Other Documents*, 86).

17 Gil, "Introducción," 27–8. "One can see very clearly that Columbus assigns names to rivers based on the day of the week on which he reaches them, and that on Sunday he does remember not the Lord but the sun, in agreement with the oldest astrological concepts ... At the same time, when one revisits the *Diario*, [it becomes evident that] Columbus himself, his sons, or Las Casas were

afraid that this astrological influence was becoming too evident; therefore, the relevant passages were obscured, and [the names] are distributed in this manner:

Day	River	*Diario*
Monday	Luna	Monday 30 Oct.
Tuesday	Mares	Monday 30 Oct.
Sunday	Sol	Monday 12 Nov."

(my translation)

18 Ibid., 25.
19 Ibid., 27. Slightly confusing is Gil's statement that the two rivers, Río de la Luna and Río de Mares, were named on Monday, *30* October. In the *Diario*, both place names appear for the first time on Monday, *29* October, while 30 October is a Tuesday. However, this minor incoherence, a typographical error, perhaps, does not detract from Gil's fundamental argument.
20 Varela and Gil, 134–5. "All that coast was heavily populated around the river, to which he gave the name *Rio del Sol.* He says that the Sunday before, 11 November, it had seemed well to capture some of the people of that river to take to the Sovereigns to learn our language, in order to find out what there is in the country" (Morison, *Journals and Other Documents*, 92).
21 For a discussion of these authors, see Cañizares-Esguerra, "New World, New Stars."
22 D. Torres Villaroel, *El ermitaño y Torres: Conversaciones Físico-Médicas y Chímicas*, quoted in García Font, *Historia de la alquimia en España*, 281. "Superior astronomy deals with true stars, both fixed and wandering ones, and with their movements, whereas inferior astronomy deals with 'inert stones' which in the vocabulary of alchemists are also called *stars* and which are Sun, Moon, Mars, Saturn, Jupiter, Venus, niter, anthrax, emerald and other stones that do not avoid fire" (my translation).
23 Chaucer, *The Canterbury Tales*, 425 (lines 825–9).
24 Las Casas, *Obras Completas*, vol. 6, *Apologética Historia*, 353. "Of all the things that have been said about this island one can infer that it is very healthy and temperate, as much because of its location in relation to the manners and shapes of the sky as because of the shapes and disposition of the lands themselves" (my translation).
25 Ibid., 353. "And so just as doctors say that in order to understand the nature and the disposition of the human body it is necessary to consider not only the superior and universal reason or cause (that is, the sky or the celestial bodies and their positions and movements), but also the doctor needs to consider inferior causes or reasons (and these are the composition and the disposition of the person). In the same way, in order to know whether the lands are

appropriate and favourable for human habitation, whether they are temperate or of disagreeable weather, healthy or sick, whether they are inhabited or visited frequently or infrequently, it is necessary to have knowledge about the universal cause which is the sky ... as well as the particular or specific causes that have to do with the land and its potential" (my translation).

26 Geber, *Summa perfectionis magisterii*, ed. and trans. Newman, 678.

27 Ibid., 672–3.

28 According to different interpretations, *goanin*, or *guanín*, refers to gold of low quality, gold, copper, an alloy of gold and copper, or an alloy of gold, silver, and copper. It also refers to plates made of one of those metals or alloys that the chieftains wore around their necks (Coll y Toste, *Prehistoria*, 221). Another word for gold was *caona* (Cambiaso, *Pequeño diccionario*, 49). According to Las Casas, *goanin* was made up of thirty-two parts, of which eighteen were of gold, six of silver, and eight of copper: "halló que de treinta y dos partes las diez y ocho eran de oro y las seys de plata y las ocho de cobre" (Symcox, 153).

29 *Cabo de Luna* was, most probably, named during the fourth voyage, eleven or twelve years after the other eleven toponyms in this toponymic cluster were named during the two and a half months of the first voyage; it does not participate in the pattern that Columbus consciously created during the first voyage.

30 Varela and Gil, 143. "He saw on the beach many other stones of the color of iron, and others that some said were from silver mines; all of which the river brought down" (Morison, *Journals and Other Documents*, 101).

31 Varela and Gil, 28. "When one revisits the *Diario*, [it becomes evident that] Columbus himself, his sons, or Las Casas were afraid that this astrological influence was becoming too evident; therefore, the relevant passages were obscured" (my translation).

32 Varela and Gil, 399. "This gulf he named Golpho de las Perlas" (my translation).

33 Coll y Toste, *Prehistoria*, 189–90.

34 According to Morison, *Baveque* "undoubtedly was Great Inagua Island" (Morison, *Admiral of the Ocean Sea,* 262), while Varela states with less certainty, "quizá [fue] Inagua Grande" (Varela and Gil, 134).

35 Coll y Toste, *Prehistoria*, 189.

36 Varela and Gil, 134. "Left the Harbor and River of Mares at the relieving of the dawn watch, to visit an island which many of the Indians on board declare to be *Babeque*, where, they said by signs, the people gather gold on the beach by candles at night, and then (it is said) make bars of it with a hammer" (Morison, *Journals and Other Documents*, 92).

37 Morison, *Journals and Other Documents*, 92; Varela and Gil, 134.

38 According to Morison, the river Río del Sol is Puerto Sama (262). Later explorers, such as Hernán Cortés, also performed the act of naming from the ship. See Scott, "'Ver cosas nunca oídas, ni aún soñadas ...'"

39 Morison, *Journals and Other Documents*, 92; Varela and Gil, 134.

40 Varela and Gil, 189. "the evil works of Satan, who wished to hinder that voyage, as he had done up to that time" (Morison, *Journals and Other Documents*, 146).

41 Varela and Gil, 189. "Thus, lord Princes, I realize that Our Lord miraculously ordered that ship to stay there, because it is the best place of the whole island to make a settlement, and the nearest to the mines of gold" (Morison, *Journals and Other Documents*, 146).

42 Varela and Gil, 189. "And the Admiral says here that the caravel bartered much gold, so that for a lace point they gave good pieces of gold the size of two fingers, and at times of a hand" (Morison, *Journals and Other Documents*, 146).

43 Varela and Gil, 190. "And found that the sand at the mouth of the river, which is very great and deep, was, it is said, all full of gold, and of such quality that it is marvellous, but it was very fine" (Morison, *Journals and Other Documents*, 147).

44 Varela and Gil, 191. "They found bits of gold adhering to the barrel-hoops, and the same to the pipe-hoops" (Morison, *Journals and Other Documents*, 147).

45 Morison, *Admiral of the Ocean Sea*, 309.

46 Varela and Gil, 191. "The Admiral gave the river the name *Rio del Oro*" (Morison, *Journals and Other Documents*, 147). The Río del Oro is the river Yaque del Norte (Morison, *Admiral of the Ocean Sea*, 309).

47 Columbus makes one last quick reference to this toponym in his account of the third voyage, when he discusses the inferior quality of the coloured pearls he had found there (Varela and Gil, 397).

48 Varela and Gil, 134–5 (emphasis mine). "He says that the Sunday before, 11 November, it had seemed well to capture some of the people of that river to take to the Sovereigns to learn our language, in order to find out what there is in the country" (Morison, *Journals and Other Documents*, 92). Here, I disagree with Morison's translation of "en la tierra" as "in the country" as I believe that an alchemical meaning of "inside the earth" is implied.

49 Varela and Gil, 135 (emphasis mine). "Because without doubt there is in these countries a tremendous quantity of gold; for not without reason these Indians on board say that there are in these islands places where they mine gold and wear it on their necks, ears, arms and legs, and the bracelets are very large, and also they have precious stones and pearls, and endless spicery" (Morison, *Journals and Other Documents*, 92). Again, my interpretation of "es en estas tierras grandíssima suma de oro" differs from that of Morison, as I read it as "in these lands a great quantity of gold is buried."

50 Varela and Gil, 166 (emphasis mine). "After dinner a squire brought a belt ... and two pieces of worked gold which were very thin, so that I believe that

here they obtain little of it, although I hold that they are very near to where it comes from, and much exists" (Morison, *Journals and Other Documents,* 125).

51 Varela and Gil, 167 (emphasis mine). "On this day he bartered, he says, little gold; but the Admiral learned from an old man that there were many neighboring islands a hundred leagues or more away, as far as he could understand, in which very much gold was produced; he even told him of an island that was all gold, and in the others there was so great a quantity that they gather it and sift it as in a sieve, and smelt it and make bars and a thousand things of art" (Morison, *Journals and Other Documents,* 125–6). Here, my interpretation differs from that of Morison who translates "en las cuales nasçe mucho oro" as "in which much gold was produced" (Morison, *Admiral of the Ocean Sea*, 291). Instead, I believe that the word "nasçe" – which I translate as "is born," based on the alchemical tradition of the time – is essential for understanding Columbus's thinking.

52 Varela and Gil, 115.

53 Varela and Gil, 165 (emphasis mine). "The Admiral said that he thought that neither in that island Hispaniola nor in Tortuga were there mines of gold, and that they bring little from Babeque because they have nothing to give for it ... And the Admiral believed that he was very near the source, and that our Lord would show him where the gold came from" (Morison, *Journals and Other Documents*, 124).

54 Varela and Gil, 165. "They told the Admiral that in Tortuga there was much more gold than in the island Hispaniola, because it was nearer to Babeque" (Morison, *Journals and Other Documents*, 124).

55 The only two references to *Río de la Fuente* are in Columbus's letter to Miguel Ballester, 21 May 1499. We know from this letter that Columbus named the river *Río de la Fuente* on Española, and that he most probably did so during the first voyage.

56 Millares Carlo, 1:368–9.

57 Ibid., 1:384. "affirming that there was on it [Jamaica] much gold (and I think, by the way, that this is the island that they called during the first voyage *Baneque*, which they mentioned so many times, and here I do not see that the admiral makes mention of Baneque)" (my translation).

5. Iguana and Christ

1 Several of the other place names Columbus invented during the second half of the first voyage still mark the maps today: among them are today's Monte Cristi, Puerto de Plata, Samaná Peninsula, Samaná City, and Cape Las Galeras on the northern and northeastern coast of the Dominican Republic. Though

Monte Cristi today is a town on the coast of the Dominican Republic, it is not related to the *Monte Cristo* Columbus named, which is on the island known today as Isla de Cabras (Goats Island) located at the entrance of the San Juan bay in Puerto Rico, as Varela has pointed out. The aesthetic appeal of Monte Cristi is undeniable even in pixelated photos featured on promotional tourist websites; it must have been truly breathtaking when viewed from the neighbouring island or from a caravel in the sea.

2 Varela and Gil, 186 (emphasis mine). "At sunrise he weighed anchor with a light wind … very good [channel] for coming in front of the town of Navidad … the full length of the reefs, which were large and stretched from Cabo Santo to the *Cabo de Sierpe* which is more than 6 leagues, and outside in the sea [they extend] a good 3 [leagues] … He sailed to the E, on a course towards a very high mountain … and which has the shape of a very fine tent, to which he gave the name *Monte Christo*, which lay due E of Cabo Santo …" (Morison, *Journals and Other Documents*, 143–4).

3 The sixteenth-century Dutch collection of curiosities in Leiden included "a snake from Surinam with Arabic letters on its back" (Schupbach, quoted in Mason, *Infelicities*, 80). Knorr von Rosenroth in 1663 gives a detailed description (in Latin) of the contents of twelve collections in Amsterdam, where he saw the following Americana: a sloth, a club, various armadillos, American iguanas with and without beards, West Indian spiders, a parrot from Greenland, gum form Guayana, American cacao, American duck, American laurel, a Peruvian balsam tree "with the scent of sweet Asia" (Mason, *Infelicities*, 80).

4 "Carta-relación del viaje de exploración a las islas Española, Cuba y Jamaica. Isabela, 26 de febrero de 1495" in Rumeu de Armas, *Libro Copiador de Cristóbal Colón*, 1:495. "There I saw from very close up captured in many places near the bases of the trees various serpents, the most repulsive thing that one has seen; all of them had their mouths sewn, except for the ones that had no teeth" (my translation).

5 The presence of smaller animals such as iguana and the absence of large land animals is explained by the history of the formation of the islands: "All the islands in the West Indies, as here defined, are oceanic, rather than continental. They have not been attached to the mainland in geologically recent time, if at all, and therefore lack land animals larger than the hutia (a small rodent) and the iguana" (Rouse, *The Tainos*, 4).

6 "Había otra caza, según ellos muy preciada y aun según muchos de nuestros españoles después que la gustaron, y ésta fue las que llamaron *iuanas*, propias sierpes" (Millares Carlo, 328) (There was another prey that was highly valued

among them, and even some of our Spaniards liked it after trying, and that is what they called *iuanas*, which are true serpents; my translation).

7 Millares Carlo, 328. "It is as large as a lap-dog, its shape resembles that of a lizard, the patterns on it are similar to those on a lizard, but they are not green or golden saffron but instead brown which make it even uglier. A row of needles crosses its entire back from the head to the end of its tail, which makes it more horrible and frightening. When the Indians went to capture it, it inflated its jowl as do wall lizards, which became the size of a large calf's bladder, and it opened its mouth to show its teeth like a ferocious serpent does (which, as it seems, it is). But it does no harm, and they easily capture it, tie it up, and bring it" (my translation).

8 Las Casas describes the massacre of the indigenous settlement *Higuay* in his *Brevísima* with gruesome details.

9 The full sequence of place names in which *Cabo de Sierpe* appears in the *Diario del primer viaje* is as follows, based on the list of Columbian toponyms provided in the appendix: *Provinçia Caribata* (19 Dec.), *Isla Amiga* (24 Dec.), *Guarionex*, *Macorix*, *Mayonic*, *Fuma*, and *Coroay* (29 Dec.); *Villa de la Navidad*, *Cabo Sancto*, *Cabo de Sierpe*, *Monte del Cristo* (4 Jan.) and *Cabo del Bezerro* (5 Jan.); *Isla Iona*; *Isla Yamaye* (6 Jan.); *Río Yaqui* (8 Jan. [margin]); *Río del Oro* (8 Jan.); *Punta Roxa* (9 Jan.); *Río de Gracia* (10 Jan.); *Cabo Belprado*, *Monte de Plata*, *Cabo del Angel*, *Punta del Hierro*, *Punta Seca*, *Cabo Redondo*, *Cabo Françés*, *Cabo del Buen Tiempo*, and *Cabo Tajado* (11 Jan.); *Cabo de Padre y Hijo* and *Cabo del Enamorado* (12 Jan.); *Isla de Matininó*, *Isla de Goanin*, *Isla de Carib*, *Higuay*, and *Puerto de Plata* (13 Jan.); *Golfo de Samana* (margin), *Río Yuma* (margin), and *Río Tamo* (margin) (16 Jan.); *Golfo de las Flechas*, *Puerto de las Flechas*, and *Cabo Sant Theramo* (16 Jan.).

10 Oliva, *Historia de la invención de las Indias*, 74. "a frightening food to us and among them [the fishermen] highly esteemed" (my translation).

11 Ibid., 79. "There on the table of Anacaucoa they put for the Adelantado some of those serpents that the Admiral had seen in the first port of Cuba, and one of the sisters of Anacaucoa took away all the repulsiveness we had towards it because she invited us to try it with so much grace" (my translation).

12 Scott writes about naming lands from the ship in two articles, "Bernal Díaz, Meet John Smith," and "'Ver cosas nunca oídas, ni aún soñadas ...'"; Morison, who traced Columbus's voyages, also noticed that some of the shapes evoked in the toponymy could only be seen from a distance.

13 Casey explores the subject of depicting landscape shapes in his chapter dealing with landscape painting where he says further: "The painter aims at an

eidetics of the landscape, its inherent form or material essence: he describes landscape as land-shape" (Casey, *Representing Place,* 168). Other examples from the Columbian toponymy that evoke various kinds of shapes include those referring to geometric and geographic shapes such as *Cabo Boto*, *Punta Lançada*, *Isla Llana*, *Cabo Luengo*, *Cabo Redondo*, and *Cabo Tajado*. Shapes resembling animals (*El Delfín* and *El Caracol*) make it into Columbian toponymy as well, and the historian Morison, who saw these places from aboard a ship, describes them: "The next island (now Huevos) he named *El Delfín*, and when seen from the westward it is very like a dolphin fish or dorado, with a large head looking down the Gulf. The largest island, which now bears the formidable name Chacachacare, he called *El Caracol* (the Snail), probably because of its intricate outline" (*Admiral of the Ocean Sea,* 538).

14 Since the thirteenth century, the street was called *Calle de la Sierpe*. The plural form, *calle de las Sierpes*, was adopted towards the end of the eighteenth century, and the final transformation of the toponym occurred in the second half of the nineteenth century, when the article and preposition were dropped and the street became *calle Sierpes*, as it is still known today (*Diccionario histórico de las calles de Sevilla*).

15 Quoted in *Diccionario histórico*, 369: "They named it [the street] after the jawbones which they believed to be of a snake hanging on a tavern wall in the middle of the street, and thus, because of those jawbones, they named the street *De la Sierpe*" (my translation). Another well-known case when the jaws of a dead animal resulted in a proper name is the surname of the grandfather of Álvar Núñez Cabeza de Vaca, the conquistador who was to become famous for his unfortunate adventures in the lands of La Florida. He inherited his name from his maternal ancestor, Martín Alhaja, who showed King Sancho of Navarre a pass marked with a cow's skull. Use of this pass enabled Sancho to win the famous battle of Las Navas de Tolosa against the Moors in 1212, and Martín Alhaja proudly called himself Cabeza de Vaca, a name that he passed on to the later generations.

16 Quoted in *Diccionario histórico*, 369.

17 *Diccionario histórico*, 369. No information about Gil de Sierpe is available in Olson, *Historical Dictionary of the Spanish Empire*.

18 Varela and Gil, 145. "And it had seemed to him like the lands of Campana" (my translation).

19 During the second voyage, Columbus granted all of the place names inspired by Christian saints to islands. This is true for the toponymy of the third voyage as well, with the exception of *Puerto de la Navidad*.

20 Varela and Gil, 137–8 (emphasis mine). "He marvelled greatly at seeing so many and such lofty islands, and assured the Sovereigns that the mountains

which he has seen since day before yesterday, along these coasts and islands, it seems to him that there are no higher in the world, nor any so beautiful and clear" (Morison, *Journals and Other Documents*, 95). And Varela and Gil, 138 (emphasis mine). "Called it *La Mar de Nuestra Señora* ... Some of them [the islands] seem to reach to the sky, and were shaped like diamond points; others have at their highest point a top like a table, at the foot of them very great depth, so that the biggest caravel could lie alongside; all full of trees and without rocks" (Morison, *Journals and Other Documents*, 95–6).

21 Ibid., 172. "He gave it the name *Puerto de la Mar de Sancto Thomás*, for today was his feast; called it a 'sea' owing to its extent" (Morison, *Journals and Other Documents*, 130).

22 On the symbolism of the serpent in pagan religions, see Eliade, *Myth of the Eternal Return*. On the Western myths of language, hermeneutics, and rhetorical eloquence associated with the symbol of the serpent, see Jager, *The Tempter's Voice*.

23 Barreto, *The Portuguese Columbus*, 284.

24 This idea is consistent with Nicolás Wey Gómez's general argument in *The Tropics of Empire* that Columbus sailed south to the Indies.

25 Beazley, "Review of *Alcuni Cimelli della Cartografia Medievale*," (694).

26 Coexistence of such contrasting ideas was frequently found in medieval religious art, as Gertrud Schiller points out: "The antithesis between the Fall and the Redemption, between death and resurrection occurs frequently and the theme of the church in various aspects was linked with that of the Crucifixion" (*Iconography of Christian Art*, 1:107). Other allegorical meanings that relate the serpent with Christ are the serpent being the devil, thus, the antihero of Christ, as well as the serpent *being* Christ, when it is elevated by Moses: "No one has ascended into heaven but he who descended from heaven, the Son of man. And as Moses lifted up the serpent in the wilderness, so must the Son of man be lifted up, that whoever believes in him may have eternal life" (John 3:13–15).

27 According to the definition in the *Oxford English Dictionary*.

28 Mignolo, *The Darker Side of the Renaissance*, 264.

6. Infernal Imagery: Spirituality and Cosmology in the Final Two Voyages

1 In the *Relación del tercer viaje*, the second mention of *Boca del Drago* or *Boca del Dragón* is very soon after the first: "Después que yo salí de la boca del Dragón, qu'es una de las dos aquella del Septentrión, a la cual así puse nombre " (Varela and Gil, 381) (After I came out of the Boca del Dragón, which is the northern one of the two [mouths], which I had thus named; my

translation). In his *Décadas del Nuevo Mundo*, Peter Martyr refers to *Boca del Dragón* only once and he does not even mention *Boca de la Sierpe*. Oliva, in his *Historia de la invención de las Indias*, breezes through the description of the navigation through the *bocas* without even mentioning their names.

2 Varela and Gil, 379 (emphasis mine). "In the southern mouth, which I called *De la Sierpe*, I found that, as the night approached, the North Star was almost at the height of five degrees, and in the other one in the north, which I called *Del Drago*, it was at almost seven" (my translation). The critic Enrique Gandía questions Columbus's authorship of *Boca del Drago*: "En realidad, no sabemos si este nombre de Boca del Dragón lo impuso Colón o lo halló entre los naturales o tiene otro origen" (386) (In reality we do not know whether Columbus imposed this name, Boca del Dragón, or whether he heard it from the natives or whether it has yet another origin; my translation). Columbus's statement in *Relación del tercer viaje* is unambiguous in this regard: "la boca del Dragón ... a la cual así puse nombre" (Varela and Gil, 381) (*Boca del Dragón* ...which I so named; my translation).

3 Díaz, 267. "These mouths are formed by the two western points of Trinidad and two points issuing from the mainland, and they lie almost due north and south of each other" (Keen, *Life of the Admiral*, 183).

4 See map in Morison, *Admiral of the Ocean Sea*, 530–1.

5 Morison states that the Bocas del Dragón "are four in number, formed by the three islands placed like giant steppingstones between Trinidad and the mainland" (*Admiral of the Ocean Sea*, 538). Columbus speaks of one mouth, in the singular, *Boca del Drago* (or *Boca del Dragón*), and he occasionally refers to it in the plural, *bocas*.

6 According to Morison, Columbus named *Golfo de la Ballena* "for no apparent reason" (*Admiral of the Ocean Sea*, 534).

7 Ibid., 529.

8 Gandía refers to the pre-eminence of the dragon as a symbol in the Asian and the American continents: "El dragón era un animal legendario y también mítico, respetado por todo el Oriente asiático: China, India, etcétera. Su leyenda pasó a América bajo diferentes formas de tradiciones y de figuras de serpientes y otros animales fabulosos" (386) (The dragon was a legendary animal and also a mythical one, which was respected in all the Asian Orient: China, India, etc. Its legend was passed to America in forms of various traditions as well as in the shapes of serpents and of other miraculous animals; my translation).

9 According to Gil, "la entrega [del libro de Marco Polo] tuvo lugar precisamente en 1497" (*El libro de Marco Polo anotado por Cristóbal Colón*, viii) (Columbus received [the book of Marco Polo] precisely in 1497; my translation).

10 Barbara Fick, in her *El libro de viajes en la España medieval*, comments that lyricism in these accounts is scant and that instead they aim to be objective and informative: "El viajero medieval ha dejado, en general, observaciones muy objetivas de la naturaleza, y se refiere a ellas solo en cuanto tienen relación a su viaje ... Muy pocas veces, poquísimas, aflora en estas narraciones una nota lírica" (17) (Medieval travellers left, generally speaking, very objective observations of nature, and they referred to them only in those instances in which they were relevant to the narrative of the travel ... Few times, very few indeed, these narratives are adorned with lyrical notes; my translation).

11 Marco Polo's description of a huge serpent may explain, if not the naming of the *bocas*, then that of *Punta del Arenal*. The Venetian traveller includes a notable description of the hunting of a great serpent. (For discussion of the influence of his *Travels* on the imagination of the American landscape, see Rabasa, *Inventing A-M-E-R-I-C-A*, chapter 2.) Marco Polo advises that to capture a gigantic serpent, one should first bury a sharp knife in the sand so that when the serpent slithers over the sandy strip, the hidden knife would cut its belly: "Así, cuando pasa de noche, el ofidio se arroja según su costumbre sobre el arenal y, al clavarse en su impetus el hierro oculto y agudo, muere en el acto o recibe una herida gravísima" (104) (Thus, when the snake slithers at night, it stretches its body over the sandy strip according to its custom and, as the body strikes the hidden and sharp iron object, the snake dies in the act or it receives a very serious wound; my translation). Notable in the Castilian translation is the use of words related to "arena" (sand), including "arenal" (sandy strip) and "arenoso" (sandy), when Marco Polo describes a sandy strip which gives away the serpent's den hidden behind it: "hay allí un paso arenoso" (103) (there is a passage on a sandy strip), and the serpent's heavy body that leaves an unmistakable trace in the sand: "parece que se han arrastrado por el arenal grandes toneles llenos de vino" (104) (it seems as though they have dragged across the sand great barrels filled with wine). Columbus paid attention to these passages and he wrote in the margin of his personal Castilian edition of Marco Polo's *Travels*, next to the description of unusually large serpents found in the region of Carayam, a note that said: "grandes serpientes" (great serpents). Next to the passage describing how to hunt them, he wrote, "manera de cazarla" (way of hunting it).

12 *Livro de Lisuarte de Abreu* (c. 1558–65), the Morgan Library and Museum, New York, shelfmark MS M.525; Georg Braun and Franciscus Hogenbergius, *Civitatis Orbis Terrarum* (*Atlas of Cities of the World*) (1572, Cologne), the Morgan Library and Museum, New York, shelfmark PML 77078.2.

13 1519, Bibliotèque Nationale, Paris, shelfmark Ge DD 683 Rés, folio 3v.

14 The photographs of these artefacts are displayed in the catalogue of the exhibit: *Kunst und Kultur um 1492. Weltausstellung. Expo 92*. Seville: Sociedad Estatal para la Exposición Universal Sevilla 92, S. A., 1992.

15 Gandía writes: "No queremos extendernos a la parte arqueológica precolombina, con el estilo llamado draconiano y otros dibujos que se hallan en las grandes culturas de los mayas, aztecas, chibchas e incas, y exhiben animales que pueden definirse como dragones u otros semejantes" (386) (It would not be worth getting into the subject of the pre-Columbian archaeology, the style that was called "draconian," and drawings left by the great cultures of the Maya, the Aztecs, the Chibchas, and the Incas, in which figures of animals are found that could be defined as dragons, in addition to other examples; my translation).

16 "Duas ligneas statuas, rudes tamen, singulis anguibus ipsis inhaerentibus elevates conspicati simulacra quae colerent arbitrate sunt sed ad decorum ibi posita postmodum didicerunt" (Peter Martyr, 228) ("Having noticed two wooden, roughly hewn statues, each with climbing snakes on top, they thought that might be of worshipped gods; later they learned that the statues were merely ornamental"; ibid., 229).

17 For a discussion on the meaning of "India" which Columbus employed, see Wey Gómez, *The Tropics of Empire*, "The Meaning of India in Pre-Columbian Europe," 159–228.

18 Levillier, *América, la bien llamada*, 1:7.

19 Nunn, in *The Columbus and Magellan Concepts of South American Geography*, describes the parts of the body of the dragon in Enricus Martellus Germanus's map, in which "The Marco Polo section of Asia is the rump and tail. *Mangi* is one hind leg and the *Aurea chersonesus* is the other leg" (45). Whether or not Galvão's mysterious map with a dragon's tail can be identified with Enricus Martellus Germanus's map was a topic of debate between Nunn and Enrique Gandía (*Nueva historia del descubrimiento de América*). In addition to Levillier, who was interested in the dragon's tail as a geographical concept, more recently Paul Gallez studied the antecedents of Martellus's map and demonstrated that the dragon shape can be traced back as far as medieval maps, and even ancient Greek and Egyptian maps (*La cola del dragon*). In his recent study, Wey Gómez explores the meaning of the concept of India for Columbus.

20 Varela and Gil, 195. "The Admiral says further that in the islands passed they were in great fear of the Carib … that the Indians on board understood [no?] more; but that they found a difference of languages, owing to the great distance of the lands" (Morison, *Journals and Other Documents*, 151–2).

21 Columbus states that the Mango province borders with the Cathay province (Varela and Gil, 493).
22 In more rare cases, they were associated with something positive: for example, the Portuguese King Manuel I (1469–1521) adopted the dragon as a regal symbol for his crest.
23 George and Yapp, in *The Naming of the Beasts*, distinguish five basic forms of serpent in medieval bestiaries.
24 Oviedo, *Sumario de la natural historia de las Indias*, 129. "Finally, that these lizards are very frightening dragons based on their appearance: some claim that they are basilisks, but this is not true" (my translation).
25 Varela and Gil, 267 (emphasis mine). "After they entered the one that they needed, the admiral decided to leave the other mouth behind ... which he would later name *Boca del Dragón, in order to distinguish it* from the other mouth where they were at that time, which was *Boca de Sierpe*" (my translation and emphasis).
26 For further commentary, see Rowland, *Animals with Human Faces*, 16.
27 Its Greek name is derived from "both ways" and "to go" (Rowland, *Animals with Human Faces*, 3). The real life limbless lizards of the modern family *amphisbaenidae* are found in tropical and subtropical regions including countries bordering the Mediterranean and they are much less harmful than their imaginary monstrous twin from the medieval bestiaries. The unusual real appearance of these "worm-like creatures" inspired the imagination of medieval authors who wrote: "Their head is rounded and so is the tail, they burrow, and can move in both directions, so that they appear to have two heads" (George and Yapp, *The Naming of the Beasts*, 199–200).
28 Openshaw, "Weapons in the Daily Battle," 19. According to Openshaw, "The theme is spiritual warfare or the battle between good and evil ... is one of the earliest themes to be isolated and emphasized in Western medieval psalter decoration." She also tells us that "the Book of Psalms was perhaps the most frequently copied and consulted book of the Middle Ages" (17).
29 1573, Archivo Nacional de la Torre, Lisbon.
30 Varela and Gil, 372. "Even today I feel the fear in my body that [a wave of water as tall as a ship] would bury the ship under it" (my translation). After retracing the trajectory of Columbus's caravels, Morison describes the currents the latter experienced in Boca de la Sierpe as "the swift tideway," and he attributes them to "a volcanic disturbance" rather than to a tidal bore (Morison, *Admiral of the Ocean Sea*, 532, 537). For analysis of Portuguese and Spanish shipwreck narratives, see Blackmore, *Manifest Perdition*: "The *discurso* as an itinerary that is diverted or undone and represented as such

narratively – the discourse of shipwreck – underlies the axiomatic notion to the writing and reading of shipwreck literature that it is a narrative of rupture, breakage, and disjunction in which the context of maritime expansion plays a critical role" (39–40). Similarly, due to the overwhelming fear of a shipwreck, the paradisiacal discourse in the *Relación del tercer viaje* is ruptured, disjointed, and instead replaced by a new discourse tainted with infernal imagery.

31 Oliva, *Historia de la invención de las Indias*, 176–7.

32 Peter Martyr, 314. "since he began to sail as a child, in no place had he been more afraid then here" (ibid., 315).

33 Díaz, 267. "They named it the Boca de la Sierpe on account of the fright that it gave them" (Keen, *Life of the Admiral*, 184).

34 Symcox, 160 and 175. "Because of this great danger he named this mouth Serpent's Mouth" (ibid., 32) and "the mouth that he called the Dragon's Mouth for the following reason and because of the danger which he had been in there" (ibid., 46).

35 d'Anghiera, *Décadas*, 1:56.

36 For an extensive analysis of this map, see P.D.A. Harvey, *Hereford World Map: Medieval World Maps and Their Context* (London: British Library, 2006).

37 For an informative discussion of this, see Scafi, *Mapping Paradise*. In fact, Scafi reminds us that medieval theologians believed the Garden of Eden, or Paradise, to lie in the East, and thus, in Asia.

38 Varela and Gil, 380. "but rather that it [the Earthly Paradise] is on the top of the pear's nipple" (my translation).

39 Zamora argues in *Reading Columbus* that Columbus's ultimate goal, "marked by such spiritually charged names as Isla de la Trinidad, Tierra de Gracia, and Paraíso Terrenal – is the reconquest of the earthly Jerusalem, understood as the anagogical promise of the Heavenly City. The profound religious symbolism of such names suggests that the phrase 'otro mundo,' which has so exercised scholars of the Discovery, has strong mystical connotations, as it does in the discourses of pilgrimage" (145).

40 Quoted in Scafi, *Mapping Paradise*, 48.

41 Varela and Gil, 380. "Not that I believe that to the summit of the extreme point is navigable ... or that it is possible to ascend there, for I believe that the earthly paradise is there and to it, save by the will of God, no man can come" (translated in Scafi, *Mapping Paradise*, 242).

42 Zamora, *Reading Columbus*, 143.

43 For the eschatological implications of the last place name, see Gil (1977 and 1989) and Kadir, *Columbus and the Ends of the Earth*.

44 Edson and Savage-Smith, "An Astrologer's Map," 14.

45 Ulysses made a voyage to the Mount of Purgatory via Gibraltar and the South Atlantic, which was believed to be located opposite Jerusalem (*Inferno* 26:85). Since no one was allowed there, God punished Ulysses by sinking him. According to Dante, the gates to Hell were located in Jerusalem, at the top of the earth, and Purgatory was at the Antipodes of Jerusalem where you could get from Rome with an angel.

46 "One Pole is always high above us, but the other, / beneath our feet, black Styx observes, and the countless dead. / Above, mighty Draco snakes a course that winds / like a river around and amid the two Bears, / the Bears afraid to dive beneath the Ocean's surface" (Virgil, *The Georgics*, 1.242–6).

47 Woodward, "Reality, Symbolism, Time, and Space in Medieval World Maps," 513.

48 Girolamo Benivieni, *Dialogo di Antonio Manetti*, quoted in Woodward, *History of Cartography*, 3:454.

49 Varela and Gil, 489. "I had never seen the sky so frightening: day and night it burned like a furnace, and it threw down flames with the rays" (my translation).

50 Ibid., 486. "I did not enter the port nor could I because of the storm, the rain pouring down from the sky, the continuous thunder and lightning, and it seemed to be the end of the world" (my translation).

51 Díaz, 267–8. "This mountainous wave came toward the ships to the great terror of all, who feared to be swamped" (Keen, *Life of the Admiral*, 184).

52 *Décadas*, 166. Peter Martyr's full description of the struggle between fresh and salty waters is as follows: "Ulterius aliquantulum per id discrimen procedens, fauces reperit quasdam octo mihiarum, veluti alicuius maximi portus introitum, ad quas aquarum ille defluxus ruebat; *Os draconis* fauces appellavit et insulam ori oppositam *Margaritam*. Ex faucibus autem non minor impetus aquarum dulcium, venientibus salsis occurrens, egredi conabatur ita quod ibi esset inter utrasque undas non leve certamen" (Peter Martyr, *Discovery of the New World*, 314) ("Proceeding a little farther, in the midst of such danger, he found a strait eight miles long, with a mouth of a very wide port, toward which the current rushed; he named this *Boca del Dragon* and the island opposite to it *Margarita*. Now, from the strait a fresh water current just as large was flowing out against the rushing salt water, making for a great clash of the two currents"; ibid., 315–17).

53 Symcox, 176. "They say that the admiral said at this time – even though I did not find it written in his hand as I found the above – that if they escaped from here, they could tell stories about how they escaped from the dragon's mouth. And because of this, the name stuck, and with good reason" (Symcox, 46). Morison also observes that Columbus named the channel *Boca del*

Dragón "because they had escaped, as it were, from a dragon's mouth" (*Admiral of the Ocean Sea*, 550).

54 Symcox, 170. "He wanted then to leave the Golfo de la Ballena, where he was sailing surrounded by the mainland and Trinidad" (Symcox, 42).

55 Varela and Gil, 381 (emphasis mine). "And because [the water] had devoured such a large piece of land, this is why so many islands were created, and they are the testimony of this" (my translation).

56 The popular collection from the Middle Ages entitled *Physiologus* contains moralized beast tales by various authors, among which is the commentary about the violently sexual nature of the female viper's mouth: "Indeed, the woman [that is, female viper] has no secret place, that is, genitals for giving birth, but has only a pinhole. If the male lies with the female and spills his seed into her mouth, and if she drinks his seed, she will cut off the male's necessaries [that is, his male organs] and he will die. When, however, the young have grown within the womb of their mother who has no genitals for giving birth, they pierce through her side, killing her in their escape" (Curley, trans., *Physiologus*, 16).

57 For a discussion of the development of and variations of the iconography of Hell Mouth in medieval Europe, including northern Europe, see Pamela Sheingorn, "Who Can Open the Doors of His Face? The Iconography of Hell Mouth," in *The Iconography of Hell*, ed. Davidson and Seiler, 1–19; and for its development in England, see Schmidt, *The Iconography of the Mouth of Hell*.

58 In the New Testament, Mark describes "unquenchable fire" in Hell (9:43), while in Revelation "Death and Hades were thrown into the lake of fire. This is the second death, the lake of fire" (20:14). Curiously, the Portuguese had already named a place after Hell: *Ilha do Inferno ou Tanariffe* (Baião, *O manuscrito "Valentim Fernandes"*). In a different context, fire also symbolizes God and the divine truth.

59 Varela and Gil, 369, "I entered into such great heat that I thought that my ships and people would burn" (my translation); Varela and Gil, 376, "I found such great heat and the rays of the sun so hot that I thought I would burn" (my translation); Oliva, *Historia*, 175, "they were afraid that their ships would catch on fire" (my translation); Peter Martyr, 310, "the ships almost caught fire" (311).

60 Varela and Gil, 371. "there were great currents that crossed that mouth and they caused a great noise" (my translation). Columbus later concluded that this extraordinary noise was the cause of the deafness of those born in the vicinity of the Earthly Paradise: "la cual agua que sale del Paraíso Terrenal para este lago trahe un tronido y rogir muy grande, de manera que la gente

que naze en aquella comarca son sordos" (Varela and Gil, 380) (that water, which comes out of the Earthly Paradise to this lake, makes a thunder and a very great noise, so much so that the people who are born in that region are deaf; my translation).

61 Varela and Gil, 375. "and that was the struggle between fresh and salty waters: the fresh streams pushed so that the other stream could not enter, and the salty stream pulled so that the other could not leave" (my translation). These were the fresh waters of the Amazon River meeting the salty ones of the Atlantic Ocean.

62 Consuelo Varela also scrutinizes the downfall of Columbus during the third voyage in her book, *La caída de Cristóbal Colón: El juicio de Bobadilla*.

63 My summary is based on the description of events in the *Diario* as well as on Morison's reconstruction of the course of navigation during the third voyage and fourth voyages and on his interpretation of the geographic location of the places mentioned in the *Diario*. For a full description of the navigation during the third voyage, see Morison, *Admiral of the Ocean Sea*, chapters 37–41 (503–72), and during the fourth voyage, chapters 42–9 (573–671).

64 For a discussion of Columbus's devotion to the Holy Trinity, see Milhou, *Colón y su mentalidad mesiánica.*

65 *El Gallo* appears in Ferdinand Columbus (Díaz, 267).

66 Mignolo writes: "las obsesiones personales – que nada tienen de literario en un momento en que lo poético se determina por sus grados de verosimilitud y no de expresión (en el sentido romántico) – se manifiestan en dos direcciones: por un lado en la imaginería, paralela a la comprobación empírica, que le lleva a pensar en las puertas del paraíso, por otro, en la manifestación de la quiebra del sujeto, notable en su cuarta carta" ("Cartas, crónicas y relaciones del descubrimiento y la conquista," 62). (His personal obsessions, which are associated with nothing literary at the time when the poetic is determined by its degree of verisimilitude and by its expression [in the Romantic sense], are manifested in two directions: on the one hand in the imaginary, parallel to the empirical proof, which moves him to think of the gates to Paradise, and on the other hand, in the manifestation of the breaking of the subject, notable in his fourth letter; my translation). He further comments: "Quiebra del sujeto relacionada, obviamente, con el desplazamiento que Colón va sufriendo en el desarrollo de la empresa que él mismo comenzó" (62) (This breaking of the subject is obviously related to the displacement that Columbus suffers from the enterprise which he himself had begun; my translation). On the subject of Columbus's messianic and eschatological outlook, see Gil, "Colón y la Casa Santa"; Kadir, *Columbus and the Ends of the Earth*; and Milhou, *Colón y su mentalidad mesiánica*.

67 The toponym *Puerto Gordo* could be based on the variation of the name of the Virgin, "Virgen Gorda," or it could be an optimistic statement about the abundance of provisions available, synonymous in that sense with *Puerto de Bastimentos*; lack of any further toponymic context limits the expressiveness of these toponyms and leaves them more isolated than many of the toponyms named during all other voyages.

68 Varela and Gil, 489. "I found the way to *Retrete* where I arrived suffering great dangers and obstacles, and I, the ships, and the people were all greatly exhausted" (my translation). Interestingly, the concept of the inhospitable and infertile areas being associated with the marginal regions was established in the Taino language as well: for example, they said that the non-Taino people of Haiti lived in Guacayarima, "which in Arawak meant the 'anus of the world'" (Rodríguez Ramos, "From the Guanahatabey to the Archaic of Puerto Rico," 407).

69 Millares Carlo, 2:302–3 and Millares Carlo, 2:321. "Navigating from this small island [Beata] to come to this port of *Sancto Domingo* is very difficult" (my translation).

70 See the appendix for notes regarding the circumstances of naming the last two toponyms.

71 On the subject of Columbus's voyages as pilgrimage, see Zamora, *Reading Columbus*, 136–51.

72 V.A. Kolve, in *Chaucer and the Imagery of Narrative*, in a chapter titled "The Man of Law's Tale: The Rudderless Ship and the Sea," analyses the images of sea and ship from four angles: literal, allegoric (concerning the life of Christ), moral (telling us how we should behave and avoid evil), and anagogical (regarding the mysteries of death and judgment, heaven and hell and eternity), according to the well-known memory tag: "Littera gesta docet; quid credas, allegoria; / Moralis, quid agas; quo tendas, anagogia" (quoted in Kolve, *Chaucer and the Imagery of Narrative*, 301). Applying the four principles to the image of Custance in a rudderless ship on a tormented sea allows Kolve to draw upon a range of iconographic meanings associated with the tormented sea and the ship tossed on its waves. He discusses the medieval notion of the sea with rising and falling waves as God's instrument through which he expresses his judgment. Lady Fortune is often represented in visual art standing in the sea of life with her wheel and facing a pilgrim. The pilgrim, battling satanic temptations, attempts to rise up. The sea is a symbol of quickly changing fortune: "The waves of the sea present a restless motion – a raising high and casting low – symbolically equivalent to that figured by Fortune's wheel" (326).

73 Physiologus tells us: "when he [the serpent] grows old, his eyes become dim and, if he wants to become new again, he abstains and fasts for forty days

until his skin becomes loosened from his flesh. And if it does become loosened with fasting, he goes and finds a narrow crack in the rock, and entering it he bruises himself and contracts and throws off his old skin and becomes new again. We, too, throw off for Christ the old man and his clothing through much abstinence and tribulation. And you, seek out Christ the spiritual rock and the narrow crack. 'The gate is narrow and there is tribulation on the way which leads towards life, and few are those who enter through it'" [Matt. 7:14] (16).

74 Oliva, *Historia de la invención de las Indias*, 175 (emphasis mine). "Thus exhausted they finally reached a gentle, temperate climate and from the topsails they saw high mountains, the view of which liberated them from the great fear that they had that they could not get a break from the storm" (my translation).

75 *Décadas,* 60 (emphasis mine). "And thus he affirms and believes that *at the top of those three mountains*, which the sailor saw from afar who was keeping watch from the watchtower, is located *the Earthly Paradise*" (my translation).

76 Varela and Gil, 370. "A sailor [Alonso Pérez] climbed up the mainmast and saw to the west three hills together. We sang the *Salve Regina* and other devotional hymns and we thank our Lord. And later … I turned back to the land … after I had named *Isla de la Trinidad*" (my translation).

77 Morison quotes: "He named this land *la ysla de la Trinidad* because he had determined that the first land he should discover should be so named" (*Admiral of the Ocean Sea*, 528).

78 Varela and Gil, 369 (emphasis mine). "Everything came all of a sudden and in such a *disorderly fashion* that no one dared to go below the cover to arrange the vessels and the supplies" (my translation and emphasis).

79 In the book of Revelation, Satan, in the shape of a dragon, destroys the Church in the apocalyptic battle.

80 Eliade, *Myth of the Eternal Return*, 59. The motif of heroes being swallowed by or entering the mouths of great monsters and defeating them can be found in various cultures. They begin as early as in the ancient Etruscan culture: "An Etruscan vase pictures a hero, probably Hercules rescuing Hesione, stepping into the open mouth of a sea monster whose toothy jaws closely match those of the mouth of hell" (Schmidt, *Iconography of the Mouth of Hell*, 51).

81 Columbus named two places during the third voyage after two female saints associated with the dragon, St Catherine and St Margaret: *Isla Margarita* and *Isla Santa Chaterina*. However these toponyms are unlikely to have any connection with the toponyms *Boca del Drago* and *Boca de la Sierpe*. *Isla Santa Chaterina* is likely an echo of *Puerto de Santa Catalina*, which appears for the first time on 24 November in the ship log of the first voyage. *Isla Margarita* is associated with pearls and the toponym *Golfo de las Perlas*,

which Columbus also assigned to the gulf in the vicinity of the *bocas* during the third voyage. *Isla Santa Chaterina* could be a reference to either of two saints: St Catherine of Alexandria and St Catherine of Siena. Catalina was also a popular female name, and the name of Isabel and Ferdinand's daughter, who married Arthur, the heir to the throne of England. However, Columbus did not name the port after the member of the royal family, as he only made a passing effort to honour the main members of the royal family with a handful of place names among the many he invented during the first voyage. St Catherine of Alexandria was tempted by the serpent but, after having visions of Christ, the Virgin Mary, and the saints, was able to resist and became the bride of Christ; St Catherine of Siena, a Dominican patron saint of the poor, protected the faithful from fire and sexual temptations. In "Carta a los Reyes," dated in 1501, Columbus makes a reference to a saint, *Santa Catalina*, who is most likely St Catherine of Alexandria (Varela and Gil, 448). Since Columbus mentions St Catherine of Alexandria in his correspondence soon after the third voyage, her name may have possibly inspired the naming of *Isla Santa Chaterina*.

82 Both mentioned in *O manuscrito "Valentim Fernandes."* According to the manuscript, Infante Dom Pedro ordered that the island be named so in 1445 (Baião, ed., *O manuscrito "Valentim Fernandes,"* 116). Columbus makes reference to *Isla San Miguel* in the *Diario*; elsewhere it is also known as *Insula Sancti Michaelis*.

83 G.R. Crone believes that what the historian Babcock interpreted as an island on Beccario's 1435 map was most likely a "displaced representation of the Gates of Hercules." The legendary "newly reported" islands to which Babcock refers are the Azores. See Crone, "The Origin of the Name 'Antillia,'" 260–1, and Babcock, "Antilia and the Antilles," 109–24.

84 Oliva, *Historia de la invención de las Indias*, 143. "They left ... with greater confidence than Hercules had, and leaving behind them the pillars that he had built they sailed thirty days to the west" (my translation).

85 The first of such coins was found in Mexico and was produced during the reign of Carlos I and Doña Juana la "Loca" (1536–56), while similar coins were produced as late as the nineteenth century.

86 Eliade, *Myth of the Eternal Return*, 11.

87 Díaz, 330. "But the people ... are almost black in color, ugly in aspect, wear no clothes, and are very wild in all respects. According to the Indian who was our prisoner they eat human flesh and raw fish, and pierce holes in their ears large enough to insert hen's eggs; that is why the Admiral named that country Costa de las Orejas" (Keen, *Life of the Admiral*, 234).

88 Ferdinand Columbus, 331 (emphasis mine). "They tattoo their arms and bodies by burning in Moorish-style designs that give them a strange aspect … When they adorn themselves for some festivity, some paint their faces black or red, others draw stripes of various colors on their faces or put on a beak like an ostrich, and still others blacken their eyes. They do this to appear beautiful, but they really *look like devils*" (Keen, *Life of the Admiral*, 235; emphasis mine).

Conclusion

1 One of the longer considerations of such maps is in the *Relación del segundo viaje*. See Varela and Gil, 239–40.
2 "I do not understand how he said above that he had assigned to this bay the name *Puerto María* and now he says that he named it *De San Nicolás*" (my translation).
3 Delgado, 302. "Navigating along the coast Columbus discovered many capes; he named one of them *Del Ángel*, another *Punta del Hierro*, another *Redondo*, another *French*, another *Cabo del Buen Tiempo*, and yet another *Tajado*. Of all these names of capes none remain today" (my translation). Las Casas also expresses repeatedly his frustration regarding the inconsistency in the use of individual place names or the lack of information about the circumstances of granting a particular place name in the context of various place names: "De allí pasaron arriba del puerto del Retrete, a una tierra que tenía junto muchas isletas, que el Almirante llamó las Barbas, y creo que hoy es el que pintan en las cartas el Golfo de San Blas; y cuando no nos catáremos, éstos que hacen cartas les pornán de Sant Nicolás, *según cada día se escriben novedades*" (Millares Carlo, 2:301, emphasis mine) (From there they navigated north from Puerto del Retrete to a land next to which there were many small islands, which the admiral called *Las Barbas*, and I believe that they mark this area today as *Golfo de San Blas*; and it might be that these are the same which they called *De Sant Nicolás* on navigational charts, since every day they come up with something new; my translation). And again: "Tornando adonde quedó el hilo de hystoria en este passo, haze mención el Almirante de munchas puntas de tierra e islas y nombres que les avía puesto, pero no parece cuándo, y en esto y en otras cosas que hay en sus itinerarios, parece ser natural de otra lengua, porque no penetra del todo la significación de los vocablos de la lengua castellana ni del modo de hablar della. Haze mención aquí de la Punta Seca, de la isla Isabeta, [de la isla Tramontana], de la Punta Llana, de la Punta Sara, suponiéndolas. Empero, ninguna cosa a dicho dellas o de algunas dellas" (Symcox, 170) ("At the point where we left

the thread of the story, the admiral mentions many capes and islands and the names that he had given them, but he does not say when. And in this and other things in his itineraries, he appears to be a native speaker of some other language, because the meaning of the Castilian words is not at all clear, nor is his way of using the language. He mentions here the Punta Seca, the Isla Isabeta, the Isla Tramontana, the Punta Llana, assuming that they are known, even though he has said nothing about them or about any one of them"; Symcox, 41–2).

4 Morison, *Admiral of the Ocean Sea*, 601, 383.

5 Michel de Cuneo claims that the admiral named the island in his honour because he saw it first, as he himself claims in his infamous letter. The letter became popular because of the passage in which he describes, in rich detail, his raping of a native woman. It may have been Columbus's brother Bartholomew who assigned the name: "una isleta que los indios llaman Adamaney, que agora llamamos Saona, el cual nombre creo que lo puso el mismo Almirante o su hermano el Adelantado [Bartolomé]" (Millares Carlo, 1:277) (a small island which the Indians called *Adamaney* and which we call now *La Saona*; and I believe that the admiral himself or his brother the *Adelantado* [governor] assigned this name; my translation).

6 Francisco de Bobadilla, appointed as the chief justice and the royal commissioner by the Spanish Crown in the spring of 1499, arrived in Santo Domingo on 23 August 1500, arrested Columbus, and, in October 1500, sent him as well as his brothers Diego and the Adelantado Bartolomé in chains to Spain. For an in-depth study of Columbus's downfall, see Varela, *La caída de Cristóbal Colón*.

7 Morison, *Admiral of the Ocean Sea*, 568.

8 Millares Carlo, 2:301–2. "From which it seems that the admiral did not assign the name to the port that we call today *De Cartagena*, as some have said … I think that Rodrigo de Bastidas and Juan de la Cosa or perhaps Cristóbal Guerra imposed this name as they were the first to discover, explore, and disturb this land" (my translation). In addition to the geographical facts such as the distances between the places, Las Casas bases his supposition on the lack of the mention of the name by Ferdinand Columbus: "que pues decía otros nombres que ponía el Almirante a lugares no tan principales, D. Hernando éste no callara" (since he recorded the other names that the admiral had assigned to places that were not as central, Don Hernando would not have omitted this one; my translation).

9 Millares Carlo, 2:156. "very frequently mentioned *Marañón*; I do not know who or for what reason assigned this name" (my translation).

10 Millares Carlo, 2:274. "All these islands and many bays and places on mainland are now unknown because those who make navigational charts constantly change their names, and this causes much confusion and frequently even results in mistakes and losses of ships" (my translation).
11 The noun in the toponym is spelled differently in different manuscripts: *Bocas* in the version of the *Diario* in Castilian; *Pozzas* in the Italian version and in Ferdinand Columbus's *Historia del Almirante* (Varela, *Textos y documentos completos*, 1982, 300). Based on the toponymic context, both interpretations are plausible.

Appendix: A Comprehensive List of Columbian Place Names

1 Morison, *Admiral of the Ocean Sea*, 239.
2 Bidó, *Voces de bohío*, 142.
3 Millares Carlo, 2:273.
4 Morison, *Admiral of the Ocean Sea*, 254.
5 Varela and Gil, 127. "Describing the disposition of the river and the harbor, which he mentioned above and named San Salvador, [he says] that it has beautiful and lofty mountains like the *Pena de los Enamorados*; and one of them has on its summit another little peak like a pretty little mosque" (Morison, *Journals and Other Documents*, 84).
6 Varela and Gil, 127. "and he saw a cape full of palm trees, and he named it Cape of Palm Trees" (my translation).
7 Varela and Gil, 206. "After that, the Admiral and all the people made a vow that, upon reaching the first land, they would all go in their shirts in procession to make a prayer in a church that was dedicated to Our Lady" (Morison, *Journals and Other Documents*, 164).
8 Varela and Gil, 138. "Called it *La Mar de Nuestra Señora* and the harbor which is near the mouth of the entrance of the said islands he named *Puerto del Príncipe*, toward which he stood in no more than to see it from the outside, until another visit, which he made on Saturday of the next week, as will then appear. He says so many and such things of the fertility and beauty and altitude of these islands that he found in this harbor, that he tells the Sovereigns not to wonder at his praise of them, for he assures them that he thinks he tells not the hundredth part. Some of them seem to reach to the sky, and were shaped like diamond points; others have at their highest point a top like a table, at the foot of them very great depth, so that the biggest caravel could lie alongside; all full of trees and without rocks" (Morison, *Journals and Other Documents*, 95–6).
9 Symcox, 195, 61.

10 Varela and Gil, 145. “And because the tide and currents had set him that night more than 5 or 6 leagues to the SE beyond where he had hove-to at nightfall, and where the land of Campana had appeared” (Morison, *Journals and Other Documents*, 103).
11 Díaz, 117. “The island that he next found, Cuba, he named Juana in memory of Prince Juan, heir apparent to the throne of Castile. Thus he aimed to honor both the spiritual and temporal powers” (Keen, *Life of the Admiral*, 67).
12 Díaz, 117–18. “That country has many streams and lakes, and near one of these they saw a serpent seven feet long and a foot wide in the middle … The Indians call it *iguana*” (Keen, *Life of the Admiral*, 67).
13 Covarrubias, *Tesoro*, 494, 497.
14 Varela and Gil, 154. “At the hour of vespers he entered the said harbor, and gave it the name Puerto de San Nicolao, because it was the feast of St. Nicholas, for his honor; and at the entrance thereof he marvelled at its beauty and graciousness” (Morison, *Journals and Other Documents*, 112).
15 Varela and Gil, 156; Morison, *Admiral of the Ocean Sea*, 283.
16 Varela and Gil, 172. “He gave it the name *Puerto de la Mar de Sancto Thomás*, for today was his feast; he called it a ‘sea’ owing to its extent” (Morison, *Journals and Other Documents*, 130).
17 Covarrubias, *Tesoro*, 497. “The roundness of the earth and its provinces, and the many forces, the great courage and extreme wisdom needed to conquer them” (my translation).
18 Varela and Gil, 187.
19 Covarrubias, *Tesoro*, 214–15.
20 Varela and Gil, 242. “which the Indians call Samaná” (my translation).
21 Díaz, 149. “Bay of Arrows, now called Samaná” (my translation).
22 Varela and Gil, 199. “This is Cape Sant Theramo, and I believe it is the one that they call today Cape of Deceit” (my translation).
23 Cambiaso, *Pequeño diccionario*, 68.
24 Coll y Toste, *Prehistoria*, 212.
25 Ibid., 195.
26 Ibid., 209; Cambiaso, *Pequeño diccionario*, 49.
27 Coll y Toste, *Prehistoria*, 229.
28 Millares Carlo, 1:384. “affirming that there was on it [Jamaica] much gold (and I think, by the way, that this is the island that they called during the first voyage *Baneque*, which they mentioned so many times, and here I do not see that the admiral makes mention of Baneque)” (my translation).
29 Coll y Toste, *Prehistoria*, 189–90.
30 Ibid., 233; Cambiaso, *Pequeño diccionario*, 123.
31 Coll y Toste, *Prehistoria*, 223.

32 Ibid., 239.
33 Cambiaso, *Pequeño diccionario*, 65.
34 Coll y Toste, *Prehistoria*, 211.
35 Ibid., 259; Cambiaso, *Pequeño diccionario*, 124.
36 Coll y Toste, *Prehistoria*, 221.
37 Symcox, 153. "of thirty-two parts, eighteen were of gold, six of silver, and eight of copper" (Symcox, 25).
38 Cambiaso, *Pequeño diccionario*, 49.
39 Coll y Toste, *Prehistoria*, 205.
40 Cambiaso, *Pequeño diccionario*, 80.
41 Coll y Toste, *Prehistoria*, 229.
42 Ibid., 205, 252.
43 Cambiaso, *Pequeño diccionario*, 126.
44 Bidó, *Voces del bohío*, 118–19.
45 Cambiaso, *Pequeño diccionario*, 124; Bidó, *Voces de bohío*, 142.
46 For a listing of sources and spelling variations, see Coll y Toste, *Prehistoria*, 195–6.
47 Millares Carlo, 1:384. "which he named during the first voyage, when he discovered it, *Alpha et Omega*, and which is now called *Punta de Bayatiquiri*, in the language of the Indians" (my translation).
48 Ibid., 1:396. "which is now called *Cabo del Engaño*, and the admiral during the first voyage had assigned it the name *Cabo de San Rafael*" (my translation).
49 Coll y Toste, *Prehistoria*, 212.
50 Ibid., 240.
51 Ibid., 191.
52 Varela and Gil, 236. "I arrived on Sunday … to an island on which was a very high mountain, and I named it [the island] La Dominica in memory of that day" (my translation).
53 Peter Martyr, 226. "Since chance had them run into this island on a Sunday, they decided to call it *Domínica*" (227). Díaz, 178. "because it was discovered on Sunday morning" (Keen, *Life of the Admiral*, 110).
54 Symcox, 155. "or one of the Cannibal Islands which today are called the Caribes" (Symcox, 127).
55 Díaz, 178; Keen, *Life of the Admiral*, 111.
56 Peter Martyr, 230. "They named this island *Guadalupa* [Guadeloupe] because it resembled mount *Guadalupa*, where we honor a beautiful statue of the Immaculate Virgin. The natives call it *Caracueria*, it is the main Carib location" (231).
57 Ibid., 232. "since it had high mountains, [they] called it Montserrat" (233).

58 Ibid., 236. "Proceeding from this place half way into the sea there is an island called *Burichena* by the natives: Columbus named this the island of *San Juan*" (237).
59 Ibid., 232. "The next day, another island appeared, which the Admiral named *Santa María la Redonda*, because it was round" (233).
60 Symcox, 277, 296.
61 Highfield, "Some Observations on the Taino Language," 161.
62 Peter Martyr, 234. "they reached another island, bigger than all the previous ones, and wanted this one named *Santa Cruz*, whereas the natives called it *Ay Ay*" (235).
63 Millares Carlo, 1:368. "The admiral ordered that certain noblemen go ahead with the workers up the mountain range ... and for this reason he named that port *Puerto de los Hidalgos*" (my translation).
64 Ibid., 1:368–9. "Which the admiral named *Río de las Cañas* without realizing that during the first voyage he had named it *Rio del Oro*, when he was at its mouth, which empties into *Monte Christi*" (my translation).
65 Coll y Toste, *Prehistoria*, 221; Millares Carlo, 1:390. "I believe that this is the island that we later called *Isla de Pinos* and this is how it is known today" (my translation).
66 Millares Carlo, 1:390. "*Cabo de Cuba* ... which he had called *Fin de Oriente* and by another name *Alpha et Omega*" (my translation).
67 Ibid., 1:394. "which he named *Cabo de Sant Miguel* and which is now called *Cabo* or *Punta del Tiburón*" (my translation).
68 Symcox, 219. "This was a tiny islet which he called Madama Beata, and which today is commonly known as Beata ... He believed that Beata was an islet that he had called Santa Caterina when he came along this southern coast after the discovery of Cuba" (Symcox, 79).
69 Symcox, 219. "Next to it [La Beata] is another even smaller islet which has a somewhat high mountain range, which from far away looks like a candle, and he gave it the name Alto Velo" (Symcox, 79).
70 Millares Carlo, 2:11.
71 Ibid., 1:394–5. "This must be the land that is now called *De Cathalina*, in honor of a *cacica* (woman chieftain) or woman ruler whom the Christians later met and who rules that land" (my translation).
72 Ibid., 1:369. "Which the Christians, as the time passed, called *Río Seco*" (my translation).
73 Coll y Toste, *Prehistoria*, 210.
74 Millares Carlo, vol. I, 395. "A small island which the Indians called *Adamaney* and which we call now *La Saona*; and I believe that the admiral himself or his brother the *Adelantado* [governor] assigned this name" (my translation).

75 Oliva, *Historia de la inuención de las Yndias*, 41. "Christopher Columbus, Genovese, born in Saona" (my translation).

76 Cambiaso, *Pequeño diccionario*, 28. "This name is not a corruption of the name Savona (the city in Liguria, which claimed for some time to be the birthplace of the immortal Genoese) assigned by Columbus in the memory of his ancestors, as some have believed. *Adamanaí* owes its name to a cacique who had lived in this island" (my translation).

77 Coll y Toste, *Prehistoria*, 182.

78 Ibid., 245.

79 Millares Carlo, 2:302. "At the vespers of St John they arrived at a port of Jamaica, called *Puerto Bueno*, and although it was a good place to hide from the storm on the sea, it was bad for easing thirst and hunger because there was not on it any fresh water nor a settlement of Indians" (my translation).

80 Díaz, 214. "a channel that he named the Boca de las Vacas, which contained nine little islands close to land" (Keen, *Life of the Admiral*, 143). Known today as Portland Bight.

81 Díaz, 214. "This does not seem to be sufficient reason to justify such a name. It was probably assigned because the explorers saw there many manatees which the Europeans believed to be a kind of sea cows" (my translation).

82 Ibid., 195.

83 Cambiaso, *Pequeño diccionario*, 48; Coll y Toste, *Prehistoria*, 209.

84 Peter Martyr, 242–4. "He thought this could be the large outlet of a river and saw in it a favorable and safe harbor; the men decided, therefore, to call it Puerto Real" (243–5).

85 Coll y Toste, *Prehistoria*, 204.

86 Ibid., 237–40.

87 Cambiaso, *Pequeño diccionario*, 96.

88 Highfield, "Some Observations on the Taino Language," 161.

89 Varela and Gil, 370. "I arrived … at a cape which I named de la Galea, having named the Trinidad island" (my translation).

90 Morison, *Admiral of the Ocean Sea*, 529.

91 Symcox, 156. "a cape that appeared to be toward the west, which he named Cabo de la Galera because of a large rock which, from far away, looked like a galley under sail" (Symcox, 28).

92 Ibid., 155. "He named this island of Trinidad, because he had determined to give the first land he discovered that name. 'And our Lord pleased,' he says, 'through his great majesty, that the first sight of it was three knolls joined together. I mean three mountains all at one time and in a single view. His immense power through his mercy guides me,' he says, 'in such a way that he receives much service and your highnesses much pleasure, for it is certain that

finding this land in this place was a great miracle, as was the discovery on the first voyage.' These are his words" (Symcox, 27).

93 Varela and Gil, 371. "They found the ground all marked by certain animals the footsteps of which looked like those of a goat" (my translation).

94 Ibid., 374. "I called this place Jardines because it corresponds to this name" (my translation).

95 Ibid., 379. "the gulf that I mentioned before, which I called *de las Perlas* " (my translation).

96 Symcox, 170–1. "To this Gulf he gave the name Golfo de las Perlas, even though, I believe, there are not any pearls there" (Symcox, 42).

97 Ibid., 165–70.

98 Varela and Gil, 379; Symcox, 160. "In this southern boca, which I called Serpent's Mouth" (my translation) and "Because of this great danger he named this mouth Serpent's Mouth" (Symcox, 32).

99 Varela and Gil, 379. Symcox, 176. "They say that the admiral said at this time – even though I did not find it written in his hand as I found the above – that if they escaped from here, they could tell stories about how they escaped from the dragon's mouth" (Symcox, 46).

100 Symcox, 156, 159, 178. "This is the mainland, which, since he saw only a small part, looked like an island to him. He named it Isla Sancta. He says here that he did not want to take any Indians because he did not want to raise an alarm" (Symcox, 29); "between the two islands (Trinidad and the one he called Santa and afterwards another that he called Isla de Gracia" (Symcox, 31); "Finally, of all of the names that he gave to islands and capes of the mainland, which he knew as Isla de Gracia, none remain or are known today except the Island of Trinidad, the Dragon's Mouth, the Testigos, and Margarita" (Symcox, 48).

101 Morison, *Admiral of the Ocean Sea*, 537.

102 Ibid., 538.

103 Symcox, 160, 154. "He saw near the cape two islets in the middle of another opening which form that cape of the mainland, which he named Cabo Boto because it was thick and blunt, and another cape on Trinidad island which he named Cabo de Lapa" (Symcox, 32); "And some fish appeared that are called *votos*, which are a little smaller than large calves, with heads that are very blunt (or *boto*)" (Symcox, 26).

104 Morison, *Admiral of the Ocean Sea*, 538.

105 Cambiaso, *Pequeño diccionario*, 45.

106 Symcox, 160. "He called one of the little islands Caracol and the other Delfín" (Symcox, 32).

107 Morison, *Admiral of the Ocean Sea*, 538.

108 Ibid., 540; Symcox, 161. "He named it Belaforma, because from far away it must have seemed attractive" (Symcox, 33).
109 Morison, *Admiral of the Ocean Sea*, 545.
110 Symcox, 163.
111 Luzzana, *The History of the Life and Deeds of the Admiral Don Christopher Columbus*, 191.
112 Symcox, 163. "Arriving at the Punta del Aguja, he says that he saw another island fifteen leagues toward the south, running from southeast to north-west, very large and high, and he called it Sabeta" (Symcox, 35).
113 Morison, *Admiral of the Ocean Sea*, 545.
114 Symcox, 170. "He mentions here the Punta Seca, the Isla Isabeta, the Isla Tramontana, the Punta Llana, the Punta Sara, assuming that they are known, even though he has said nothing about them or about any one of them" (Symcox, 41–2).
115 Morison, *Admiral of the Ocean Sea*, 549.
116 Symcox, 177. "Along the lower coast he saw many islands toward the north and many capes on the mainland, which he named: Cabo de Conchas; Cabo Luengo; Cabo de Sabor; and Cabo Rico, a high and very beautiful land" (Symcox, 47).
117 Morison, *Admiral of the Ocean Sea*, 550.
118 Ibid., 551.
119 Symcox, 178.
120 Morison, *Admiral of the Ocean Sea*, 551.
121 Ibid., 551.
122 Ibid., 551.
123 Peter Martyr, 242–3.
124 Díaz, 274. "He stood to the eastward for Santo Domingo, putting in to this port on August 30th. The Adelantado had founded the city on the east bank of the river, where it stands today, naming it in memory of his father, who bore the name Domingo" (Keen, *Life of the Admiral*, 189–91).
125 Symcox, 164. "Regarding the pearls that the admiral says were found in the islands of Babueca, I had never heard about the pearls that were found in the islands of Babueca, which are close to the harbor of Plata on Hispaniola and are lower in the water than any islands, which creates a lot of danger for ships that pass by there, if they are not aware of the danger, and therefore they are called Abre-el-ojo, 'Open your eyes'" (Symcox, 36).
126 Ibid., 177. "The one is called Coche, which means deer" (Symcox, 47).
127 Ibid., 178. "And this is the islet in the area to the north, close to Margarita, which is now called Isla Blanca, which lies eight or nine leagues from Margarita, as I said" (Symcox, 47–8).

128 Ibid., 222. "This province lies some twenty leagues from Santo Domingo, and ten from the Vega Grande, or rather, from the fortress Concepción, which is in the Vega" (Symcox, 81).

129 Bidó, *Voces de bohío*, 113.

130 Symcox, 160. "From Point Arenal, which is at the end of the island of Trinidad, he saw a cape or point on the mainland toward the north, a quarter from the northeast at a distance of fifteen leagues, and this was the one which is called Paria. The admiral called it Isla de Gracia, since he believed that it was a different island" (Symcox, 32).

131 Ibid., 186. "Amerigo himself confesses in his account of his first voyage that he had arrived in Paria on his first voyage, saying: 'And this province Paria was named by them. This is what he says.'" (Symcox, 54).

132 Ibid., 276. "He planned to do more in this year of 1500: to order a fortress to be constructed in the land of Paria for the pearl fishery, from where he could send a great quantity of pearls to their highnesses every year, because their number, weight, and value could not be told. He said that if his provisions had not been spoiling when he discovered the pearls, he certainly could have sent a cask filled with them" (Symcox, 122).

133 Ibid., 164, 177–8. "And they spoke the truth, for twenty-five or thirty leagues from there, toward the west, is the island of Cubagua, of which more will be said later, where they harvested them" (Symcox, 36); "The one is called Coche, which means deer, and the other Cubagua, which is the one I mentioned above in chapter 135, where an enormous number of pearls have been gathered. So even though he did not know that pearls were produced in this little gulf, the admiral appears to have guessed as much in calling this islet Margarita, and he was very near to it, even though he does not say so" (Symcox, 47).

134 Ibid., 177. "the Yuyaparí, through the river that empties near there that today we call Camarí" (Symcox, 47).

135 Coll y Toste, *Prehistoria*, 195.

136 Cambiaso, *Pequeño diccionario*, 37.

137 Symcox, 221–2. "And so he came toward the province of Bonao, where there is a very fertile and cultivated plain, well-populated with Indians and abundant with food and cassava bread, where some Christians had already settled and where afterwards the village of Bonao was established" (Symcox, 80–1).

138 Millares Carlo, 2:283. "The port which we call *Nombre de Dios*, which the admiral had called *Puerto de Bastimentos* because all those regions and the three small islands nearby are full of farmland and maize fields" (my translation).

139 Ibid., 2:283. "a small port, which the admiral named *Retrete*, due to its being narrow because no more than five or six ships could fit in it at once" (my translation). Díaz, 341. "A little harbor that the Admiral named Retrete" (Keen, *Life of the Admiral*, 245).
140 Millares Carlo, 2:287.
141 Coll y Toste, *Prehistoria*, 204.
142 Ibid., 252.
143 Cambiaso, *Pequeño diccionario*, 43; Coll y Toste, *Prehistoria*, 251.
144 Millares Carlo, 2:275. "[Cyguare] must have been a city or a province in the kingdom of the Great Khan, since at a distance of ten days travel from there was the river Ganges" (my translation).
145 Ibid., 2:273.
146 Ibid.
147 Ibid., 2:274. "Because there were on them [the islands] many pine trees, the admiral named it *Isla de Pinos*" (my translation).
148 Morison, *Admiral of the Ocean Sea*, 596.
149 Millares Carlo, 2:274. "The cape which they call now *De Honduras* is the place where the city that the Spaniards called *Trujillo* is or was located" (my translation).
150 Ibid., 2:277. "There were other peoples on that coast who had their ears pierced and the holes were so large that through them a chicken's egg would have easily passed, and [the admiral] assigned to that coast the name *Costa de la Oreja*" (my translation); Díaz, 330. "But the people … are almost black in color, ugly in aspect, wear no clothes, and are very wild in all respects. According to the Indian who was our prisoner they eat human flesh and raw fish, and pierce holes in their ears large enough to insert hen's eggs; that is why the Admiral named that country Costa de las Orejas" (Keen, *Life of the Admiral*, 234).
151 Millares Carlo, 2:277.
152 Ibid.
153 Ibid., 2:287. "Because of all this adverse and diverse weather that the navigators had never experienced before during such a short journey as they did from *Bel Puerto* until *Veragua*, he assigned to that coast the name *Costa de los Contrastes*" (my translation).
154 Ibid., 2:288–9. "The very high mountains that are above Veragua, which the admiral called *De Sant Cristóbal* because the tip of the highest mountain seems to go past the region that has air since one never sees above it any clouds; instead all the clouds remain below and it resembles a hermit's chapel" (my translation).

155 Ibid., 2:301. "From there they proceeded up from *Puerto del Retrete*, to a land near which there were many small islands, which the admiral called *Las Barbas*, and I believe that today they draw them on maps near *Golfo de San Blas*; and if we look, those who make the maps will mark them as islands of *Sant Nicolás* since every day they invent something new" (my translation).
156 Ibid., 2:301–2.
157 Ibid., 2:302.
158 Ibid., 2:302–3.
159 Ibid., 2:321. "Navigating from this small island [Beata] to come to this port of *Sancto Domingo* is very difficult" (my translation).
160 Ibid., 2:274. "In the end, after great difficulties, dangers and indescribable suffering, he discovered a small island which the Indians called *Guanaja*, near which there are three or four more even smaller islands, which the Spaniards later called *Las Guanajas*" (my translation).
161 Cambiaso, *Pequeño diccionario*, 70.
162 Díaz, 329. "A point of the mainland that he called the Caxinas Point, from the name of a tree that grew there; this tree produces fruit resembling wrinkled olives with a spongy core that are good to eat, especially when cooked; the Indians of Española call these fruit 'caxinas'" (Keen, *Life of the Admiral*, 234).
163 Millares Carlo, 2:287. "Above this river there is another one, one or two leagues away, which the Indians called *Veragua*" (my translation).
164 Ibid., 2:289.
165 Ibid., 2:290.
166 Ibid., 2:302.
167 Ibid., 2:319.
168 Díaz, 333–4. "the wind having freshened from seaward and the sea become heavy, such a surf built up at the mouth that one boat was swamped and her crew drowned" (Keen, *Life of the Admiral*, 236).
169 Díaz, 338. "On arrival at the Guayga, which is a river twelve leagues distant from Alburemá, the Admiral sent his boats ashore. As they approached they saw over one hundred Indians on the beach, and these rushed at them with fury, entering the water up to their waists brandishing spears, blowing horns, beating a drum, splashing water toward the Christians, and squirting towards them the juice of some herb that they were chewing" (Keen, *Life of the Admiral*, 242).
170 Díaz, 343. "which is the same name of another place situated between Veragua and Ciguare" (Keen, *Life of the Admiral*, 244).
171 Coll y Toste, *Prehistoria*, 219.
172 Ibid., 257.

Bibliography

Abrams, Janet, and Peter Hall Abrams, eds. *Else/where: Mapping New Cartographies of Networks and Territories.* Duluth: University of Minnesota Design Institute, 2006.

Adorno, Rolena. *The Polemics of Possession in Spanish American Narrative*. New Haven, CT: Yale University Press, 2007.

Akerman, James R., ed. *The Imperial Map: Cartography and the Mastery of Empire.* Chicago: University of Chicago Press, 2009.

Alavez Chávez, Raúl G. *Toponimia mixteca*. Mexico: Centro de Investigaciones y Estudios Superiores en Antropología Social, 1988.

Alvar, Manuel, ed. *Diario del descubrimiento*. 2 vols. Madrid: Editorial la Muralla, 1976.

Anghiera, Peter Martyr d'. *Décadas del Nuevo Mundo*. Vol. 1. Mexico: José Porrúa e Hijos, Sucesores, 1964.

Arias, Santa, and Mariselle Meléndez, eds. *Mapping Colonial Spanish America: Places and Commonplaces of Identity, Culture and Experience*. London: Associated University Presses, 2002.

Arrom, José Juan. "The Creation Myths of the Taíno." In *Taíno: Pre-Columbian Art and Culture from the Caribbean*, edited by Fatima Bercht, Estrellita Brodsky, John Alan Farmer, and Dicey Taylor, 68–79. New York: El Museo del Barrio, 1997.

– "La lengua de los taínos: Aportes lingüísticos al conocimiento de su cosmovisión." In *La cultura taína*, 53–64. Madrid: Turner Libros, S.A., 1989.

Augustine, St. *Expositions on the Book of Psalms*. Vol. 4. *Psalms 76–101*. London: John Henry Parker; Oxford: F. and J. Rivington, 1850.

Austin, John Langshaw. *How to Do Things with Words*. 2nd ed. Edited by J.O. Urmson and Marina Sbisà. Cambridge, MA: Harvard University Press, 1975.

Babcock, William H. "Antilia and the Antilles." *Geographical Review* 9, no. 2 (1920): 109–24.
Bachelard, Gaston. *The Poetics of Space*. Translated by Maria Jolas. New York: Orion Press, 1964.
Baião, António, ed. *O manuscrito "Valentim Fernandes."* Lisbon: Academia Portuguese da História, 1560.
Bailey, Gauvin Alexander. *Art of Colonial Latin America.* London: Phaidon Press, 2005.
Bakhtin, Mikhail M. *The Dialogic Imagination: Four Essays*. Edited by Michael Holquist. Austin: University of Texas Press, 1981.
Barnes, Trevor J., and James S. Duncan, eds. *Writing Worlds: Discourse, Text and Metaphor in the Representation of Landscape*. New York: Routledge, 1992.
Barreto, Mascarenhas. *The Portuguese Columbus: Secret Agent of King John II.* Translated by Reginald A. Brown. New York: St Martin's Press, 1992.
Barthes, Roland. *S/Z: An Essay*. Translated by Richard Miller. New York: Hill and Wang, 2000.
Bartosik-Vélez, Elise. "The First Interpretations of the Columbian Enterprise." *Revista Canadiense de Estudios Hispánicos* 33, no. 2 (2009): 317–34.
– "The Three Rhetorical Strategies of Christopher Columbus." *Colonial Latin American Review* 11, no. 1 (2002): 33–46.
Beazley, Raymond. Review of *Alcuni Cimelli della Cartografia Medievale esistenti a Verona*, by Giuseppe Crivellari. *Geographical Journal* 22, no. 6 (1903): 693–4.
Beckjord, Sarah. *Territories of History: Humanism, Rhetoric, and the Historical Imagination in the Early Chronicles of Spanish America*. University Park: Pennsylvania State University Press, 2007.
Bedini, Silvio A., ed. *Christopher Columbus and the Age of Exploration: An Encyclopedia*. New York: Da Capo, 1998.
Benítez Rojo, Antonio. *El mar de las lentejas*. Barcelona: Editorial Casiopea, S.L., 1979.
Berg, Lawrence D., and Jani Vuolteenaho, eds. *Critical Toponymies: The Contested Politics of Place Naming*. Burlington, VT: Ashgate, 2009.
Berggren, Lennart J., and Alexander Jones, eds. *Ptolemy's* Geography*: An Annotated Translation of the Theoretical Chapters.* Princeton: Princeton University Press, 2000.
Bidó, Rafael García. *Voces de bohío: Vocabulario de la cultura taína*. Santo Domingo, Dominican Republic: Archivo General de la Nación, 2010.
Blackmore, Josiah. *Manifest Perdition: Shipwreck Narrative and the Disruption of Empire*. Minneapolis: University of Minnesota Press, 2002.

Bordieu, Pierre. *Language and Symbolic Power*. Edited by John Thompson. Translated by Gino Raymond and Matthew Adamson. Cambridge, MA: Harvard University Press, 1991.
Boucher, Philip P. *Cannibal Encounters: Europeans and Island Caribs, 1492–1763*. Baltimore: Johns Hopkins University Press, 1992.
Brading, D.A. "The Two Cities: St. Augustine and the Spanish Conquest of America." *Revista Portuguesa de Filosofia* 44, no. 16 (1988): 99–126.
Branch, Michael P., ed. *Reading the Roots: American Nature Writing before* Walden. Athens, GA: University of Georgia Press, 2004.
Brincken, Ann-Dorothee von den. "Mappa mundi und Chronographia." *Deutsches Archiv für die Erforschung des Mittelalters* 24 (1968): 118–86.
Brokaw, Galen. "Ambivalence, Mimicry, and Stereotype in Fernández de Oviedo's *Historia general y natural de las Indias*: Colonial Discourse and the Caribbean Areíto." *CR: New Centennial Review* 5, no. 3 (2005): 143–65.
– "Indigenous and European Discursive Modes in Colonial Mexican Land Documents." *Indiana Journal of Hispanic Literatures* 13 (1998): 105–10.
Cabeza de Vaca, Álvar Núñez. *Los naufragios*. Edited by Enrique Pupo-Walker. Madrid: Editorial Castalia, 1992.
Cambiaso, Rodolfo Domingo. *Pequeño diccionario de palabras indo-antillanas*. 3rd ed. Santo Domingo, Dominican Republic: Ediciones La Trinitaria, 1998.
Cañizares-Esguerra, Jorge. "New World, New Stars: Patriotic Astrology and the Invention of Indian and Creole Bodies in Colonial Spanish America, 1600–1650." *American Historical Review* 104, no. 1 (1999): 33–68.
Carpentier, Alejo. *El arpa y la sombra.* Mexico: Siglo Veintiuno Editores, 1979.
Carter, Paul. *The Road to Botany Bay: An Exploration of Landscape and History*. Minneapolis: University of Minnesota Press, 1987.
Casey, Edward S. *Earth-Mapping: Artists Reshaping Landscape*. Minneapolis: University of Minnesota Press, 2005.
– *Representing Place: Landscape Painting and Maps*. Minneapolis: University of Minnesota Press, 2002.
Certeau, Michel de. *The Practice of Everyday Life*. Berkeley and Los Angeles: University of California Press, 1975.
– *The Writing of History.* Translated by Tom Conley. New York: Columbia University Press, 1988.
Chaucer, Geoffrey. *The Canterbury Tales*. Edited by Winthrop Wetherbee. Cambridge: Cambridge University Press, 2004.
Coll y Toste, Cayetano. *Prehistoria de Puerto Rico*. Bilbao: Editorial Vasco Americana, S.A., 1897.
Colón, Hernando. *Historia del Almirante*. Edited by Manuel Carrera Díaz. Barcelona: Ariel, 2003.

Cook, Karen Severud. "Benjamin Franklin and the Snake that Would Not Die." In *Images and Icons of the New World: Essays on American Cartography*, edited by Karen Severud Cook, 88–111. London: British Library, 1996.

Corominas, Joan. *Diccionario crítico etimológico de la lengua castellana*. Berna: Editorial Francke, 1954.

Cosgrove, Denis, ed. *Mappings*. London: Reaktion Books, 1999.

Cosgrove, Denis. "Maps, Mapping, Modernity: Art and Cartography in the Twentieth Century." *Imago Mundi* 57, no. 1 (2005): 35–54.

Cosgrove, Denis, and Stephen Daniels, eds. *The Iconography of Landscape: Essays on the Symbolic Representation, Design and Use of Past Environments*. New York: Cambridge University Press, 1988.

Covarrubias Horozco, Sebastián de. *Tesoro de la lengua castellana o española*. Edited by Martín de Riquer. Barcelona: S.A. Horta, I.E., 1943.

Crisciani, Chiara, and Michela Pereira. *L'arte del sole e della luna: Alchimia e filosofia nel Medioevo*. Florence: Centro Italiano di studi sull'alto medioevo, 1996.

Crone, Gerard Roe. "The Origin of the Name 'Antillia.'" *Geographical Journal* 91, no. 3 (1938): 260–2.

Crosby, Alfred W. *The Columbian Exchange: Biological and Cultural Consequences of 1492*. Westport, CT: Praeger, 2003.

Curtius, E.R. *European Literature and the Latin Middle Ages*. Translated by Willard Trask. New York: Pantheon Books, 1961.

– *The Discovery of the New World in the Writings of Peter Martyr of Anghiera*. Ed. Ernesto Lunardi et al. Trans. into English by Felix Azzola. *Nuova Raccolta Colombiana*. Vol. 2. Rome: Istituto Poligrafico e Zecca dello Stato, 1992.

Dante Alighieri. *La Divina Commedia*. Vols 1 and 2, *Inferno* and *Purgatorio*. Edited by Natalino Sapegno. Florence: La Nuova Italia, 1955 and 1956.

Darcy, Jean. "Visualizing Discovery: Christopher Columbus's Maps." In *Writing the Visual: A Practical Guide for Teachers of Composition and Communication*, edited by Carol David and Anne R. Richards, 168–82. West Lafayette, IN: Parlor Press, 2008.

Davidson, Clifford, and Thomas H. Seiler, eds. *The Iconography of Hell*. Kalamazoo, MI: Medieval Institute Publications, Western Michigan University, 1992.

Deagan, Kathleen, and José María Cruxent. *Columbus's Outpost among the Taínos: Spain and America at La Isabella, 1493–1498*. New Haven, CT: Yale University Press, 2002.

Delacampagne, Ariane, and Christian Delacampagne. *Here Be Dragons: A Fantastic Bestiary*. Princeton: Princeton University Press, 2003.

Díaz. See Colón, Hernando.

Di Camillo, Ottavio. *El humanismo castellano del siglo XV*. Valencia: Fernando Torres, 1976.
Diccionario histórico de las calles de Sevilla. Vol. 2. Edited by Antonio Collantes de Terán Sánchez, Josefina Cruz, et al. Seville: Consejería de Obras Públicas y Transportes, Exemo Ayuntamiento de Sevilla, 1993.
Eco, Umberto. *Serendipities: Language and Lunacy*. Translated by William Weaver. New York: Columbia University Press, 1998.
Edson, Evelyn. *Mapping Time and Space: How Medieval Mapmakers Viewed Their World*. London: British Library, 1997.
Edson, Evelyn, and Emilie Savage-Smith. "An Astrologer's Map: A Relic of Late Antiquity." *Imago Mundi* 52 (2000): 7–29.
Eliade, Mircea. *The Forge and the Crucible*. Chicago: University of Chicago Press, 1978.
– *The Myth of the Eternal Return: or, Cosmos and History*. Translated by Willard R. Trask. Princeton: Princeton University Press, 1954.
Elliott, J.H. *The Old World and the New: 1492–1650*. Cambridge: Cambridge University Press, 1970.
Evans, Jonathan. "Dragons, Texts, and History." *Semiotica* 59, no. 3–4 (1986): 303–28.
Fernández de Oviedo y Valdés, Gonzalo. *Historia general y natural de las Indias*. Bogota: Instituto Caro y Cuervo, 1995.
– *Sumario de la natural historia de las Indias*. Edited by Manuel Ballesteros. Madrid: Historia 16, 1986.
Fernández de Palencia, Alfonso. *Universal vocabulario en latín y romance*. Madrid: Comisión Permanente de la Asociación de Academias de la Lengua Española, 1967.
Fick, Barbara W. *El libro de viajes en la España medieval*. Santiago de Chile: Editorial Universitaria, 1976.
Flint, Valerie. *The Imaginative Landscape of Christopher Columbus*. Princeton: Princeton University Press, 1992.
– "The Medieval World of Christopher Columbus." *Parergon* 12, no. 2 (1995): 9–27.
Foucault, Michel. *Archaeology of Knowledge*. New York: Pantheon Books, 1972.
– *The Order of Things: An Archaeology of the Human Sciences*. New York: Vintage Books, 1994.
Galarza, Joaquín. *Estudios de escritura indígena tradicional (azteca-náhuatl)*. Mexico: Archivo General de la Nación, 1979.
Gallez, Paul. *La cola del dragón: América del Sur en los mapas antiguos, medievales y renacentistas*. Bahía Blanca, Argentina: Instituto Patagónico, 1990.

Gandía, Enrique. *Nueva historia del descubrimiento de América*. Buenos Aires: Universidad del Museo Social Argentino, 1989.

García Berrio, Antonio. *Teoría de la literatura: La construcción del significado poético*. Madrid: Cátedra, 1989.

García Font, J. *Historia de la alquimia en España*. Barcelona: Creación y Realización Editorial, S.L., n.d.

Geber. *Summa perfectionis magisterii*. Edited and translated by William R. Newman. New York: E.J. Brill, 1991.

Genette, Gérard. *Mimologics*. Translated by Thaïs E. Morgan. Lincoln: University of Nebraska, 1995.

George, Wilma, and Brunsdon Yapp. *The Naming of the Beasts: Natural History in the Medieval Bestiary*. London: Ebenezer Baylis & Son, 1991.

Gerbi, Antonello. *The Dispute of the New World: The History of a Polemic, 1750–1900*. Revised and enlarged edition. Translated by Jeremy Moyle. Pittsburgh: University of Pittsburgh Press, 1973.

Giamatti, Bartlett A. *The Earthly Paradise and the Renaissance Epic*. Princeton: Princeton University Press, 1966.

Gil, Juan. "Colón y la Casa Santa." *Historiografía y bibliografía americanistas* 21 (1977): 125–35.

– "Introducción." In *Cristóbal Colón: Textos y documentos completos*, edited by Consuelo Varela and Juan Gil, 15–79. 3rd ed. Madrid: Alianza, 2003.

– *Mitos y utopías del descubrimiento*. Vol. 1, *Colón y su tiempo*. Madrid: Alianza Editorial, 1989.

– "Pedro Mártir de Anglería, intérprete de la cosmografía colombina." *Anuario de estudios americanos* 39 (1982): 487–502.

Gil, Juan, and Consuelo Varela. *Cartas de particulares a Colón y relaciones coetáneas*. Madrid: Alianza Editorial, 1984.

González Echevarría, Roberto. "Garcilaso y Garcilaso." *Hofstra Hispanic Review: Revista de literaturas y culturas hispánicas* 1, no. 1 (2005): 15–27.

– *Myth and Archive: A Theory of Latin American Narrative*. Durham, NC: Duke University Press, 1998.

Greenblatt, Stephen. *Marvelous Possessions: The Wonder of the New World*. Chicago: University of Chicago Press, 1991.

Greene, Ronald. *Unrequited Conquests: Love and Empire in the Colonial Americas*. Chicago: University of Chicago Press, 1999.

Gregory, Derek. *Geographical Imaginations*. Cambridge, MA: Blackwell, 1994.

Gruzinski, Serge. *Images at War: Mexico from Columbus to Blade Runner (1492–2019)*. Translated by Heather MacLean. Durham and London: Duke University Press, 2001.

– *The Mestizo Mind: The Intellectual Dynamics of Colonization and Globalization.* New York and London: Routledge, 2002.

Guadalupi, Gianni. *Land of the Bible: Places and Stories.* New York: Barnes and Noble, 2003.

Hallock, Thomas, Ivo Kamps, and Karen L. Raber, eds. *Early Modern Ecostudies: From the Florentine Codex to Shakespeare.* New York: Palgrave Macmillan, 2008.

Hanke, Lewis. *Aristotle and the American Indians.* London: Hollis & Carter, 1959.

– *The Spanish Struggle for Justice in the Conquest of America.* Philadelphia: University of Pennsylvania Press, 1949.

Harley, J.B., and David Woodward, eds. *The History of Cartography.* Vol. 1. *Cartography in Prehistoric, Ancient, and Medieval Europe and the Mediterranean.* Chicago: University of Chicago Press, 1987.

Hassig, Debra. *Medieval Bestiaries: Text, Image, Ideology.* New York: Cambridge University Press, 1995.

Highfield, Arnold R. "Some Observations on the Taino Language." In *The Indigenous People of the Caribbean*, edited by Samuel M. Wilson, 154–68. Gainsville: University Press of Florida, 1997.

Horsfall, Nicholas. "The Poetics of Toponymy." *Literary Imagination: Review of the Association of Literary Scholars and Critics* 4, no. 3 (2002): 305–17.

Hulme, Peter. *Colonial Encounters: Europe and the Native Caribbean, 1492–1797.* London and New York: Methuen, 1986.

Isidore. *Etymologiae.* Edited by Wallace Martin Lindsay. 2 vols. Oxford: Clarendon Press, 1911.

Jacob, Christian. *The Sovereign Map: Theoretical Approaches in Cartography throughout History.* Edited by Ed Dahl. Translated by Tom Conley. Chicago: University of Chicago Press, 2006.

Jager, Eric. *The Tempter's Voice: Language and the Fall in Medieval Literature.* Ithaca, NY: Cornell University Press, 1993.

Jáuregui, Carlos A. *Canibalia: Canibalismo, calibanismo, antropofagia cultural y consumo en América Latina.* Madrid: Iberoamericana; Frankfurt: Vervuert, 2008.

Jiménez, Antonio Núñez. *Colón, Cuba y el tabaco.* Madrid: Tabacalera, 1992.

Jung, C.G. *The Collected Works of C.G. Jung.* Vol. 13, *Alchemical Studies.* Translated by R.F.C. Hull. Bollingen Series 20. Princeton: Princeton University Press, 1967.

Kadir, Djelal. *Columbus and the Ends of the Earth: Europe's Prophetic Rhetoric as Conquering Ideology.* Berkeley: University of California Press, 1992.

Kagan, Richard L. *Urban Images of the Hispanic World, 1493–1793.* New Haven, CT: Yale University Press, 2000.

Katchor, Ben. "Literary Legends: The Realm of the Literary Map." *Civilization* (February / March 2000): 66–71.

Keegan, William, and Lisabeth A. Carlson. *Talking Taíno: Essays on Caribbean Natural History from a Native Perspective*. Tuscaloosa: University of Alabama Press, 2008.

Keen, Benjamin, trans. and ed. *The Life of the Admiral Christopher Columbus by His Son Ferdinand.* 2nd ed. New Brunswick, NJ: Rutgers University Press, 1992.

Kolve, V.A. *Chaucer and the Imagery of Narrative: The First Five Canterbury Tales*. Stanford: Stanford University Press, 1984.

Kripke, Saul. *Naming and Necessity*. Cambridge, MA: Harvard University Press, 1981.

Kunst und Kultur um 1492. Weltausstellung. Expo 92. Seville: Sociedad Estatal para la Exposición Universal Sevilla 92, S.A., 1992.

Las Casas, Bartolomé de. *Las Casas on Columbus: The Third Voyage.* Edited by Geoffrey Symcox and Jesús Carrillo. Translated by Michael Hammer and Blair Sullivan. Repertorium Columbianum 11. Turnhout: Brepols, 2001.

– *Historia de las Indias*. Edited by Agustín Millares Carlo. Preliminary study by Lewis Hanke. 3 vols. Mexico: Fondo de Cultura Económica, 1951.

– *Obras completas*. Vol. 6, *Apologética Historia Sumaria I*. Edited by Paulino Castaneda Delgado. Madrid: Alianza Editorial, 1992.

Le Goff, Jacques. *Your Money or Your Life: Economy and Religion in the Middle Ages*. Translated by Patricia Ranum. New York: Zone Books, 1988.

Leonard, Irving A. *Los libros del conquistador*. Mexico: Fondo de cultura económica, 1953.

León Pinelo, Antonio de, ed. *Recopilación de las Indias*. 2 vols. Mexico: Miguel Angel Porrua, 1992.

León-Portilla, Miguel, ed. *The Broken Spears: The Aztec Account of the Conquest of Mexico*, Boston: Beacon Press, 1962.

Levillier, Roberto. *América, la bien llamada*. Vol. 1, *La conquista de occidente*. Buenos Aires: Editorial Guillermo Kraft, 1948.

Lévi-Strauss, Claude. *The Raw and the Cooked: Mythologiques*. Vol. 1. Chicago: University of Chicago Press, 1983.

Lima, Robert. "The Mouth of Hell: The Iconography of Damnation on the Stage in the Middle Ages." In *European Iconography: East and West*. Selected Papers of the Szeged International Conference June 9–12, 1993, edited by György E. Szőnyi, 35–48. New York: E.J. Brill, 1996.

Lind, Ivan. *De Portugal ao Brasil: Um pequeno estudo de toponímia brasileira*, Lisbon: Casa Portuguesa, 1963.

López Pérez, Miguel. *Asclepio renovado: Alquimia y medicina en la España moderna (1500–1700)*. Madrid: Ediciones Corona Borealis, 2003.

Luzzana, Ilaria Caraci, ed. *The History of the Life and Deeds of the Admiral Don Christopher Columbus Attributed to His Son Fernando Colón*. Translated by Geoffrey Symcox and Blair Sullivan. Turnhout: Brepols, 2004.

MacCormack, Sabine. "Limits of Understanding: Perceptions of Greco-Roman and Amerindian Paganism in Early Modern Europe." In *America in European Consciousness: 1493–1750*, edited by Karen Ordahl Kupperman, 79–129. Chapel Hill: University of North Carolina Press, 1995.

Mâle, Émile. *The Gothic Image: Religious Art in France of the Thirteenth Century*. New York: Harper & Row, 1972.

– *Religious Art from the Twelfth to the Eighteenth Century*. New York: Pantheon Books, 1949.

Mann, Charles C. *1491: New Revelations of the Americas before Columbus*. New York: Vintage, 2005.

Manzano Manzano, Juan. *Colón y su secreto*. Madrid: Ediciones Cultura Hispánica, 1976.

Marañón, Gregorio. "Ruiseñores en el mar." Opening essay in *Diario de Colón* by Christopher Columbus and Bartolomé de Las Casas. Madrid: Instituto de Cultura Hispánica, 1968.

Marrero-Fente, Raúl. *Al margen de la tradición: Relaciones entre la literatura colonial y peninsular en los siglos XV, XVI y XVII*. Madrid: Editorial Fundamentos, 1999.

– *La poética de la ley en las Capitulaciones de Sante Fe*. Madrid: Editorial Trotta, 2000.

Mason, Peter. *Infelicities: Representations of the Exotic*. Baltimore: Johns Hopkins University Press, 1998.

Mayers, Kathryn M. *Visions of Empire in Colonial Spanish American Ekphrastic Writing*. Lewisburg, PA: Bucknell University Press, 2012.

Mazín Gómez, Oscar, ed. *México y el mundo hispánico*. Zamora, Michoacán: El Colegio de Michoacán, 2000.

Mazzotti, José Antonio. *Agencias criollas: La ambigüedad "colonial" en las letras hispanoamericanas*. Pittsburgh: Instituto Internacional de Literatura Iberoamericana, 2000.

– *Coros mestizos del Inca Garcilaso: Resonancias andinas*. Lima: Fondo de Cultura Económica, 1996.

Menéndez Pidal, Ramón. *La lengua de Cristóbal Colón: El estilo de Santa Teresa y otros estudios sobre el siglo XVI*. 6th ed. Madrid: Espasa-Calpe, 1978.

Mignolo, Walter D. "Cartas, crónicas y relaciones del descubrimiento y la conquista." In *Historia de la literatura hispanoamericana*. Vol. 1, *Época colonial*, edited by Luis Íñigo Madrigal, 57–116. Madrid: Cátedra, 1998.

– *The Darker Side of the Renaissance: Literacy, Territoriality, and Colonization*. Ann Arbor: University of Michigan Press, 1995.

Milani, Virgil I. *The Written Language of Christopher Columbus.* Forum Italicum, Supplement. New York: State University of New York at Buffalo, 1973.

Milhou, Alain. *Colón y su mentalidad mesiánica en el ambiente franciscanista español.* Valladolid: Casa Museo de Colón, 1983.

Millares Carlo. See Las Casas, Bartolomé de, *Historia de las Indias.*

Morison, Samuel Eliot. *The Admiral of the Ocean Sea.* Boston: Little, Brown and Company, 1942.

– trans. and ed. *Journals and Other Documents on the Life and Voyages of Christopher Columbus.* New York: Heritage Press, 1963.

Mundy, Barbara E. *The Mapping of New Spain: Indigenous Cartography and the Maps of the* Relaciones Geograficas. Chicago: University of Chicago Press, 1996.

Nader, Helen, and Luciano Formisano, eds. *The Book of Privileges Issued to Christopher Columbus by King Fernando and Queen Isabel 1492–1502.* Berkeley: University of California Press, 1996.

Nebrija, Antonio de. *Gramática Castellana.* Edited by José Ibañez Martín. Madrid: La Junta del Centenario, 1946.

Nunn, George E. *The Columbus and Magellan Concepts of South American Geography.* Glenside, PA: privately printed, 1932.

O'Gorman, Edmundo. *The Invention of America: An Inquiry into the Historical Nature of the New World and the Meaning of Its History.* Bloomington: Indiana University Press, 1961.

Oliva, Fernán Pérez de. *Historia de la invención de las Indias: Historia de la Conquista de la Nueva España.* Edited by Pedro Ruíz Pérez. Textos e Instrumentos, no. 29. Cordoba: Universidad de Córdoba, n.d.

Oliva, Hernán Pérez de. *Historia de la inuención de las Yndias.* Edited by José Juan Arrom. Bogota: Instituto Caro y Cuervo, 1965.

Olson, James S. *Historical Dictionary of the Spanish Empire, 1402–1975.* New York: Greenwood Press, 1992.

Openshaw, Kathleen M. "Weapons in the Daily Battle: Images of the Conquest of Evil in the Early Medieval Psalter." *The Art Bulletin* 75, no. 1 (1993): 17–38.

Oviedo. See Fernández de Oviedo y Valdés, Gonzalo.

Padrón, Ricardo. *The Spacious Word: Cartography, Literature, and Empire in Early Modern Spain.* Chicago: University of Chicago Press, 2004.

Pagden, Anthony. *The Fall of Natural Man: The American Indian and the Origins of Comparative Ethnology.* Cambridge: Cambridge University Press, 1982.

Pagels, Elaine. *Adam, Eve, and the Serpent.* New York: Vintage Books, 1989.

Paiewonsky, Michael. *Conquest of Eden, 1493–1515: Other Voyages of Columbus; Guadeloupe, Puerto Rico, Hispaniola, Virgin Islands.* Rome: Mapes Monde Editore, 1991.

Pané, Fray Ramón. *Relación acerca de las antigüedades de los indios*. Edited by José Juan Arrom. Mexico: Siglo Veintiuno Editores, 1974.

Panofsky, Erwin. *Studies in Iconology: Humanistic Themes in the Art of the Renaissance*. New York: Icon Editions, 1939.

Pastor, Beatriz. *Discursos narrativos de la conquista: Mitificación y emergencia*. 2nd ed. Hanover: Ediciones del Norte, 1988.

Patai, Raphael. *The Jewish Achemists: A History and Source Book*. Princeton: Princeton University Press, 1994.

Pelikan, Jaroslav. *Jesus throughout the Centuries: His Place in the History of Culture*. New Haven, CT: Yale University Press, 1985.

– *Mary throughout the Centuries: Her Place in the History of Culture*. New Haven, CT: Yale University Press, 1996.

Pérez de Guzman, Juan. "Sobre el nombre de América y los demás que se dieron a las tierras occidentales descubiertas por Cristóbal Colón y los españoles." *El Centenario* 2 (1892): 249–69.

Pérez de Tudela y Bueso, Juan. *Mirabilis in altis*. Madrid: Consejo Superior de Investigaciones Científicas, 1983.

Peter Martyr. See Anghiera, Peter Martyr d'.

Petersen, Ronald H. *New World Botany: Columbus to Darwin*. Konigstein, Germany: A.R.G. Gantner Verlag, 2001.

Physiologus. Translated by Michael J. Curley. Austin: University of Texas Press, 1979.

Pistarino, Geo. *Cristoforo Colombo: L'enigma del criptograma*. Genoa: Accademia Ligure di Scienze e Lettere, 1990.

Plato. *The Collected Dialogues*. Edited by Edith Hamilton and Huntington Cairns. Princeton: Princeton University Press, 1961.

Pliny the Elder. *Natural History*. Vol. 1. Cambridge, MA: Harvard University Press, 1949–62.

Polo, Marco. *El libro de Marco Polo anotado por Cristóbal Colón: El libro de Marco Polo versión de Rodrigo de Santaella*. Edited by Juan Gil. Madrid: Alianza Editorial, 1987.

Portuondo, María M. *Secret Science: Spanish Cosmography and the New World*. Chicago: University of Chicago Press, 2009.

Potter, Jonathan. *Collecting Antique Maps: An Introduction to the History of Cartography*. London: Jonathan Potter, 1988.

Pratt, Mary Louise. *Imperial Eyes: Travel Writing and Transculturation*. New York: Routledge, 1992.

Puerto Sarmiento, Francisco Javier. "La alquimia española durante el siglo XVI: Los manuscritos alquímicos seudolulianos conservados en la Biblioteca Nacional de Madrid." In *América y la España del siglo XVI*, edited by

Francisco de Solano and Fermín de Pino, 1:253–71. Madrid: Instituto Fernández de Oviedo de Historia de América, 1982.

Rabasa, José. *Inventing A-M-E-R-I-C-A: Spanish Historiography and the Formation of Eurocentrism*. Norman: University of Oklahoma Press, 1993.

Ramos Pérez, Demetrio. *Las variaciones ideológicas en torno al descubrimiento de América: Pedro Mártir de Anglería y su mentalidad*. Valladolid: Seminario Americanista de la Universidad de Valladolid, 1981–2.

Ramsay, Raymond H. *No Longer on the Map: Discovering Places that Never Were*. New York: Viking Press, 1972.

Read, John. *Prelude to Chemistry*. London: G. Bell & Sons, 1939.

Ricoeur, Paul. *The Symbolism of Evil.* Translated by Emerson Buchanan. Boston: Beacon Press, 1967.

Rivera-Barnes, Beatriz, and Jerry Hoeg. *Reading and Writing the Latin American Landscape*. New York: Palgrave Macmillan, 2009.

Rodríguez, Ileana. *Transatlantic Topographies: Islands, Highlands, Jungles*. Minneapolis: University of Minnesota Press, 2004.

Rodríguez Ramos, Reniel. "From the Guanahatabey to the Archaic of Puerto Rico: The Nonevident Evidence." *Ethnohistory* 55, no. 3 (2008): 393–415.

Rouse, Irving. *The Tainos: Rise and Decline of the People Who Greeted Columbus*. New Haven, CT: Yale University Press, 1992.

Roux, Rodolfo R. de. *Cómo se legitima una Conquista: Fe y Derecho en la conquista española de América*. Bogota: Editorial Nueva América, 1998.

Rowland, Beryl. *Animals with Human Faces: A Guide to Animal Symbolism*. Knoxville: University of Tennessee Press, 1973.

Ruiz Pérez, Pedro, ed. *Gramática y humanism: Perspectivas del Renacimiento Español*. Madrid: Ediciones Libertarias, 1993.

Rumeu de Armas, Antonio. *Libro copiador de Cristóbal Colón: Correspondencia inédita con los Reyes católicos sobre los viajes a América*. Madrid: Testimonio Compañía Editorial, 1989.

– *Nueva luz sobre las Capitulaciones de Santa Fe de 1492 concertadas entre los Reyes Católicos y Cristóbal Colón*. Madrid: Consejo Superior de Investigaciones Científicas, 1985.

Russell, Jeffrey Burton. *Medieval Society.* New York: John Wiley & Sons, 1968.

Sale, Kirkpatrick. *The Conquest of Paradise: Christopher Columbus and the Columbian Legacy*. New York: Alfred A. Knopf, 1990.

Sanz, Carlos. *El nombre América: Libros y mapas que lo impusieron*. Madrid: Suarez, 1959.

Scafi, Alessandro. *Mapping Paradise: A History of Heaven on Earth*. Chicago: University of Chicago Press, 2006.

Schiller, Gertrud. *Iconography of Christian Art*. Vols 1 and 2. Translated by Janet Seligman. Greenwich: New York Graphic Society, 1969.

Schmidt, Gary D. *The Iconography of the Mouth of Hell: Eighth-Century Britain to the Fifteenth Century*. London: Associated University Presses, 1995.

Scott, Nina. "Bernal Díaz, Meet John Smith." *Américas* 33, no. 6–7 (1981): 32–9.

– '"Ver cosas nunca oídas, ni aún soñadas...': Bernal Díaz's Initial Impressions of Mexico." Special issue, *El paisaje en la literatura hispánica. Cuadernos de ALDEEU* 1, no. 2–3 (1983): 469–79.

Seed, Patricia. *Ceremonies of Possession in Europe's Conquest of the New World, 1492–1640*. New York: Cambridge University Press, 1998.

Sluyter, Andrew. *Colonialism and Landscape: Postcolonial Theory and Applications*. New York: Rowman & Littlefield, 2002.

Smith, Pamela H., and Paula Findlen, eds. *Merchants and Marvels: Commerce, Science, and Art in Early Modern Europe*. New York: Routledge, 2002.

Stevens-Arroyo, Antonio M. *Cave of the Jagua: The Mythological World of the Taínos*. Scranton, PA: University of Scranton Press, 2006.

Stewart, George R. *Names on the Land: A Historical Account of Place-Naming in the United States*. Boston: Houghton Mifflin, 1958.

Stone, Cynthia. *In Place of Gods and Kings: Authorship and Identity in the "Relación de Michoacán."* Norman: University of Oklahoma Press, 2004.

Subirats, Eduardo. *El continente vacío: La conquista del Nuevo Mundo y la conciencia moderna*. Madrid: Anaya & Mario Muchnik, 1994.

Symcox. See Las Casas, Bartolomé de, *Las Casas on Columbus*.

Tato, Julio F. Guillén. *La parla marinera en el Diario del primer viaje de Cristóbal Colón*. Madrid: Instituto Histórico de Marina, 1951.

Taviani, Paolo Emilio. *Christopher Columbus: The Grand Design*. London: Orbis, 1985.

Taylor, Douglas. *Languages of the West Indies*. Baltimore: Johns Hopkins University Press, 1977.

Thacher, John Boyd. *The Continent of America: Its Discovery and Baptism*. New York: Benjamin, 1896.

Todorov, Tzvetan. *The Conquest of America: The Question of the Other*. Translated by Richard Howard. Norman: University of Oklahoma Press, 1984.

– *The Morals of History*. Translated by Alyson Waters. Minneapolis: University of Minnesota Press, 1995.

Toynbee, J.M.C. *Animals in Roman Life and Art*. Baltimore: Johns Hopkins University Press, 1973.

Tucker, Gene Rhea. "Place-Names, Conquest, and Empire: Spanish and Amerindian Conceptions of Place in the New World." PhD diss., University of Texas at Arlington, 2011.

Ulloa, Luis. *El predescubrimiento hispano-catalán de América en 1477: Xristo-Ferens Colom, Fernando el Católico y la Cataluña española*. Paris: Maisonneuve Frères, 1928.

Val Julián, Carmen. "Albores de la toponimia indiana: Colón y Cortés." In *La etapa inicial.* Vol. 1, *La formación de la cultura virreinal*, edited by Karl Kohut and Sonia V. Rose, 289–97. Madrid: Iberoamericana, 2000.

– "La toponomía conquistadora." *Relaciones* 70 (1997): 41–61.

Vance, Eugene. *From Topic to Tale: Logic and Narrativity in the Middle Ages.* Theory and History of Literature 47. Minneapolis: University of Minnesota Press, 1987.

Varela, Consuelo. *La caída de Cristóbal Colón: El juicio de Bobadilla.* Madrid: Marcial Pons, Ediciones de Historia, 2006.

– *Cristóbal Colón: Textos y documentos completos.* Madrid: Alianza, 1982.

Varela, Consuelo, and Juan Gil, eds. *Cristóbal Colón: Textos y documentos completos.* 3rd ed. Madrid: Alianza, 2003.

Vega, Lope de. *El nuevo mundo descubierto por Cristóbal Colón.* Edited by Robert M. Shannon. New York: Peter Lang, 2001.

Verdera, Nito. *De Ibiza y Formentera al Caribe: Cristobal Colón y la toponimia.* Ibiza: privately published, 2000.

Virgil. *The Georgics.* Translated by Janet Lembke. New Haven, CT: Yale University Press, 2005.

Vizenor, Gerald. "Manifest Manners: The Long Gaze of Christopher Columbus." *Boundary 2* 19, no. 3 (1992): 223–35.

Vogel, Joseph Henry, and Camilo Gomides. "Ecological Debt and the Existence Value of Biodiversity: The Evidence Begins with the *Diario of Columbus' First Voyage to America, 1492–1493.*" *Ometeca* 9, no. 1 (2005): 206–19.

Wachtel, Nathan. *The Vision of the Vanquished: The Spanish Conquest of Peru through Indian Eyes, 1530–1570.* Translated by Ben and Siân Reynolds. Hassocks, UK: Harvester Press, 1977.

Watts, Pauline Moffitt. "Prophecy and Discovery: On the Spiritual Origins of Christopher Columbus's 'Enterprise of the Indies.'" *American Historical Review* 90, no. 1–2 (1985): 73–102.

West, Delno C., and August Kling. *The* Libro de las Profecías *of Christopher Columbus: An* en face *edition.* Gainesville: University of Florida Press, 1991.

Wey Gómez, Nicolás. *The Tropics of Empire: Why Columbus Sailed South to the Indies.* Cambridge, MA: Massachusetts Institute of Technology Press, 2008.

White, Hayden. *The Content of the Form: Narrative Discourse and Historical Representation.* Baltimore: Johns Hopkins University Press, 1987.

– "The Historical Text as Literary Artifact." In *The Writing of History: Literary Form and Historical Understanding*, edited by Robert H. Canary and Henry Kozicki, 41–62. Madison: University of Wisconsin Press, 1978.

Wilson, Samuel M. *Hispaniola: Caribbean Chiefdoms in the Age of Columbus.* Tuscaloosa and London: University of Alabama Press, 1990.

– ed. *The Indigenous People of the Caribbean.* Gainsville: University Press

of Florida, 1997.
Woodward, David, ed. *The History of Cartography.* Vol. 3, *Cartography in the European Renaissance*. Part 1. Chicago: University of Chicago Press, 2007.
– "Reality, Symbolism, Time, and Space in Medieval World Maps." *Annals of the Association of American Geographers* 75, no. 4 (1985): 510–21.
Zamora, Margarita. "'If Cahonaboa Learns to Speak ...': Amerindian Voice of the Discourse of Discovery." *Colonial Latin American Review* 8, no. 2 (1999): 191–205.
– *Reading Columbus.* Berkeley: University of California Press, 1993.
Zelinsky, Wilbur. "By Their Names You Shall Know Them: A Toponymic Approach to the American Land and Ethos." *New York Folklore* 8, no. 1–2 (1982): 85–96.
– "Slouching toward a Theory of Names: A Tentative Taxonomic Fix." *Names* 50, no. 4 (2002): 243–62.

Index

TORONTO IBERIC

1 Anthony J. Cascardi, *Cervantes, Literature, and the Discourse of Politics*
2 Jessica A. Boon, *The Mystical Science of the Soul: Medieval Cognition in Bernardino de Laredo's Recollection Method*
3 Susan Byrne, *Law and History in Cervantes' Don Quixote*
4 Mary E. Barnard and Frederick A. de Armas (eds), *Objects of Culture in the Literature of Imperial Spain*
5 Nil Santiáñez, *Topographies of Fascism: Habitus, Space, and Writing in Twentieth-Century Spain*
6 Nelson Orringer, *Lorca in Tune with Falla: Literary and Musical Interludes*
7 Ana M. Gómez-Bravo, *Textual Agency: Writing Culture and Social Networks in Fifteenth-Century Spain*
8 Javier Irigoyen-García, *The Spanish Arcadia: Sheep Herding, Pastoral Discourse, and Ethnicity in Early Modern Spain*
9 Stephanie Sieburth, *Survival Songs: Conchita Piquer's* Coplas *and Franco's Regime of Terror*
10 Christine Arkinstall, *Spanish Female Writers and the Freethinking Press, 1879–1926*
11 Margaret Boyle, *Unruly Women: Performance, Penitence, and Punishment in Early Modern Spain*
12 Evelina Gužauskytė, *Christopher Columbus's Naming in the* diarios *of the Four Voyages (1492–1504): A Discourse of Negotiation*

www.ingramcontent.com/pod-product-compliance
Lightning Source LLC
Chambersburg PA
CBHW020812030725
29016CB00012B/123/J

* 9 7 8 1 4 4 2 6 4 7 4 6 6 *